HARPER'S NEW TESTAMENT COMMENTARIES

GENERAL EDITOR: HENRY CHADWICK, D.D.

THE GOSPEL ACCORDING TO ST. LUKE

A COMMENTARY ON

THE GOSPEL ACCORDING TO ST. LUKE

A. R. C. LEANEY

HENDRICKSON
PUBLISHERS
PEABODY, MASSACHUSETTS 01961-3473

A COMMENTARY ON THE GOSPEL ACCORDING TO ST. LUKE

Copyright © 1966, 1958 by Alfred Robert Clare Leaney

Hendrickson Publishers, Inc. edition

ISBN: 0-913573-54-X

reprinted by arrangement with
A. & C. Black (Publishers) Limited

First printing — February, 1988

Printed in the United States of America

ALFRED HENRY LEANEY
OPTIMO PATRI
PIENTISSIMUS FILIUS
ALFRED ROBERT CLARE LEANEY

CONTENTS

GOSPEL ACCORDING TO ST. LUKE

PREFACE TO THE FIRST EDITION

LUKE a theologian—to scholars of a generation ago the conception would have been impossible: he was the accurate reporter, the trustworthiness of whose facts was illustrated by the investigations of modern historians and archaeologists; all his departures from the simplicity of Mark must be departures of his alternative sources, rivalling or superior to Mark in their antiquity.

Recognition has been long accorded to Mark as more than the composer of a basic record for subsequent use by other evangelists, and understanding of his status as a theologian is now common. Recent studies have extended to Luke a like recognition as a theologian, with ideas peculiarly his own; the inevitable corollary is a question: how far may he still be regarded as a historian?

The present work attempts to assess the character and value of Luke both as theologian and historian, endeavouring both to give an account for university students and others of the present stage of the debate, and to make some contribution to it.

My sincere thanks are due to the editors of the *Expository Times*, of *New Testament Studies*, and of *Novum Testamentum* for permission to include parts of the Introduction which have appeared in those journals.

Many debts are acknowledged in the course of the book, but I wish specially to thank Professor G. D. Kilpatrick, D.D., of the University of Oxford, for invaluable help and encouragement given over a number of years, and the Rev. H. Chadwick, D.D., of Queens' College, Cambridge, for many patient and helpful criticisms and suggestions.

ROBERT LEANEY

The University,
  Nottingham
Ascension Day, 1957.

ix

ABBREVIATIONS

Bauer	*Wörterbuch zum Neuen Testament,* by W. Bauer.
BC	*The Beginnings of Christianity,* edited by Foakes-Jackson and Kirsopp-Lake.
Black	*An Aramaic Approach to the Gospels and Acts,* by Matthew Black (2nd edn.).
Brownlee	See under *Man. Disc.*
C.I.G.	*Corpus Inscriptionum Graecarum.*
Conzelmann	*Die Mitte der Zeit,* by H. Conzelmann.
Daube	*The New Testament and Rabbinic Judaism,* by D. Daube.
ET	*The Expository Times.*
HTR	*The Harvard Theological Review.*
Hobart	*The Medical Language of St. Luke,* by W. K. Hobart.
ICC	*International Critical Commentary.*
JRLB	*John Rylands Library Bulletin.*
JRS	*The Journal of Roman Studies.*
JTS	*The Journal of Theological Studies* (NS = New Series).
LS	Liddell and Scott's *Greek Lexicon.*
LXX	*Septuagint.*
Man. Disc.	*The Manual of Discipline* from Qumran. The translation chiefly used is that of W. H. Brownlee in *Bulletin of the American Schools of Oriental Research,* Supplementary Studies, Nos. 10-12.
MC	*The Modern Churchman.*
Mysticism	*The Mysticism of Paul the Apostle,* by Albert Schweitzer.
NTS	*New Testament Studies* (The Journal of Studiorum Novi Testamenti Societas).
Quest	*The Quest of the Historical Jesus,* by Albert Schweitzer.
S	The Sinaitic Codex (often referred to by the Hebrew letter, *Aleph*).
SB	Strack and Billerbeck's *Kommentar zum Neuen Testament aus Talmud und Midrasch.*
Schürer	*A History of the Jewish People in the Time of Jesus Christ,* by E. Schürer.

Streeter	*The Four Gospels*, by B. H. Streeter.
syr. cur.	The Curetonian version of the Syriac text.
syr. sin.	The Sinaitic version of the Syriac text.
TWNT	*Theologisches Wörterbuch zum Neuen Testament*, edited by Kittel and Friedrich.

The references to Creed are to his edition and commentary; those to Klostermann to the commentary in the series, *Handbuch zum Neuen Testament*; those to Plummer to his commentary in the *ICC* series.

INTRODUCTION

The Author and the Writing of the Gospel

i. THE AUTHOR

At the beginning of the gospel the author addresses a certain Theophilus; and when referring at the very beginning of Acts to his 'former word' the author of Acts addresses a person of the same name. There is no evidence against the natural conclusion that the same man is author of both the gospel and Acts.

Who was this author? The external evidence consists of:

1. The Gospel Prologues, extant in 38 Latin biblical manuscripts; only the Prologue to the gospel of St. Luke has survived in Greek—and this is in a single manuscript. The date of the prologues has for long been put between 160 and 180. It has recently been argued[1] that the Greek prologue to Luke may contain genuine old tradition in its first, biographical paragraph, but the ascription of the gospel and Acts to Luke, which follows, may depend upon Irenaeus (who died about 202).

This prologue tells us that Luke was an Antiochene Syrian and a physician; the further biographical details are mentioned below, in the discussion on the place of composition of the gospel.

2. The fragment of the Muratorian Canon, embodied in Codex 101 in the Ambrosian Library, once at Bobbio, now at Milan.[2] This manuscript was probably written in the eighth century; but the work of which it was part was originally composed a little before A.D. 200 and refers to 'the third book of the gospel, according to Luke', who was a physician and stood in some relation to Paul: this much is clear, though the text is difficult and must be further discussed below.

3. Irenaeus (*Adv. Haer.* iii. 1) says that Luke was a follower of Paul and he regards Luke's gospel as the written form of

---

[1] R. G. Heard in *JTS*, NS, vi. 1 (Apr. 1955), pp. 7 ff.
[2] For a description see Buchanan in *JTS*, viii (1907), pp. 537 ff.

that which Paul preached. The fathers from Tertullian onwards repeat this kind of statement.

The next step is to consider any NT evidence for a Luke who fulfils the conditions suggested by this external evidence. The references are Col. iv. 14; 2 Tim. iv. 11; Philem. 24. In these we read of Luke the beloved physician, whom Paul clearly regards as a faithful companion, and who is a fellow-worker. It is possible that we might add either the Lucius of Rom. xvi. 21 (a suggestion mentioned, but not as his own view, by Origen) or that of Acts xiii. 1, since Ramsay found at Antioch two inscriptions, in one of which a man is called Lucius and in the other Loukas, Ramsay concluding that the Antiochian Greeks regarded the two forms of the name as equivalent.[1] The two can hardly be identified, as Paul is unlikely to have had a kinsman (Rom. xvi. 21) who was a Cyrenian (Acts xiii. 1); again, if Luke was an Antiochene, as stated by the Gospel Prologue and Eusebius (*H.E.* iii. 4, 7), the identification with Lucius the Cyrenian of Acts xiii. 1 is less likely. Origen also suggested that Luke might be 'the brother whose praise is in the gospel', of 2 Cor. viii. 18; but the words do not imply that the brother had written a gospel but that he was praised for his services to the gospel, and while this does not exclude Luke, it makes this reference less germane to the discussion. (It should be noticed that to take a written gospel as implied would mean a very early date for the composition of the Gospel according to St. Luke, since it would have been in circulation by A.D. 55, an impossibly early date in view of the apparently clear reference to the events of 66–70 in Luke xxi. 20.)

Discussion of the authorship of Acts must take full account of the 'we-passages' of that work:[2] for our purpose it is enough to show that (a) the author of the gospel and of the Acts were very probably indeed the same person; (b) the 'we-passages' make a prima facie case for believing that this author was at least on occasions a companion of St. Paul; (c) St. Paul himself refers to a companion named Luke; (d) tradition (not earlier than *c.* 160) calls the author Luke. But we cannot conclude from this that Luke, Paul's companion, was certainly the author of both

---

[1] See Clark, *The Acts of the Apostles*, p. 392.
[2] Acts xvi. 10-17; xx. 5-15; xxi. 1-17; xxvii. 1-xxviii. 16.

works: the facts (a), (b), and (c) do not prove this, though they
are consistent with it; and the tradition which calls the author
Luke may be no more than an inference from these facts. This
point may now conveniently be discussed in connexion with the
possibility that Luke was a native of or a dweller in Antioch,
perhaps even Lucius the Cyrenian (cf. Acts xi. 20; xiii. 1).

ii. LUKE AND ANTIOCH

If Luke was an Antiochene, Paul might have indeed met him
early in his ministry. This is clear from Acts xi. 25-26, whether
or not Luke is the Lucius of Acts xiii. 1. Harnack argues that
Luke 'was most probably a native of Antioch'.[1] His arguments
might be said to warrant a conclusion rather less than this,
namely, that Antioch was a very important city in the history
of the early church, and that Luke was well aware of this importance and of the facts which accounted for it; but Harnack
is justified in saying that 'the testimony of the Acts is not only
not opposed to the tradition that its author was a native of
Antioch, but even admirably accommodates itself thereto'.[2]
Cadbury cites further evidence:[3] the fifth-century Codex Bezae
and Augustine have a variant reading at Acts xi. 28 which implies the presence of Luke at Antioch on the occasion when
prophets came from Jerusalem to Antioch and prophesied a
coming famine; but even if this reading is original, it does not
actually demand the conclusion that the author was an Antiochene, although it is perfectly consistent with it.

We may add at this point the puzzle raised by Luke iii. 1:[4]
why does Luke mention Philip as well as Herod Antipas, and
above all the mysterious Lysanias of Abilene? The question may
be answered by Koh's suggestion[5] that the gospel was destined
to circulate particularly in the rather remote and unexpected
regions mentioned; this would be consistent with Luke's special
interest in the regions near Antioch.

We may continue with the rest of the evidence mentioned
by Cadbury:[6] the Pseudo-Clementine *Recognitions* (x. 71) mention Theophilus as an Antiochene, but it is far from certain that

---

[1] *Luke the Physician*, pp. 20-24. [2] *Op. cit.* p. 23. [3] *BC*, ii, p. 248.
[4] See Introd., p. 48. [5] In *The Writings of St. Luke*. [6] *Ibid.*

this romance has any basic source earlier than the third century, and it may well be that the Lucan writings themselves suggested the name Theophilus for a character in the story.

Lastly, Bacon[1] has pointed out that Basilides (the gnostic of the second century) and Marcion's teacher Cerdo, both Antiochenes, used only Luke's gospel.

It is clear that each of these pieces of evidence is inconclusive; Koh's suggested solution to the problem of the mention of Iturea, Trachonitis, and especially Abilene, may be right. If not, we must admit that the belief that Luke was connected with Antioch may have arisen from his text, and have no independent value.

We can therefore do no more than set side by side the NT references to Luke, a companion of St. Paul, and the external evidence of the tradition; but we can say that nothing in our review of the evidence makes it impossible to identify the Luke of tradition with Luke, Paul's companion. In this connexion it is fair to mention the facts that the latest date implied in the writings themselves is *c.* A.D. 70 and that the author does not mention the death of St. Paul, facts which, however they be interpreted, are consistent with the author being a companion of the Apostle.

It remains to mention the argument from the vocabulary of Luke to an identification with St. Paul's 'beloved physician'. Hobart published in 1882 *The Medical Language of St. Luke*, an exhaustive study of aspects of Luke's vocabulary, which satisfied the author that Luke was a physician. Harnack thought that Hobart had overstated his case[2] but that traces in the gospel could be found to show that the character of the narrative as a whole is determined by 'views, aims, and ideals which are more or less medical', that marked preference is shown for stories about the healing of diseases, and lastly, that the language is coloured by the language of physicians.

Against this we may urge that the character of the narrative may be said to be theological or religious rather than 'more or less medical'; this we hope the various sections of the introduction and many passages in the commentary will all assist in showing. Luke's themes are the reign of Christ, how it is estab-

---

[1] *Expositor*, Oct. 1920, p. 291.   [2] *Op. cit.* p. 175, n. 1.

lished and how it may be entered. They include an interest in healing as they are bound also to include an 'interest in' the forgiveness of sins. The preference for stories about healing is exaggerated and must in any case be seen as integral to Luke's theological presentation.

On the language, it will be enough to refer, for a typical contemporary verdict, to Cadbury[1] who concludes that 'the words that he shares with the medical writers are found too widely in other kinds of Greek literature for us to suppose that they point to any professional vocabulary'.

iii. THE OCCASION OF THE GOSPEL AND ACTS

There can be little doubt that Luke was influenced, among other considerations, by the desirability of showing that Christianity was politically innocent; he probably also wished to show that Paul in particular was wrongly regarded as a political offender. Sahlin has argued[2] that Luke was providing a document to aid a literal and actual plea in a Roman court. Lagrange[3] also appears thus to interpret 'iuris studiosum'[4] of Luke in the Muratorian Fragment on the Canon in the difficult passage referred to above; this reads 'cum eo paulus quasi ut iuris studiosum secundum adsumsisset numeni suo ex opinione concriset', etc., usually emended with Hort (as in *BC*, ii. p. 210, n. 1) to 'cum eum Paulus itineris sui socium secum adsumsisset',[5] etc. But we may, like Sahlin and Lagrange, try to make sense of the text as we have it: it is not necessary to take 'iuris studiosum'[6] literally as they do, but to accept the help suggested by 'quasi

---

[1] *The Making of Luke-Acts.* The quotation is from p. 358.
[2] *Der Messias und das Gottesvolk,* pp. 11 ff.
[3] *S. Luc,* p. xii; cf. p. xxii.   [4] 'a legal expert.'
[5] 'when Paul had added him to his company as a companion on his journey.'
[6] See Ehrhardt on the Muratorian Fragment in *Ostkirchliche Studien,* ii. 2 (July 1953); he shows that *iuris studiosus* can apply 'to a legal expert who acts on behalf of a Roman official, provincial governor and the like', and from *Dig. Just.* I. 22. 1. *Paul.* we learn that 'an *adsessor* or *iuris studiosus* issued an *edictum decretum,* or *epistola* either in the name of the Roman official to whom he was attached, or else *suo nomine ex opinione* of his superior. The appointment of such a member of his staff by a Roman official was technically described as *in consilium adsumere. . . .*'
But due regard must be paid to the words *quasi ut.*

ut' and to imagine that Paul may have obtained Luke's help 'as a kind of legal counsel' before both Jews and Gentiles: in other words, before the entire public. Such a metaphorical use is suggested by 'quasi ut' and accords with Luke i. 2 when we reflect that 'logos' in the gospel often carries with it a well-developed theological meaning.[1] But 'logos' is used of legal cases (as at Acts xix. 38) and the theory must be further examined.

It is an important part of the argument that Acts xxviii. 30 ('he stayed on two whole years') is a deliberate implication that Paul was set free, διετία being a legal technical term. Mommsen's *Römisches Strafrecht*[2] is quoted in support of this view, and to the effect that an accuser must be ready to present his case against the accused within two years of laying the original charge. Otherwise, it was assumed that the charge was withdrawn. Thus the point of 'when two years were fulfilled' in Acts xxiv. 27 is that the action of Felix in leaving Paul a prisoner was illegal.

The theory can hardly stand unless it can be shown that διετία was a technical legal term bearing the implication claimed at any date when Paul could have been tried or Luke have been writing. Unfortunately this cannot be established, for the all-important opening words of the passage in Mommsen's *Strafrecht* are not mentioned; these tell us that it was only in later times that this custom obtained, and that it became law under Constantine I.[3] Thus if Luke intended to convey some special point by the use of 'two whole years' at Acts xxiv. 27 and xxviii. 30, it can have been only that the detention for two years of a prisoner whose case remained 'pending' during that time was contrary to custom, not to actual law; but Mommsen's authority seems to imply that even the custom did not exist at the time when Luke was writing. We are left with the conclusion that Luke cannot have meant anything special by his mention of 'two years' in this connexion.

We must return to a more conservative interpretation of Luke i. 1-4, and suggest that the description of Luke as 'iuris studiosum' in the Muratorian Fragment is metaphorical to the

---

[1] See commentary on iv. 32.　　　　[2] Leipzig, 1899, p. 488.
[3] The authority quoted by Mommsen is Paulus, *Digest* 48. 16. 6. 2.

extent that the 'logos' in Luke i. 2 is the case for Christianity rather than for Paul alone.[1]

A further point may now be urged: prefaces or prologues are notoriously written after the main work has been completed, and Luke's may be no exception,[2] the language being certainly consistent with this view; and the ἐγένετο (without particle) of verse 5 makes in fact an excellent beginning. A study of the main work, therefore, beginning at Luke i. 5, is a legitimate and desirable way of obtaining evidence for interpreting the prologue; in other words, we may well read Luke to see what were his purposes in writing. These are revealed only partly in the gospel, but what is revealed there is entirely consistent with what emerges from a study of Luke-Acts: the author's purpose seems to be to make, explain, and defend the claim that Jesus was a king. Luke writes as if he meant to say in effect, 'We Christians do indeed claim that our Lord was a king, but it is impossible to understand—and very easy to misunderstand—what we mean by his kingship and his kingdom unless you hear the story from the very beginning'. It is not only Paul who is on trial. Many passages, of which Acts xxviii. 21 is a significant example, show that he personally is no disturber of the peace. But Christianity itself is on trial: Acts xxviii. 22 is spoken by Jews but might have been uttered by any who knew about 'this sect', and a summary answer is given at Acts xxviii. 28.

If therefore due weight is given to the fact that the prologue may well have been written after the work had been completed, the conclusion is unavoidable that interpretation of the main part of Luke-Acts does not depend upon, but supplies the means for understanding this prologue, which accordingly may be taken as addressed to someone interested in but not convinced by what he had heard of the Christian story, to whom Luke undertakes to supply the 'real facts' from the very beginning. But it is impossible to hold that the gospel and Acts were

---

[1] For a full discussion of the vocabulary of the prologue see Cadbury in BC, ii. Appx. C, pp. 489-510; and for a summary of an almost identical view see the commentary ad loc.

[2] The opening words of Herodotus read like those of a man who has finished his work and now adds his reflexions; while the beginning of Thucydides' Peloponnesian War clearly refers to the experience gained when writing the work which the author now introduces.

composed only for Theophilus: Luke bears in mind a mixed audience, part Jewish, part Gentile.

If this account of Luke's motives is so far sound, the question may well arise, how far do his anxiety to argue the Christian case, his desire to convince both Jew and Gentile, his very loyalty and enthusiasm as a Christian, cause him to write in a manner detracting from his claim to be accounted a careful historian? To this question Morgenthaler[1] would answer that Luke not only relies upon 'eye-witnesses and ministers of the word', but he 'too, having given minute attention to everything from the beginning', is a literary witness. As such, Morgenthaler claims,[2] he obeys the scriptural rule about witness in Deut. xix. 15 which Matt. xviii. 16-17 represents Jesus himself as acknowledging, and respect for which is shown at John viii. 17; 2 Cor. xiii. 1; 1 Tim. v. 19; Heb. x. 28; 1 John v. 6 ff. Thus, for example, Peter at the beginning of Acts is accompanied by the otherwise inactive John,[3] and even the introduction of Herod into the trying of Jesus may be due to the desire for two 'official' witnesses to his innocence.[4]

This principle has not affected Luke's literary form as much as Morgenthaler believes:[5] but the witness principle is certainly present in the gospel and Acts, and we must see clearly how far this fact affects the question of the historicity of Luke. It is true that it is to the actuality of the events that Luke's witnesses give their testimony, and a particular style and arrangement do not make the material unhistorical; it was the evangelist's intention to write a history just as certainly as to be a witness to that history, or rather to its Lord. His earnest desire to be a witness is inseparable from his belief in the historical truth of his material, and his belief in this truth is an indispensable factor to account for his desire to bear witness to it; but fidelity to such a 'witness' principle whose particular form is prescribed may betray a writer, however sincere, into forcing his material into a framework which was not native to it. Moreover, the final composition, by disposing parts in a pattern chosen by the

[1] *Die lukanische Geschichtschreibung als Zeugnis* (Zwingli-Verlag, Zürich, 1948).   [2] *Op. cit.* ii. p. 9.
[3] *Op. cit.* ii. pp. 7 ff.   [4] *Op. cit.* ii. p. 10.
[5] E.g. the pair, Annas and Caiaphas (iii. 2), need hardly be explained in this way.

author, may falsify the picture in some of the details and in general. We can vindicate Luke's sincerity and conscientiousness but not the claim—which he would perhaps have found difficult to conceive—that he wrote with scientific objectivity: for Luke's claim to historicity cannot exempt him from a judgment based on comparison of his work with the data afforded by the Pauline epistles and Josephus. It is idle to refer to the correct introduction of names or titles known to be used in the period and places with which he is dealing: a writer may introduce impeccable 'local colour' without accuracy in chronology or even in fact. Luke is not a 'scientific' historian. He writes as one for whom Christ alone makes history intelligible.

iv. DATE

Cadbury, after referring to 'our uncertainty about the author's identity', adds: 'As to the exact date and place of writing the evidence is equally indefinite, within certain obvious quite wide limits. I refrain from the thankless process of confuting arguments which purport to answer these questions more precisely.'[1] We can indeed do little more than set out the facts: Acts, with an ending which to our minds is almost abrupt, seems to possess knowledge of no event later than c. A.D. 60 (the close of Paul's two years in Rome), and it is the gospel which bears signs in Luke xxi. 20 of knowledge of the events of 66–70 and in xix. 39-44 specifically of the destruction of Jerusalem in 70, while the retention of Mark xiii. 30-31 at xxi. 32 may be some slight indication that the distress of these times had not yet passed when Luke wrote the gospel (but see note on xxi. 32). It is natural to emphasize the strangeness of the fact that whereas the gospel shows knowledge of events as late as A.D. 70, Acts makes no reference to the martyrdom of St. James the brother of the Lord in 62,[2] nor to the Neronian persecution in Rome in 64 in which, as tradition holds, both St. Paul and St. Peter perished. The solution that Acts was written first is contrary to the clear reference at the opening to the 'former treatise'; this makes very difficult the ingenious attempt to identify the latter

---

[1] *The Making of Luke-Acts*, p. 360.
[2] Josephus, *Ant.* xx. 9. 1.

with Proto-Luke, making the final gospel Luke's third composition, an attempt made by C. S. C. Williams[1] and Koh[2] independently, the latter leaning more heavily than the former on the existence of Proto-Luke (in Streeter's sense); such a theory will not satisfy those who distrust the evidence for Proto-Luke's existence.

Another important consideration is Luke's dependence on or independence of Josephus. Commentators on Acts v. 36 ff. have conjectured that Luke's careless misreading of *Ant.* xx. 5 will account for his placing the rebellion of Judas (A.D. 6–8) after that of Theudas (A.D. 44–45), and for his allowing Gamaliel to speak of the latter in a debate anticipating him by about fifteen years. The implication for our purpose would be that Acts was written after A.D. 93 when Joseph published the *Antiquities*. But it is hazardous in the extreme to deduce dependence from a supposed mistaken understanding, especially as there is no obscurity in *Ant.* xx. 5. We are therefore left with the facts which we have stated, the only reliable internal evidence suggesting a date after A.D. 70 but without any decisive indication (such as certain identification of the author with Luke, the companion of St. Paul would have given) for a date soon after that catastrophic year.

V. PLACE

There is little to say about the place of composition. R. G. Heard (*JTS*, NS, vi, 1 (April 1955), pp. 7 ff.) believes that 'the first, biographical, paragraph' of the Gospel Prologue 'gives a number of facts about Luke credible in themselves, and not at all to be deduced from the New Testament. In particular his virginity, which is not stressed like that of John in the Monarchian Prologues,[3] his age, and the place of his death seem to reflect a genuine tradition.' Indeed, we may say that it is only these last items which may reflect a genuine, independent tradition. Heard regards the rest of the Lucan prologue as on a different level and less valuable, even the interesting piece of

---

[1] *ET*, June 1953, pp. 283 f. and Williams' commentary on Acts in this series, pp. 12-13.

[2] *The Writings of St. Luke*, pp. 26 ff.

[3] These represent a Roman tradition a little later than that of the Muratorian Canon.

information that Luke wrote the gospel in the regions of Achaea, being an 'easy deduction from his death in Boeotia', and he sensibly ends by saying, 'We can only guess at where it was written, but an origin in Greece itself is possible'. We may echo these words with regard to the gospel itself.

II. Luke and his Sources

vi. general

In the main central block, Luke iv. 31-xxi. 38, Mark is the chief source of iv. 31-44; v. 12-38; vi. 1-19; viii. 4-ix. 50; xviii. 15-43; xix. 28-38; xix. 45-48; xx. 1-xxi. 38. For iv. 14-30 and v. 1-11 see pp. 50 and 54.

Luke's editorial additions and changes are often noted in the commentary, especially in connexion with the Passion Narrative, the view being taken that non-Marcan material in that section may be reduced to the small compass of xxii. 31; xxii. 36-38; xxii. 49, and xxiii. 27-31, though xxiii. 6-16 may also belong to this category. Nevertheless a few characteristic passages may be noticed to illustrate Luke's treatment of Mark: thus in iv. 31-44; v. 17-26; viii. 40-48, 53 the power wielded by Jesus is emphasized more strongly than in Mark; greater reverence is paid to Jesus, both by characters in the narrative and by Luke himself at v. 12, 29, 30; vi. 1, 2, 6-11; viii. 22; ix. 48; Luke introduces prayer on the part of Jesus four times at v. 16; vi. 12; ix. 18; ix. 28, 29; Jesus is protected by Luke from the accusation of being a revolutionary in xix. 38, 47; xx. 19; 'Christ' is identified with 'Son of God' before Peter's confession at iv. 41; and the Lord's popularity is strongly emphasized at iv. 42; viii. 40; ix. 18-21; xviii. 15a.

Among other doctrinal influences may be mentioned as operative in this part of the work the importance in Luke's eyes of the Apostles, shown by his treatment in vi. 12 ff.; viii. 22-25; ix. 13; ix. 46-48; ix. 22 (by omission—cf. Mark viii. 32-33); ix. 49-50; xviii. 15-17; xviii. 27; xviii. 31 (by omission—cf. Mark x. 32).

vii. the q element

In the *Four Gospels* Streeter set out in full the arguments for the view that the non-Marcan element common to Matthew and Luke was best explained as due to a source, now lost, to which both had access, rather than to the use of the work of either by the other. Scholars had already agreed to call this hypothetical document 'Q', and in this country discussion of gospel sources has very widely assumed its existence.

This commentary follows the same tradition, but it is necessary to take account of arguments recently brought forward by Dr. A. M. Farrer which urge that the right explanation is that Luke possessed and used a copy of Matthew, and that there is no need to suppose the existence of Q.[1]

A full refutation of Farrer's arguments is not offered here, but the position adopted must be explained: this is that Luke did not know Matthew, and that the non-Marcan material common to the two gospels is due to one or more common sources. Part of this material shows such remarkable verbal agreement as to suggest a document known to both writers, slight differences between them being readily intelligible as due to editing;[2] other parts agree as to substance, but the details and vocabulary suggest the possibility of different versions available to each evangelist, without making this explanation essential.[3] It is the former kind of material which has led to the Q hypothesis, and it might be argued that the symbol Q should be confined to it; but it is more convenient to follow the usual practice of classifying under Q both types of material, but leaving the question open as to how much was contained in an actual document accessible to both evangelists.

Such a position is held because it is thought unlikely that Luke knew Matthew, and something further must be said upon this point: Farrer argues that the incredibility of Luke having read Matthew 'depends in turn on the supposition that St. Luke was essentially an adapter and compiler'. This is hardly the case: we may appreciate that Luke was a creative artist and a skilful author, but still believe that it is unlikely, had he known Matthew, that he would either have omitted certain portions of Matthew, or used his Matthaean material in the way in which he has used it. For example, what could be his objection to the Resurrection narratives of Matthew? His desire to convey to

[1] 'On Dispensing with Q', in *Studies in the Gospels: Essays in memory of R. H. Lightfoot*, ed. Nineham (Oxford: Blackwell), pp. 55 ff.

[2] E.g. cf. Luke vii. 18-28 with Matt. xi. 2-11 and Luke vii. 31-33 with Matt. xi. 16-19.

[3] E.g. cf. Luke xiv. 15-24 with Matt. xxii. 1-10.

Theophilus the 'certainty' of what he had heard might well have led him to use Matthew's refutation of the Jewish story that the disciples had stolen the Lord's body. For if Luke had read Matthew, he thereby knew of this accusation and that it was current; it was an accusation which he needed to meet; for this report depends largely on the witness of the Apostles,[1] who disbelieve the women but are convinced by the Lord's appearances: the reader might know the Jewish story and need an answer to the contention that the Apostles, when witnessing to these appearances, were untrustworthy.

Such an argument cannot of course show that Luke had not read Matthew, but is valid to show that his observed aims might lead us to expect him to use elements in Matthew which are absent from his gospel.

Farrer argues further that 'St. Matthew and St. Luke both emanate from the same literary regions'. This is not certain. There are good reasons for believing that Matthew originated from somewhere in Syria. There is no clear indication of the provenance of Luke, but the gospel could have been written, as the ancient Gospel Prologue says,[2] in Greece. One would then belong to the Judaistic, the other to the Hellenistic milieu.

Perhaps the most difficult part of Farrer's theory is his admission that Luke used Mark in some passages for which Matthew was available. He writes: 'Anyone who holds that St. Luke knew St. Matthew is bound to say that he threw over St. Matthew's order (where it diverged) in favour of St. Mark's'. Such a person is equally bound to say that he sometimes threw over Matthaean material in favour of the Marcan (e.g. Mark v. 1-20; Luke viii. 26-39). Farrer does not find surprising either the abandonment of Matthew's order or of Matthew's material in favour of that of Mark. Yet it surely is surprising, for: (a) the possessor of Matthew did not need Mark, since Matthew incorporated almost the whole of Mark. (If it be answered that Luke sometimes preferred Mark, even where he had Matthew, what is this but admission that there is no proof that he knew Matthew?) (b) the way in which Luke is believed to have 'laid his plan on Marcan foundations and quarried St. Matthew for

---

[1] Cf. Luke xxiv. 48; Acts i. 8, 22; ii. 32; iii. 15; v. 32; x. 39, 41; xiii. 31.
[2] See pp. 10-11.

materials' is not only surprising, but very nearly incredible. To quote W. H. Blyth Martin in *Theology*[1], when Luke 'lays aside Mark at ix. 40 and embarks on his central section', 'he must, on Dr. Farrer's view, have laid down his own MS., collated Matt. xix-xxv with Mark ix-xiii, extracted various non-Marcan passages from Matthew and inserted them at different points. . . . Let us take the Woes on the Scribes and Pharisees. Luke is going to follow Mark xii. 38-40 when he gets to it, but we are now asked to believe that he compares Matthew's 39 verses with Mark's 3, leaves out a number of rabbinical sayings not to his liking, and copies the remaining Matthaean verses in the following order, Matt. xxiii. 25-26, 23, 6-7, 27, 4, 29-31, 34-36, 13.'

A few further points may be made: Farrer says that 'St. Luke was not interested in the detail of the anti-Pharisaic controversy'; several passages suggest the contrary.[2] Here, again, Luke might have been expected to use some of the rabbinic material of Matthew if he had known it. The hypothesis that each had access to non-Marcan material and used it in his own way is in the circumstances at least as likely as that 'St. Luke let alone what he did not care for'.

The Lord's Prayer is an interesting case: Farrer agrees that the prayer as known to Luke was more primitive than that known to Matthew but does not believe that this casts any light on the literary relation between the two evangelists; but he neglects the observations of Kilpatrick that Matthew's version shows signs of his editing; the removal of these additions leaves a prayer nearer that of the Lucan form, and it is therefore possible either that Matthew used Luke or that both used a common source.[3] It is noteworthy that in the instance of the Lord's Prayer Farrer admits the probability that each evangelist knew his own version: here, then, is a piece of non-Marcan material which Luke did not obtain from Matthew.

Farrer refers with approval to the thesis of Evans in the same volume, on 'The Central Section of St. Luke's Gospel', that this section (ix. 51-xviii. 14; or, according to Farrer, x. 25-xviii.

---

[1] 'The Indispensability of Q', in *Theology*, vol. lix, no. 431 (May 1956), p. 187.
[2] E.g. vii. 36 ff.; xi. 37 ff.; xii. 1; xiv. 1 ff.; xv. 2; xvi. 14; xvii. 20 ff.; xviii. 10 ff.   [3] See p. 59.

30) is a Christian Deuteronomy. This reveals part of the process by which Luke must have used Matthew, extracting from the latter non-Marcan elements and using them in blocks, in an entirely different order: here, at least, the exemplar of Deut. i-xvii provides the order. The view that Luke's central section is a Christian Deuteronomy depends on the likenesses between this section and Deut. i-xxvi and cannot be said to be more than possible; and in any case it must be observed that this interpretation does no more than assist a hypothesis alternative to that of Q, by explaining Luke's treatment of non-Marcan material in one part of his work without recourse to the Q hypothesis. It does not make that hypothesis any less possible, nor does it establish a rival one.

Farrer dislikes hypotheses, but that Luke knew Matthew and used him is a hypothesis. The alternative, that Matthew used Luke, is another: Farrer may well be right not to believe it; it may be that others are right not to believe his. That Luke and Matthew both used Q, that Luke used Matthew, that Matthew used Luke, these three hypotheses remain possible, and all remain hypotheses. Farrer for his part dispenses with Q but does not show it to be more of a hypothesis by choosing another.

viii. Q—THE EXTENT IN LUKE

If the existence of Q be supposed or if Q be the symbol used to denote the non-Marcan material which is not peculiar to Luke, the following passages may be assigned to this category (the references in brackets can be only speculatively assigned to Q if this symbol is interpreted as the name of a document which once enjoyed a separate existence):

iii. 2 (end)-9, 16b-22 (John the Baptist and the Baptism of Christ).
iv. 1-13 (The Temptation).
vi. 20b-22a, 23b, (24), 25-49 (Sermon on the plain).
vii. 6b, 7b-10 (parts of the centurion's servant story).
vii. 18-28, 31-35 (The Baptist's question and Christ's testimony to the Baptist).
ix. 57-60a (Claimants to discipleship).

x. 2-3, 13-15, 21-28 (Material in the sending out of the seventy).

xi. 2b-4, (5-8), 9-13, 14b (The Lord's Prayer and teaching on prayer).

xi. 17-26 (Beelzebub controversy and the return of the evil spirit).

xi. 29b-35, 39b-44, 46-52 (The sign for this generation, about light, against the Pharisees).

xii. 2-12 (Exhortation to fearless confession), 22-34 (Cares about earthly things), (35-38), 39-46 (Watch!), (47-48) (The servant's wages), (49-50), 51-53 (Signs for this age), 57-59 (Agree with your adversary).

xiii. 18-21 (Mustard seed), 24-29 (30) (Condemnation of Israel), 34-35 (Lament over Jerusalem).

xiv. 11 =xviii. 14b (Humility); xiv. 15-24 (The great supper), 26-27, (28-35) (The cost of discipleship).

xv. 4-10 (The lost sheep and lost coin).

xvi. (10), (13), 16-18 (The law and the prophets, divorce).

xvii. 1b, 3, 4, 6, 21-29, 31-37 (Offences, forgiveness, faith, the kingdom, the days of the Son of Man).

(xviii. 2-5) (Prayer teaching in the unjust judge story).

xix. 15 (part), 16-26 (The pounds), (41-44) (Prediction of the destruction of Jerusalem).

xxii. 30b (Twelve thrones).

Such a list must be at many points tentative, but we may proceed to review the peculiar material which is left after setting the above list aside.

ix. PECULIAR MATERIAL

Of the material peculiar to Luke, iv. 14-30 and v. 1-11 may be claimed to be composite. They have been discussed elsewhere in the Introduction (pp. 50 and 54).

xxiv. 13-53 presents interesting features of its own: see pp. 28 ff. The substantial elements remaining are: i-ii; vii. 11-17, 36-50; viii. 1-3; ix. 51-56, ? 61-62; x. 17-20, 29-42; xii. 13-21; xiii. 1-5, 6-9, 10-17, 31-33; xiv. 1-14; xv. 11-xvi. 15; xvi. 19-31; xvii. 7-10, 11-19; xviii. 1, 6-8; 9-14; xix. 1-10.

This list assumes the assignment of a few short passages to

Q, presuming for this purpose the existence of an independent document so designated.

The peculiar elements in the composite passage iv. 14-30, viz. iv. 16-22a, 23a, 25-30, together with some of the passages in the above list, i.e. vii. 11-17, 36-50; ix, 51-56, 61-62; x. 1, 4-11, 17-20 appear to be influenced by the LXX version of the stories of Moses and of Elijah and Elisha. Certain other features also are noticeable: in iv. 25-30 the point is made that a prophet might be sent to one who was not an Israelite, and Samaritans are both shown mercy and yet represented as hostile (ix. 51-56). Thus the main concern is with Israel, but a tension is introduced by the thought that Israel is unworthy. Other passages may be claimed as showing an affinity both of subject-matter and style: xiii. 6-9 is a warning to the unfruitful tree of Israel, but this is followed by xiii. 10-17, when a woman is healed because she is a 'daughter of Abraham'. The phrase reminds us of the appellation given to Zacchaeus and the reason for his salvation. We may therefore add xix. 1-10; and as continuing the Samaritan theme, x. 29-37, xvii. 12-19, and finally xiv. 1-6, owing to its similarity to xiii. 10-11.

Much of what remains is in the form of story, the Prodigal Son (xv. 11-32), the Unjust Steward (the original elements of which may be reduced to xvi. 1-8a, 9, 15), the Rich Man and Lazarus (xvi. 19-31), and the Pharisee and the Taxgatherer (xviii. 9-14). In the first there may be, in the second there is without doubt, a hint of opposition to the Pharisees, and this element is quite clear in the last example. xvi. 19-31 contains much which shows an appeal intended for Christians nurtured in Judaism: the Law and the Prophets are dramatically commended through the mouth of Abraham. Here is a link with the appearance of Moses the lawgiver and Elijah the prophet at the Transfiguration, Resurrection, and Ascension. (For the identification of the 'two men' on the two latter occasions see pp. 68 ff.)

But the Lord specifically refuses to take the political authority of Moses (xii. 13b, 14), a political leader of Israel being indeed characterized as their destroyer (Herod the fox, xiii. 31-33), while their religious leaders are selfish and proud. Indeed the whole collection of sayings now being considered is marked by a particular type of criticism and appeal addressed to the Pharisees. In xiii. 31-33 certain Pharisees are even friendly. The type of appeal made is summarized in xvii. 7-10: the Pharisees must beware of supposing that their religion is adequate (cf. xviii. 9). Again, an appeal is made to renounce the growing alliance with the Sadducees and the Temple (xv. 11-32; xvi. 1-8a, 9, 15; xviii. 9-14). We may now include xiv. 7-10 and xiv. 12-14 in this collection of sayings which may have been originally addressed to Pharisees.

The peculiar material, therefore, apart from some small elements hard to classify, falls into two main blocks: one is marked by an affinity with the stories of Moses and of Elijah and Elisha, and by the strong interest in the redemption of Israel along with mercy to Samaria (the type of a 'mixed multitude'). These passages are iv. 16-22a, 23a, 25-30; vii. 11-17, 36-50; ix. 51-56, ? 61-62; x. 1, 4-11, 17-20, 29-37; xiii. 6-9, 10-17; xiv. 1-6; xvii. 12-19; xix. 1-10. It may well be under the influence of the close association of Elijah with Jesus in this source that Luke omits Mark ix. 9-13, in which Jesus himself identifies John the Baptist with Elijah.

The other main block consists of what was originally a series of appeals to the Pharisees, reflecting an early stage of their opposition. These passages are xiii. 31-33; xiv. 7-10, 12-14; xv. 11-32; xvi. 1-8a, 9, 15, 19-31; xvii. 7-10; xviii. 9-14.

These two elements are woven together, sometimes also with Q, whose denunciations of the Pharisees appear to belong to a later and fiercer stage of opposition (compare, for example, xi. 42-43 with xiv. 7-10). We may remark that xxiv. 13-35, 44-47 perhaps also shows links with the material we have been discussing, with its references to Moses and the prophets. The conception of Moses and Elijah as the unseen companions of the Lord has influenced the account of the Resurrection itself and it is under this same influence that Luke expanded the Marcan account of the Transfiguration (cf. ix. 31). Again, in xxiv. 19 Jesus is described by the two disciples on the road to Emmaus in Old Testament terms, and at xxiv. 21 he is designated as he who was expected to redeem Israel. This is a Christology less developed than that of Q (e.g. Luke x. 21-22; cf. Matt. xi. 25-27) and harmonizes with that of the passages which have been grouped together above into the first main block of peculiar material.

X. THE INFANCY NARRATIVES

Apart from the Resurrection Narratives, discussed in the next section, no substantial passages remain other than the first two chapters of the gospel. The preface, i. 1-4, clearly comes from Luke's own pen and is discussed above, under the section, 'The Occasion of the Gospel and Acts'[1] and in the commentary *ad loc*. To read on into these chapters is to plunge at once into a world of Semitic thought and phraseology. Not the least typically Semitic trait is a formal inconsistency which amounts almost to illogicality.

At i. 27 Luke brings together two important beliefs of the early church with regard to the birth of the Lord. By speaking of a 'virgin betrothed to a man whose name was Joseph, of the house of David', he refers at once both to the virginal conception of Jesus and to the formally inconsistent tradition that through Joseph Jesus was descended from the royal house of David.

Before discussing this question further, it is well to remark that Luke did not apparently regard the inconsistency as important. At i. 34 Mary protests to Gabriel that she has no husband, and this objection, while strictly accurate since Mary was as yet only betrothed to Joseph, is a strange reason for wondering at a prophecy that she would bear a child since she had the immediate prospect of marriage. i. 34 will be discussed below, but serves here to illustrate Luke's indifference to inconsistency in this matter; we may therefore rightly look for evidence that he has combined two quite incompatible traditions.

The story of the Annunciation as it now stands certainly represents Mary's conception as virginal, but at a time when she was betrothed to Joseph. As it develops, the story raises problems, the most obvious of which is that just mentioned, Mary's surprise that she is to bear a son; for, as a 'virgin betrothed to a man',[2] she would naturally suppose the promise to refer to the near future, after she was married. The story may therefore have existed in one of three forms:

[1] Pp. 5 ff.
[2] Deut. xxii. 23 is the source for the phrase denoting this status.

(a) Without reference to Mary's betrothal to Joseph; in this case, Mary's surprised question in i. 34, 'How shall this be, since I have no husband?' is quite natural, and the mention in i. 27 of her betrothal to Joseph will have been added by Luke to accommodate this tradition to that represented by ii. 1 ff., according to which Joseph and Mary have no knowledge *before* Jesus' birth of his special origin or character.

(b) As promising Mary that she would be, after her marriage to Joseph, the mother of the Messiah. Mary's surprise at the mere fact that she was destined to bear a son is hard to understand; but if we may assume that the original version did not contain the words, 'since I have no husband', her surprise will originally have been at the prophecy that the child she would bear was destined to be the Messiah. It would then be natural for her to ask, 'How shall this be?' and for Gabriel to answer with the promise of the visitation of the Holy Spirit, whose activity would lie in causing a child conceived naturally to have a special, holy character. This would make the original Annunciation story parallel to Old Testament models, e.g. Gen. xvii. 15 ff.; Judg. xiii. 2 ff.; 1 Sam. i. 1-ii. 10.

If the words 'since I have no husband' are a Lucan addition, a third explanation is also possible.

(c) That in the original story Mary was already pregnant, Joseph and Mary, following a recognized custom, having cohabited since their betrothal. According to Jewish Law, there were three alternative ways of causing a betrothal to become legally a full marriage, a money payment, a formal attestation, or cohabitation. Tobit vi-viii shows that cohabitation might follow immediately upon betrothal.

There are no convincing grounds for omitting 'since I have no husband' from the text; our argument is rather that Luke added them to his source;[1] if he did so, they may have had for

[1] The Old Latin codex b omits the words, reading 'ecce ancilla domini contingat mihi secundum verbum tuum' ('Behold the handmaid of the Lord. May it happen to me according to thy word.')—and omits these words at verse 38, reading there only 'et discessit ab illa angelus' ('and the angel departed from her'). In this variant form of verse 38, b is followed by e. But these variants may well be due to 'parablepsis', i.e. a wandering of the scribe's eye from one point in his exemplar to another where the words were similar. This explanation has been very plausibly suggested for this case by H. J. White in *JTS*, xv. pp. 600-602. The scribe of Codex Veronensis (b) allowed his eye to

3

him the added significance of reflecting the desolate state of Israel at the time when he was writing. Israel as the handmaid of the Lord cannot bring forth the Messiah without the protection of her divine husband.[1]

This theological overtone may be intended also at i. 38, in Mary's words, 'Behold the handmaid of the Lord!'—a manifestly Septuagintal phrase. David is the servant of the Lord in the Psalms, e.g. lxxviii. 70; lxxxix. 3, 20; cxxxii. 10; and Israelites are servants of the Lord in Ps. lxxix. 10. The word 'Lord' does not occur in these references, but see Ps. cxvi. 16 for the exclamation, 'O Lord, I am thy servant!' The nation Israel is identified with the servant of the Lord in Is. xlii. 1; xlviii. 20; xlix. 3, 5; and in Ezekiel we find 'Jacob my servant' (xxviii. 25), 'David my servant' (xxxiv. 23; xxxvii. 24), and 'my servant Jacob' and 'David my servant' (xxxvii. 25).

For the feminine form of this idea we must turn to 1 Sam. i. 11, clearly in the mind of Luke when writing these chapters, for it is referred to in ch. i, verses 15 and 48. (There may be also a recollection of the neighbouring verse, 1 Sam. i. 17, at Luke vii. 50.) It is therefore probable that Luke intended a double reference, on the one hand to Mary, and on the other to the nation which she represents, in the phrase, 'the handmaid of the Lord'. With this conception is allied that of the 'daughter of Zion'. Cf. Is. lii. 1-2; lxii. 11; lxvi. 7; Mic. iv. 8; Jer. iv. 31; vi. 23; viii. 19-22; xxxi. 21-22; Lam. ii. 13, 18; iv. 21-22; Zeph. iii. 14-20; Zech. ii. 10; ix. 9. In the passages from Zephaniah and Zechariah the daughter of Zion is bidden to rejoice with the word χαῖρε in the LXX, the word addressed by Gabriel to Mary. In late Judaistic literature Zion is represented as having lost her only son and to be in mourning (2 Esd. ix. 38-x. 57).[2]

---

wander from the first to the third column of a page of fifteen lines and four columns, for both verse 34, at the head of the first column, and verse 38, at the head of the third, begin with the words, 'Dixit autem Maria . . .'. Apart from manuscript evidence, some slight support for omitting 'since I have no husband' is found in the fact that ἐπεί does not occur elsewhere in Luke.

[1] Cf. John iv. 18, where the true interpretation may be that Samaria's five husbands are the gods of the nations of 2 Kings xvii. 24-34, and Yahweh is not Samaria's true husband (cf. Ezra iv. 2-3).

[2] See A. G. Hebert (on the basis of an article by Sahlin) in *Theology*, liii (Nov. 1950), p. 403.

These theological overtones illuminate only details in the narrative, and the three not wholly unified traditions remain: (a) that Mary conceived virginally, with no reference to being betrothed, (b) that Mary was divinely promised that she would be the mother of the Messiah after her marriage to Joseph, to whom she was betrothed, (c) that she conceived during her betrothal by cohabitation with Joseph. Both traditions (a) and (b) may be derived from analysis of chapter i and there is no need to suppose the existence of more than one Lucan source for them both; but tradition (c) is quite distinct: it reappears at ii. 5 where the reading adopted in the text is that with the most powerful manuscript support, 'his betrothed'. The variant readings must be briefly noticed: for example, the Sinaitic Syriac and the majority of the Old Latin manuscripts read 'his wife', and the mere fact of the survival of this variant, with so strong a doctrinal reason for its suppression, might at first sight suggest its authenticity. But if Luke understood that Mary's conception was virginal, he would naturally write 'betrothed'; and scribes might as naturally alter to 'wife', believing that Joseph would bring Mary to a census only if by now she were his wife. The Byzantine text, supported mainly by Θ and a few Old Latin mss., is rendered by the AV 'his espoused wife'; this may seem to be a composite reading, but is not impossible if Luke was briefly referring to the Jewish marriage custom by which betrothal brought the parties into a relation so close to marriage.

The question can be resolved only in the wider setting of a further consideration of the sources in these early chapters. In our search for these sources we must discuss certain difficulties arising less out of the material itself than out of its use and arrangement by Luke.

The first problem is the position of the Magnificat: this song of joy does not follow the Annunciation or the Birth, but rather curiously after the greeting between Mary and Elizabeth.[1]

---

[1] It is not surprising that for Mary at i. 46 a b l* Iren 235 Or read Elizabeth, although these fathers are not consistent, for Irenaeus 185 reads Maria. (Burkitt believed *Helisabeth* was original also in 185. See *JTS*, vii, p. 220.) These facts have led some commentators to conclude that no name was originally provided, the text reading simply 'and she said'. However this may be, verse 56 follows well upon verse 45 and the introduction of Mary (where

There are further considerations: Mary—if she is the singer—can with little suitability give thanks because God 'has looked upon the humility of his handmaid', and while Elizabeth might do so (cf. verse 25), it is strange that after the reverent greeting of the mother of the Messiah (verses 42-45) she should sing of her own cause for rejoicing. Again, at verse 50 the canticle begins to reveal its character as a hymn of Messianic joy to be sung by the nation of Israel, and this theme is strengthened and emphasized beyond all doubt in the remainder. It is above all Israel (verse 54) who has received God's mercy. Luke, then, in changing the position of the Magnificat, has shown his understanding of the dramatic identification of Israel with Mary, and there seems good reason, on the ground of this element in these chapters, to suppose that in the source, too, Mary is the singer. The objections to the present position of the canticle remain: the position in the source to which it may be assigned will be suggested later, but it may be said here that an obvious place would be some time after the Birth.

There can be little doubt that the Benedictus is really a hymn in welcome to the Messiah rather than to a forerunner. Quotations from late Jewish works (especially the *Testaments of the Twelve Patriarchs*) as well as from the Old Testament support the impression of Messianic force made by such phrases as 'visited', 'in the house of David', 'he who has risen from on high' (see note on i. 78), 'to appear', 'peace', while the evidence of verses 72-75 is overwhelming. Particularly interesting is the phrase in verse 76, 'prophet of the highest', which is found in *Test. Levi*, viii. 15, while the title of 'prophet' is given to Jesus in the gospel as well as in Acts and elsewhere.[1]

If the Benedictus is a Messianic hymn, a place for it must be found in connexion with the birth of Jesus. Sahlin suggests plausibly that it originally stood as the song of Anna, the substance of her words to those who watched for the redemption of

---

no noun is needed) in verse 56 supports the view that the Magnificat is not in its original position. Nevertheless, the testimony of the majority of the codices to the reading Mary cannot lightly be passed over, and it is likely that this is what Luke wrote, the variant Elizabeth being due to the context.

[1] Cf. Luke iv. 24; vii. 16, 39; ix. 8, 19; xiii. 33; xxiv. 19. The Lord is himself the speaker in iv. 24 and xiii. 33. vii. 16; vii. 39; xiii. 33; and xxiv. 19 all occur in the material peculiar to the gospel.

Jerusalem (ii. 38): i. 68 harmonizes excellently with this introduction of Anna and the direct address to the child in verse 76
agrees perfectly with the situation. Again, for Anna to utter a
song of praise balances Symeon's song (ii. 29-32), and there is
a sense of anticlimax in the mere 'she spoke about him' after
the elaborate description of Anna in verses 36-37.

The appropriateness which Luke felt in assigning a song to
Zacharias when his speech was restored is readily intelligible,
but it does not seem necessary to suppose that in the source a
song was already ascribed to him.

ii. 4 presents a well-known difficulty: why was it necessary
for Joseph to make the journey from Nazareth to Bethlehem?
The solution which is offered here is that in these early chapters
we have two separate sources, and that recognition of this fact
will explain a number of questions, including the problem of
Joseph's movements and the misplacement of the Magnificat.

It is unnecessary to make a detailed examination of the linguistic evidence, but it may be instructive to consider the use
of the word Nazareth. At i. 26 D and d omit 'whose name is
Nazareth'; while little can be made of this, we may observe that
at iv. 16, where the name is manifestly introduced by Luke, the
form is Nazara.[1] In the first two chapters it is Nazareth (i. 26,
ii. 4, 39, 51). It is possible, therefore, that his source for the
second chapter used this form, and that at i. 26 Luke added it
to his source there, with the reference to Joseph, which we have
already seen to raise a problem.

A further feature of our problem is the curious repetition of
opening words in verses 21 and 22. A possible explanation of this
unstylish feature is that ii. 21 is interpolated by Luke from one
source to another, and in this connexion we notice that ii. 21
refers to i. 31 and must belong to the same tradition.

We are now in a position to gather up the evidence suggested
by inconsistencies in the narrative, and that from language,
arrangement, and style, and so to formulate the theory of two
separate sources which has already been discussed in relation to
some of the problems: the reason that Joseph was bound to go
to Bethlehem for the census was that he belonged to that city,
but that he had been on a visit to Nazareth, perhaps to claim

[1] Nazara is perhaps the Q form, since it occurs also at Matt. iv. 13.

Mary, his betrothed. If this was the case, it was related in a document used by Luke only from ii. 1, the opening being discarded in favour of the other tradition in which Joseph is hardly mentioned, and there indeed possibly by 'interpolation' (i.e. not into the MS. tradition but by Luke into his source) in i. 27. The birth of Jesus and what followed immediately upon it is framed in a journey to Judaea from Galilee and back again; ii. 1-39 (except verse 21) is in fact from a source separate from chapter i of the gospel (to which ii. 21 probably belongs). This first source may be reconstructed thus: i. 5-45, 57-66, 80, 56; ii. 21 and perhaps i. 46-55. In verse 56 'with her' is a Lucan accommodation to his own rearrangement of his material, as is the whole of verse 67. Further, ii. 21, if our theory is correct, must originally have contained a statement about the Birth. It may be that the Magnificat (i. 46-55) immediately followed, and closed this section, but we have seen reason to believe that the other canticles belonged originally to chapter ii.

The second source will have comprised ii. 1-20; perhaps i. 46-55; ii. 22-38; i. 68-79; ii. 39-40 (and possibly ii. 41-52). The phrase 'all who heard' in ii. 18 appears to be a Lucan accommodation to the facts narrated in the first source, the original subject of 'heard' being Joseph and Mary (cf. ii. 33). ii. 19 may also be due to Luke who thereby excepted Mary from the general surprise, but its affinity with *Test. Levi* vi. 2 is by no means a conclusive argument for Luke having added to the source here, for the source itself may have contained this literary recollection.

The respective characteristics of the two sources may now be summarized: in the first Mary is the central figure and is the 'handmaid of God'. Her conception is virginal and it is possible that in this account there was originally no mention of Nazareth, Luke himself also abstaining from including the name, though there is no reason to think that he had doubts about the fact that Jesus was connected with that town. It is also possible that in the original source there was no mention of Joseph: if, on the other hand, the reference in i. 27 stood in the source, we may omit 'since I have no husband' in i. 34 on the assumption that the story intended the reader to understand that Joseph and Mary were betrothed and that they had, accord-

ing to custom sometimes observed, already begun to live together as man and wife. This sole occurrence of ἐπεί in Lucan
writings may be thought to add some probability to this theory.
The reference to the betrothal in i. 27 and the phrase, 'since I
have no husband' in i. 34 can hardly both be authentic: if Mary
is betrothed, she cannot be surprised at the possibility of bearing a son, but her surprise at the prophecy that he would 'be
great' is perfectly natural, even if she were already with child.
If ἐπεί is rejected with its clause (on linguistic grounds), the reference to Joseph in verse 27 may be retained. The most reasonable view may be that ἐμνηστευμένην . . . Ἰωσήφ, probably with
the addition of ἐξ οἴκου Δαυίδ in i. 27, is Luke's own accommodation to the second source, and that the first originally
narrated a virginal conception.

In the second source the signs and wonders are not centred
on Mary but on the child himself. There is no hint of a miraculous conception or of any sign before the birth of the child
that there is anything extraordinary about him. The evidences
of his Messiahship are unmistakable, but they come as a surprise
to his parents, who are mentioned frequently together, and
Joseph is himself the guarantee of Davidic descent.

The sources have been referred to as 'first' and 'second' because they occur in that order in the gospel. Although the supernatural element is present in the 'second' the miraculous does
not occur, and for this reason we may think that it is likely in
fact to be the earlier. The other source, with its account of a
virginal conception, and an ascription of relation by blood between John the Baptist and Jesus appears to be later, the earlier
containing no reference to the Baptist. Since in Q the acquaint-
ance between the Baptist and the Lord is not close, the source
which is comprised mainly in i. 5-45, 57-66 would seem to be
later than that collection. The source in chapter ii, on the
other hand, if it is correct to assign to it also the Nunc Dimittis,
the Benedictus, and the Magnificat, shows obvious affinities
with the other passages from the peculiar material: salvation has
come to Israel as promised to Abraham, his sons and daughters
can now receive it; Jesus will be called the 'prophet of the
highest' and the title 'prophet' recurs throughout these passages.

xi. THE RESURRECTION NARRATIVES

J. N. Sanders in a paper delivered to the Studiorum Novi Testamenti Societas on 10th September 1953, and published in *NTS*, vol. 1, no. 1 (Sept. 1954), pp. 29 ff., entitled 'Those whom Jesus loved (John xi. 5)', advanced the hypothesis that the authors of the Third and Fourth Gospels had access independently to the same tradition, and that certain problems connected with Martha, Mary, and the woman in Luke vii. 36 ff. and certain other questions would be thus better explained than by the view that the Fourth Evangelist used Luke directly. It had already occurred to me that this was the correct solution with regard to some of the features of the Lucan resurrection narratives, which Sanders did not discuss, and the present essay will argue that the solution which he tentatively suggested does indeed receive support from a scrutiny of these features.

The whole section, Luke xxiv (12), 13-53, is a treasury of Luke's septuagintal style and vocabulary.[1]

Some evidence suggests that a source has been rewritten, and in one instance at least without the care which the rest displays: a part of this evidence is connected with verses 12 and 24, and will be considered first, in order to establish a prima facie case for our argument. Verse 12 raises the question of text: it is given by the majority of authorities, being omitted by D e a b l r Marcion. 'Lying' is omitted by B S W 0124 syr. cur. sin. pal., sa bo Eus, and 'by themselves' by S* 579 544 69 1012 A sa. If we allow verse 12 into our text provisionally on the basis of so much authority, it may be admitted that 'lying' may be an assimilation to John xx. 5, and 'by themselves' an addition summarizing John xx. 7; but in neither case is it impossible for Luke to have written the word.

Verse 12, then, may be taken as possibly authentic, and other textual questions will be deferred till later; we shall therefore begin with a comparison of verses 12 and 24: in the Emmaus story Cleopas recounts to the unrecognized Jesus the recent events in Jerusalem, and in verses 22-23 refers to the experience of the women at the tomb early that morning (xxiv. 1-11). He

---

[1] For a detailed justification of this statement see *NTS*, vol. 2, no. 2 (Nov. 1955), p. 110.

then goes on to say, (24) 'And some of those with us went off
to the tomb and found it just as the women had said but did
not see him'. This refers to nothing in the previous narrative
if we omit verse 12. With this further reason for accepting this
verse in our text, we go on to notice that verse 24 refers to
'some', whereas verse 12 mentions only Peter, and we immediately recall that in John xx. 3-10 two disciples run to the tomb.
Unless we are to think that Luke had read the Fourth Gospel,
the natural explanation is that each was taking excerpts from a
common source. A further example, connected with Luke xxiv.
12b and John xx. 8-9, will be noticed later.

That Luke had access to a source or sources known also to
the author of the Fourth Gospel ought not to surprise us in
view not only of the arguments advanced by Sanders, but also
of the acknowledged fact that the non-Marcan material in
Luke's highly individual account of the call of Peter (v. 1-11)
appears to have close affinities with John xxi. 1-14 (p. 54).

We can now proceed to a more detailed examination of the
material: it is obvious that the Emmaus story, Luke xxiv. 13-35,
is a complete whole, only verse 34 being perhaps an insertion
into the narrative in its original form, accounted for by Luke's
having used the story of the Lord's appearance to Peter in
v. 1-11 (as argued on p. 54). Similarly, in the Fourth Gospel,
the story of the appearance to Mary Magdalene (John xx. 11-18)
has been inserted into the account of the empty tomb and first
appearance to the disciples. In neither case is there the slightest
ground for suspicion that the insertion has been made by anyone
else than the author, reasons having been given already for regarding the whole passage, Luke xxiv. 12-53, as bearing the signs
of his pen. If then we extract from Luke xxiv the Emmaus story
and from John xx the appearance to Mary Magdalene, we can
compare the homogeneous Luke xxiv. 12, 36-49 with John xx.
3-10, 19-22.

For a full discussion of the variant readings which affect the
argument see the article referred to on p. 28. The only verse
which must be discussed in this connexion here is Luke xxiv. 40,
which might be regarded as assimilation to John xx. 20; but this
is not necessarily the true account of its origin: it is at least
possible that a common tradition lay behind these two verses

which John has adapted to his own form of the Passion Narrative, mentioning the Lord's side, where Luke mentions his feet, in accordance with John xix. 34. The piercing of the Lord's side is witnessed by the disciple who may be identical with 'the other disciple' of John xx. If the material associated with this disciple in John xx is extracted, we have a story in John xx. 3-10 and Luke xxiv. 12 whose subject is Peter, from which Luke and John have each made their own selection, a story which, when rediscovered, appears perfectly coherent. It is significant that in John xx. 9 a singular verb occurs in two MS. traditions and that John xx. 9 follows logically after Luke xxiv. 12 but not after John xx. 8, a verse patently added in accordance with the tradition of the Fourth Gospel which exalts the unnamed disciple to a special position of respect.

We may now reconstruct the original thus: 'But Peter got up and ran to the tomb, and stooped down and saw the bandages lying by themselves; and he went away home wondering what had happened, for he did not yet know the scripture, that he must rise again from the dead.'

At this point each evangelist has added material of his own, Luke the Emmaus story, John the appearance to Mary Magdalene. It is possible that Luke xxiv. 33-35 were added by Luke himself to connect the Emmaus story with the remainder of the tradition shared with the Fourth Gospel.

Comparison of Luke xxiv. 36-49 with John xx. 19-22 yields similar results: compare Luke xxiv. 36 with John xx. 19, Luke xxiv. 40 with John xx. 20, and Luke xxiv. 49 with John xx. 21.

From Luke xxiv. 36 onwards it appears that Luke has preserved more nearly the original form of the appearance in the Upper Room; for it is less likely that with his respect for the Apostles he invented verses 37-39 than that John omitted them because they detracted from their reputation and the serenity of the narrative. We may suspect that Luke has added not only the link, 'while they were saying these things', at the opening of verse 36, but also in verse 41 the words 'for joy and marvelling', while John boldly removes all reference to the Apostles' doubt.

Verses 44-47 appear to be an insertion which would follow more naturally on verse 27, since in the Upper Room there has been no discourse on the Lord's fulfilment of Moses, prophets, and psalms. The account of the appearance in the Upper Room will then have continued after verse 43: 'And he said to them, "You are witnesses of these things" . . .' (verse 48; cf. Acts ii. 32; iii. 15). These words, an integral part of the account of the overcoming of the Apostles' doubt, would naturally be omitted in the Fourth Gospel. Luke xxiv. 49, compared with John xx. 21-23, suggests that here we have the close of the appearance in the Upper Room, each evangelist writing under the influence of his own convictions, Luke revealing his belief in an intermediate period between the Messiah's exaltation and the bestowal of power on the Apostles, John his 'realized eschatology'.

To sum up: the restoration into the text of Luke xxiv. 12 and 40 may be defended on the principles of textual criticism, and in this way may be reconstructed a coherent tradition in two parts which was shared, like that behind Luke v. 1-11, with the Fourth Gospel. This tradition may be roughly represented by Luke xxiv. 12, John xx. 9 for the first part, and for the second by Luke xxiv. 36-43, 48-49; but it must be observed that the representation of the beginning of the first part by Luke xxiv. 12 is indeed only rough, for xxiv. 24 indicates that Luke was aware that more than one disciple went to the tomb as a result of the women's report. (This incidentally strengthens the claim of xxiv. 12 to be authentic: interpolation from the Fourth Gospel would surely have at least mentioned two disciples.) Did the original source tell of two (or more) unnamed disciples, and was the Emmaus story originally about the same two? But speculation has perhaps gone far enough.

xii. CONCLUSION

Certain other additions may now be made to the peculiar material. For example, the genealogy, iii. 23-38, may be divided into two parts, that from Terah (verse 34) onwards being due to Luke's own researches into the LXX. On the other hand, the genealogy may equally well have been a unity when Luke received it; the notes on iii. 23-38 argue that it does not derive from Q; thus either iii. 23-34 (as far as Abraham) or the whole of the genealogy may be regarded as peculiar material and may have been attached to the early tradition among the Infancy

31

Narratives. The well-known 'as was supposed' of iii. 23 will then be yet another instance of Luke's accommodation of one tradition to another, here of that of the Davidic descent through Joseph to that of birth from a virgin. Again, there is nothing in the collection of passages reflecting an early stage in controversy with the Pharisees which makes it impossible for these to be part of the same source as those passages showing tenderness to the Jews as a nation and as individuals.[1] xiii. 31-33, where Jesus is a prophet, and xvi. 19-31, as has already been hinted, could with equal confidence have been assigned to the passages which show this patriotic outlook. We may therefore suggest that these elements in the peculiar material, possibly already woven together with Q when Luke had it before him, but exclusive of the later of the two sources in the Infancy Narratives, was originally a unit in itself. It contained an account of the birth of the Lord with the promise of greatness (the status of a prophet and of Messiahship, ii. 1-20; i. 46-55; ii. 22-38; i. 68-79; ii. 39-40), an incident in youth (ii. 41-52), a genealogy (iii. 23b-38), material for a rejection scene (iv. 16-22a, 23a, 25-30), miracles and ministry to individuals (the widow's son at Nain, vii. 11-17; the woman who was a sinner, vii. 36-50; the woman bent double, xiii. 10-17; the man with dropsy, xiv. 1-6; Zacchaeus, xix. 1-10), elements in a journey (ix. 51-56,? 61-62; x. 1, 4-11, 17-20), an interest in Samaria (x. 29-37; xvii. 12-19), and the barren fig tree (xiii. 6-9); and it seems that the passages reflecting an early stage of Pharisaic opposition may have been woven into this source when Luke found it (xiii. 31-33; xiv. 7-10, 12-14; xv. 11-32; xvi. 1-8a, 9, 15, 19-31; xvii. 7-10; xviii. 9-14). This source may have contained also the Emmaus story (xxiv. 13-35, together with 44-47). To it Luke added the Resurrection Narrative of xxiv. 12, 36-43, 48-49, which he appears to have derived from a source possessed in common with the Fourth Gospel, and upon which he has left his own mark.

Luke's peculiar materials provided him not only with much of his framework but also with very important elements in his theology, but his central theme is the kingship of Jesus, which appears to be his own contribution. It was under the combined influence of his peculiar material and this theme that Luke con-

[1] Pp. 18-19.

ceived his eschatology and rewrote Mark xiii. 5-37, manipulated much of Q, and, perhaps most important of all, recast the Passion Narrative of Mark. This source, in our judgment, is properly regarded, despite its importance, as one element in the gospel whose real author was Luke, and there is no need to suppose the existence of a 'Proto-Luke' whose lack of either an Apocalypse or a Passion Narrative would deprive it of all claim to be called a gospel. On the other hand, strong conviction as to the unsoundness of a 'Proto-Luke' theory must not make us disregard the manifest importance to Luke of Mark and Q.

Assignment of a date to sources whose very existence can be no more than inferred must be even more conjectural than attempting to date a complete work, but it may be that the material distinguished by pro-Jewish features dates from a time before the destruction of Jerusalem, which Luke regards as the rightful centre and starting-point for the new movement; it is possible that it was written in or near Jerusalem, betraying as it does such interest in the Temple and in the neighbourhood (e.g. Emmaus and Jericho). It may be earlier than Mark, since its christology and doctrine are less developed; and even earlier than Q. The other infancy tradition is probably much later: the virginal conception, or at least the enhanced importance of Mary, and the close association in the divine plan (an association expressed as kinship) of John the Baptist and the Lord, all point to this conclusion.

These considerations all deepen the impression that the Gospel of St. Luke is on the one hand unmistakably composite, and on the other unified in a masterly manner under the dominating influence of a theology thoroughly understood and held with fervent conviction.

III. Luke's Theology

Some of the features of Luke's theology are already obvious: his theme was the reign of Christ, how it is established, how it must be maintained.

When we think of the reign of Christ we have to consider its two aspects: the first presents a royal personality and that series of events by which he claimed his throne, the second his effect upon other persons in the course of that journey by which he came to his kingdom, the royal progress on which he distributed the largesse of healing and forgiveness.

The claim that Jesus was a king may be said to be in a sense an embarrassment, and many critics have so concentrated upon the apologetic motive in Luke's work as to miss the cardinal fact that this same fact is also a challenge—a challenge which Luke not only accepts but hurls back at any possible adversary: thus he introduces the Kingdom of God as the object of the Lord's work in Marcan contexts not containing it (e.g. cf. Mark i. 38 and Luke iv. 43; Mark vi. 7 and Luke ix. 2), he makes explicit the content of the *euangelion* as the kingdom (viii. 1; xvi. 16; Acts viii. 12), he narrates the birth of one who is to inherit the throne of David, he deliberately allows Jesus to enter Jerusalem as a king (xix. 38), and represents him as bequeathing a kingdom to the Apostles on the eve of his death (xxii. 18; see note *ad loc.*). Finally, Luke represents the crucifixion as a stage towards the triumph and the Resurrection as the proof of it. In retrospect the suffering of the Lord is shown to be necessary to entering his glory (xxiv. 26) and Luke alone, with his story of the Ascension, makes historically actual the enthronement of the divinely chosen king for whom Judaism has been looking throughout history: Symeon, Anna, and Joseph of Arimathaea all represent that Judaism, all bear witness to the fulfilment of their hopes; Luke, with the brilliant insight of his Christianity and with great literary boldness, sets Jesus not on the throne of Israel only, but also on the throne of the universe.

The royal progress reveals the effect which the king has upon those among whom he moves. He makes his way through angry crowds without harm, he excites the awe of his followers, he raises the dead, heals, and forgives, refuses the authority of Moses, is greater than Solomon, greater, it is hinted, than Elijah, is designated by Moses and Elijah as about to accomplish the Exodus, the deliverance valid for all people and for all time: indeed, his kingship is equivalent to, or embraces and absorbs the other titles by which he might be known, God's son, prophet, servant, chosen, Son of Man, perhaps also priest. From among the manifest works of the king, the ways in which his personality and work bear upon others, Luke selects for emphasis the power of forgiveness of sins: it is the proclamation of this which is to be the proclamation of the kingdom on its inner side (xxiv. 46-47).

Luke's eschatology is inseparable from this theological presentation: Jesus reigns by right, but not yet in full actuality. For this to be fulfilled the apostles must wield the authority which the king has delegated to them. Sometimes it is wielded, as upon Ananias and Sapphira, as stark power (Acts v. 1-11), but this is exceptional: usually its inner effects in healing are manifest (and these indeed follow in the same chapter, verses 12-16). In accordance with the importance of the Apostles' activity in the fulfilment of God's plan, their reputations are spared as much as possible; but before the crucifixion this motive is subordinate. At the second prediction of the passion, for example (Mark ix. 30-32; Matt. xvii. 22-23; Luke ix. 43b-45), Luke enlarges on Mark's report of the failure of the Apostles to understand (in contrast to Matthew's 'and they were exceeding sorry'), and at the third Luke alone mentions the Apostles' lack of understanding, and expresses it in the most emphatic way, though he excuses them at the same time by saying that this utterance (or matter) was hidden from them (Mark x. 32-34; Matt. xx. 17-19; Luke xviii. 31-34). Thus at the same time Luke insists on the value and necessity of the suffering of the Lord and excuses the apostles from not understanding this during the earthly ministry of their king.

If the suffering is the means of entering into glory and the reign thus inaugurated is delegated by the Spirit to the Apostles, both the Holy Spirit and glory accompany the very birth of the

Messiah. John the Baptist, treated by Luke from the first as herald of the Messiah, will be filled even from his mother's womb with the Holy Spirit (i. 15). The Messiah himself will reign for ever and there will be no end of his kingdom (i. 33). Around the shepherds at the Nativity the *glory* of the Lord shines and they are told that their *saviour* is born (ii. 9, 11). The close association is closer still in the Song of Symeon (ii. 30 ff.), who sings that his eyes have seen 'thy *salvation*' which is a light for revealing to the Gentiles and the *glory* of Israel. Luke alone, at iii. 6, in describing John the Baptist's proclamation, prolongs the quotation from Isaiah xl. 3 to add verses 4 and 5, which conclude with the words, '. . . and all flesh shall see the salvation of God'. Again, at xix. 9 Jesus himself says that salvation has come to a son of Abraham. All these passages are peculiar to Luke, and the theme is continued in Acts: thus Peter's sermon at Pentecost includes the verse (ii. 33), 'Exalted therefore to the right hand of God, and having received the promise of the Holy Spirit from the Father, he has poured out this which you see and hear'. God's glory and salvation come into the world with Jesus, who after his suffering is exalted to the right hand of God, whence he is able to bestow the Holy Spirit, who accompanied him through his birth and through his death which was his entrance into his glory.

It cannot be too strongly emphasized that this entrance into glory is deliberately chosen by Luke as the keystone of his theological arch, in preference to the future coming in glory apparently envisaged by Mark and Matthew. He nowhere reproduces the conception suggested by Dan. vii. 13 of the Son of Man coming with clouds of Heaven: more accurately, he nowhere reproduces the suggestion which is conveyed by the Septuagint version of Dan. vii. 13, taken over by Matthew, which envisages the Son of Man mounted *on* the clouds of heaven. Luke leaves us in no doubt as to his meaning, for he writes 'in a cloud' (xxi. 27). (The very slightly supported reading 'on the clouds' may be safely dismissed as assimilation to Matthew.) The archaic and slightly ridiculous picture suggested by Matthew may not be intended by Mark and is certainly not intended by Luke; and it is worth while observing that the presence of the clouds in the Daniel vision is not due to the necessity of a vehicle to convey the Son of Man *from heaven to earth*. This is not the only passage of the Old Testament in the use of which Matthew has excelled in naïveté.

Luke's interpretation of the cloud is clear: it is the cloud which in the J narrative of the Old Testament marked the constant presence of Yahweh (cf. Ex. xiv. 19, 24); in the E narrative his occasional presence in the tent of meeting, standing as it did from time to time at the door (e.g. Ex. xxxiii 9-10), and which in the P narrative has become a covering which conceals the glory shining through it from within (Ex. xxiv. 16-17), the glory which we have seen to accompany the Messiah throughout the gospel story in Luke.

For Luke, Jesus' glory is that of a reigning king, a king who is also a servant. He delegates his kingdom, enters his glory by his death and Resurrection, rises to his throne. The Son of Man picture is absorbed into that of the king. Since he already reigns, he has not still to come in glory, as though that coming were the first full manifestation of it, but he will manifest from time to time the glory which he already possesses, shown at the Transfiguration, Resurrection, and Ascension, and in the appearances to Stephen and Paul. Such manifestations are the 'days of the Son of Man' (Luke xvii. 22, see p. 68) and perhaps also the 'seasons of refreshing' promised by Peter in Acts iii. 20. Certainly the time of restoration of all things (Acts iii. 21) is the final manifestation which Luke envisages; and in the interval he places the present, his and our present, during which first the Apostles, then the whole church, are to convey the gospel of forgiveness of sins to the uttermost part of the earth. Luke took the account of this mission as far as Rome: his history is coninued by other hands.

IV. SPECIAL NOTES ON PARTICULAR SUBJECTS AND PASSAGES

xiii. THE HOLY SPIRIT IN ST. LUKE

(i. 15, 41, 67; iii. 16, 22)

In i. 15 a connexion is implied between abstention from strong drink and being filled with the Holy Spirit. This is deliberate. Cf. Eph. v. 18 and Acts ii. 13, 15 ff., including the quotation from Joel ii. 28-32 in Acts ii. 15 ff. In the later Midrash on Numbers, in the comment on Num. xi. 16 ff., the phrase 'the Holy Spirit' is applied to the spirit which the Lord took from Moses (without loss to him) and gave to the seventy elders. Moses and the elders are said to be 'filled with the spirit of holiness'.[1] The phrase occurs also in the Qumran *Manual of Discipline*, iii. 7, where the meaning appears to be 'by the spirit of holiness in the community'.

For Luke, as for later Judaism in general, there is a close connexion between the Holy Spirit and the spirit of prophecy. John the Baptist is like Jeremiah in being filled with the Spirit from his mother's womb (Jer. i. 5). Cf. the phrase, 'the spirit and power of Elijah', in Luke i. 17, the close connexion between the Spirit and prophesying in i. 67; and ii. 25-27. See also *Manual of Discipline*, viii. 16, where it is said that the prophets have revealed through 'the spirit of his holiness'.

For the Spirit and Jesus cf. Luke iii. 22 and the special emphasis at iv. 1 and iv. 14.

The expression 'the Holy Spirit' occurs in the OT only at Ps. li. 11 (LXX. l. 13) and Is. lxiii. 10-11; the meaning is again 'Spirit of God', or 'Spirit of Yahweh', which the LXX renders faithfully, using 'of the LORD' for 'of Yahweh'. (E.g. Gen. xli. 38; Num. xxiv. 2; 1 Sam. xvi. 13-14.) 'Spirit of holiness' occurs at Rom. i. 4 and the phrase there may be of Aramaic origin. In *Test. Levi* xviii. 7 it is taught that this spirit will rest upon the 'new priest'.

[1] Num. Rabbah 13 (172a).

INTRODUCTION

In the OT the 'Holy Spirit' is rare, as we have seen, and in rabbinic writings it is almost always the spirit of prophecy giving insight of the will of God to man, or the spirit of inspiration in authors of books of the OT. These two conceptions are very close to one another: thus in the Targums, 'spirit of God', 'spirit of Yahweh', 'Holy Spirit' are translated by 'spirit of prophecy'. The gift was thought to have been given originally to all nations, but taken from them for their hostility to Israel. At the beginning all Israelites enjoyed direct leadership from God by virtue of this gift, which was lost by the sin of the Golden Calf; after this an angel becomes their leader, and Yahweh communicates only through chosen men such as the prophets, men like David and Solomon, and the officiating high priest, who divines Yahweh's will by his official consultation of the Urim and Thummim. After the destruction of the first temple, or, according to some, after the death of Haggai, Zechariah, and Malachi, the prophetic gift in Israel was quenched, and a weak substitute was given in the *bath-qôl*, the 'little prophecy' (lit. 'daughter of a voice'). But soon rabbis held that the gift was preserved by the communication through laying-on of hands, appealing to Num. xxvii. 18 and Deut. xxxiv. 9 (P), both relating to Moses' 'ordination' of Joshua. It was also held that those who gave themselves for Israel or learnt and obeyed the Law, or taught it publicly, could receive the Holy Spirit.

Thus reception of the Holy Spirit by the promised child (as here, i.e. i. 15), by Mary according to Gabriel's promise (i. 35), Elizabeth (i. 41), Zechariah (i 67), and Symeon (ii. 25) is an entirely Judaistic notion.

When Elizabeth is filled with the Holy Spirit (i. 41) the incident begins the fulfilment of the prophecy in i. 15. The Holy Spirit is active from the very first in the events which introduce and bring the Messiah to the world; in the present passage he is associated with abnormal phenomena: Elizabeth utters a loud cry, and while her words appear to be directly addressed to Mary, they close with a promise (verse 45) which seems in part to be addressed to the reader, and which she can make only while gifted with the faculty of prophecy. Again, Elizabeth can hardly know, except by inspiration, that Mary is pregnant, still less recognize her Lord in Mary's unborn child (verse 43).

Matthew follows the same tradition in associating the Holy Spirit with the earliest beginnings of the gospel story (Matt. i. 18 ff.): this may be regarded as a natural development of the tradition represented by Mark, according to whom the Spirit first takes his part at the Baptism of Jesus (Mark i. 10).

To be filled with the Holy Spirit (i. 15) rather than with strong drink suggests being filled with some gift from God which is in some way recognizable by those who witness the experience of the person receiving it. In Ex. xix. 18 (J), 1 Kings xviii. 38, and 2 Kings i. 10 ff. fire is evidence of Yahweh's presence; in 1 Kings xix. 11-12 wind and fire precede the appearance of Yahweh, and in 2 Kings ii. 11 Elijah is taken up to heaven by fire and whirlwind. These are the outward signs of God's activity. The same ideas are used less literally in Mal. iii. 2, where God's messenger (in Mal. iv. 5 connected with Elijah) is 'like a refiner's fire'.

In Luke iii. 16 John half promises, half warns that 'one mightier' than he will baptize 'with Holy Spirit and with fire'. The original may indeed have lacked the word 'holy' (80 63 64 Clem Tert). Even if it is included, the Lucan version of this event makes the spirit seem quasi-impersonal and even violent; so also the signs of the coming of the Holy Spirit at Pentecost (Acts ii. 2-3) are fire and 'the sound as of a rushing violent wind', giving rise to ecstatic prophecy, familiar to us from the OT (e.g. 1 Sam. x. 10 ff. and xix. 24; Num. xi. 23-29). The Qumran *Manual of Discipline* (iv. 20) teaches that at the Judgment God will purge and refine (using the same verb as Mal. iii. 3) through a holy spirit. Thus, in Malachi the Lord's messenger will purify by fire, in the *Manual* God will purify by a holy spirit, in the synoptic gospels he will purify by both (Luke iii. 16; cf. Mark i. 8 and Matt. iii. 11).

Luke, then, represents John as contrasting his baptism by water with that of One to come whose baptism is to be by spirit and fire; this second baptism seems to take place at Pentecost (and perhaps answers the question, 'Why were the Apostles not baptized?'), but in Acts xix. 1-7 the contrast between John's baptism and that 'into the name of Jesus' is that of a baptism of repentance set over against a baptism where the Holy Spirit is given: the violent element has dropped out, but, as at Pentecost, ecstatic prophecy provides a recognizable token of the Spirit's presence.

xiv. JOHN THE BAPTIST

(i. 13, 15, 17, 24, 76, 80; iii. 16; vii. 18)

Luke emphasizes both the importance of the rôle of John the Baptist in the divine plan and also its subordinate character. Both are brought out in the early chapters. At i. 13 we meet his name which in its Hebrew form (*Yohanan* or *Yehohanan*) means 'Yahweh is gracious', corresponding to the situation in which he is to be born.[1]

The prohibition of wine and strong drink enjoined for John before his birth (i. 15) comes from Lev. x. 9, where it is to be obeyed by all priests when about to enter the tabernacle; it is found also in Num. vi. 3 as a rule for those who have taken a Nazirite vow, Num. vi. giving the rules for a Nazirite according to the Priestly Code. The RV mg of Num. vi. 4, 'all the days of his Naziriteship', serves the sense better; a Naziriteship as a rule lasted thirty days, but the Mishnah knows also both of a Naziriteship like Samson's, and a perpetual Naziriteship, such as that here enjoined for John the Baptist. Normally a man could devote only himself to this state, but some held that a man might so devote his son. Like Samson, John has both his birth and Naziriteship announced by an angel (Judg. xiii. 5).

In *According to the Scriptures* (p. 21) Dodd says that 'for the evangelists the "messenger" of Mal. iii. 1 and the "Elijah" of iv. 5 are identical' and 'all three synoptics more or less explicitly identify the composite figure with John the Baptist'. But Luke i. 17 and i. 76 contrast with Luke's usual presentation of this matter: in i. 17 John is indeed closely associated with Elijah, though the 'spirit and power of Elijah' work in Jesus as well as in John (see on vii. 16); and in i. 76 the words, 'to make ready his ways', are apparently a reference to Mal. iii. 1 and Is. xl. 3, the former passage certainly connecting with Elijah.

[1] Cf. Winter, *NTS*, i. 2 (Nov. 1954), p. 120.

On the other hand, apart from these two passages (i. 17 and
i. 76), Luke avoids the direct identification of John with Elijah
by omitting the whole passage Mark ix. 9-13 (cf. Matt. xvii. 9-
13), where the Lord apparently accepts the scribal teaching that
'Elijah must come first' and implies that John is Elijah who 'has
come', Matt. xvii. 13 making this quite explicit.

At i. 24 Elizabeth hides herself on learning of her pregnancy.
The verb is emphatic, perhaps meaning 'concealed herself entirely'. The reason for this close concealment is probably to be
found in Luke's desire to present John as important less in himself than as the forerunner of Jesus, and to show this as part of
the divine plan. He therefore connects Elizabeth's retirement
closely with the Annunciation to Mary: Elizabeth hides herself
'five months' (i. 24) and 'in the sixth month' (i. 26) Gabriel is
sent to Mary. When Mary visits Elizabeth, John even in the
womb acknowledges the mother of his Lord (i. 44); and after his
birth he is concealed from the public (i. 80) until the time is
ripe for him to announce the nearness of the Messiah. When
he begins his ministry Luke, along with the other evangelists,
quotes of him Is. xl. 3, and, unlike the other evangelists, prolongs the quotation to add Is. xl. 4-5; the passage from Isaiah
thus ends with the words, 'And all flesh shall see the salvation
of God'. (Luke iii. 6.) By this sentence Luke makes John prophesy the imminent appearance of the Messiah; for the phrase
'the salvation of God' is apparently equivalent to 'the Messiah'.
(See on iii. 6.)

Somewhat inconsistently Luke also preserves the primitive
tradition of Q, according to which John himself does no more
than entertain the possibility that Jesus was the Elijah who was
to come (vii. 19-20; cf. Matt. xi. 2 f.). In the same passage Jesus
pays John the tribute of identifying the Baptist himself with
Elijah (vii. 27; cf. Matt. xi. 10).

The Baptist had a considerable number of disciples (vii. 18)
and his movement was much more powerful than a superficial
reading of the NT would suggest. Josephus (*Ant.* xviii. 5. 2) represents him as influential enough to make Herod Antipas put him
to death in fear of a general insurrection. From the gospels we
can learn that John was regarded with great respect by the mass
of the people (e.g. Luke iii. 15, vii. 29; xx. 6), that he gave in-

struction on prayer and enjoined rules (Luke v. 33; xi. 1), that according to one tradition two disciples no less important than Peter and Andrew had begun by being followers of John (John i. 35-40), and that John's disciples regarded Jesus as a rival (John iii. 22-26); some interpreters have suggested that there was a dispute between John's disciples and Jesus himself, the enigmatic 'Jew' of the probably authentic text of John iii. 25 concealing this fact; even further, that Jesus had himself been originally a disciple of John, a fact shown by his acceptance of John's baptism and perhaps by his emergence as a public teacher only after the imprisonment of John (Mark i. 14). Acts shows that the early Christians regarded John's work as the beginning of theirs (i. 22; x. 37; xiii. 24), but witnesses to the persistence of John's followers as a separate movement even after Christianity had been widely established (xviii. 25).

The Fourth Gospel is nevertheless very firm on the subordination of John to Jesus (e.g. i. 6-8) and suppresses the fact of the Lord's baptism by John even while implying it (i. 32). Neither Matthew nor Luke go so far, but Matt. iii. 14-15 shows the difficulty which Matthew felt over it, and Luke hurries over it with a subordinate (genitive absolute) clause (iii. 21. See note *ad loc.*).

xv. ANGELS

(i. 11, 19)

'An angel of the Lord appeared' to Zacharias (i. 11). Luke does not say '*the* angel of the Lord'; the Hebrew corresponding to Luke's phrase could be translated either way (e.g. at Gen. xvi. 7) but this angel is named in i. 19. This naming gives a clue to the character and rôle of angels as conceived here: for names of angels appear only in the later parts of the OT. Rabbi Simeon b. Laqish (*c.* 250) explained this late appearance of the names of angels by saying that the Israelites brought these names from the Babylonian exile. He remarks also that they are all connected with the name of God (El) and carried this name on their heart like a tablet such as that hung round the neck of a slave and bearing his master's name.

The meaning of 'Gabriel' (i. 19) may be 'Man of God' (cf.

the *geber* of Dan. viii. 15 and *'ish* of Dan. ix. 21). In all lists he is one of those attendant on the throne of God, as he here claims.

The idea of 'angels of the Presence', though not the name, is found in Ezek. ix. 2. In Is. lxiii. 9 the Hebrew (though not the LXX) says 'the angel of his Presence saved them'. Cf. also the anonymous 'angel of the Presence', *Jubilees* i. 27 and 'the angels of the glory of the Presence of Yahweh', *Test. Levi* xviii. 5. For Gabriel named as Angel of the Presence or as one of the angels of the Presence see Dan. viii. 16, ix. 21; *Enoch* xx. 7; xl. 9; liv. 6; lxxi. 13. He is mentioned also in the *Targum Jerushalmi* on Gen. xxxvii. 15 and on Ex. xxiv. 10 and in the Targum to Ps. cxxxvii. 7. *Enoch* xx. 7 makes Gabriel one of those set over Paradise, the Serpent, and the Cherubs, consistently with his character as representative alike of God's primitive justice and his mercy.

Lucan angels elsewhere conform more to the earlier OT type: they have no names, their appearances are short, their conversation, if any, is confined to the message which they bring, and their interlocutors do not question them. (Luke ii. 9; xxii. 43; Acts v. 19; x. 3; xii. 7; xxvii. 23).

xvi. THE CENSUS

(ii. 1-2)

Luke tells us that the census to which Joseph took Mary at Bethlehem was a census 'of the whole empire' and that it was 'the first census, made while Quirinius was governor of Syria'. These statements raise a number of problems.

The word used by Luke for 'census' is the correct term for a provincial census, which was a register of the provincial population and excluded the Roman citizens resident in the province. Inscriptions show that such a census was repeated after an interval in an individual province and that censuses were not taken in different provinces at the same time. Their organization involved personal appearance before the authorities, and in Syria (which includes Palestine) this rule extended to women from twelve years of age upwards. Special places were assigned for wandering populations in parts of Egypt, and it is possible that, in order to include any such folk in Syria, the Romans made use of the strong tribal and family consciousness of the Jews, and ordered them to report at their ancestral city. Joseph might belong to such a category as a journeyman-carpenter,[1] but it is also possible that Bethlehem was his place of residence, as is suggested in the section on the Infancy Narratives.[2] Eusebius in his *Historia Ecclesiastica* (iii. 20) shows that even in the time of Domitian members of the Lord's family owned land in Bethlehem.

It is therefore not difficult to suggest explanations for Luke's statements that each had to go to 'his own city' and that Joseph went to 'Bethlehem, because he was of the house and clan of David' (ii. 3-4). Certain other problems may be readily solved: the decree would not literally be a decree of Augustus, but it would possess his authority, which the legate would claim when ordering the census. Again, it was not a census of the whole empire, and was confined to Syria, including Palestine; but the facts that it embraced all Syria and that other provincial censuses were held at different times would combine to cause Luke to make this mistake.

The chronology is the real difficulty: a census did take place in A.D. 6-7 under Quirinius, and Luke knew about it in another connexion, that is, the revolt under Judas which it provoked (Acts v. 37). But it is strange that he should associate the birth of Jesus with this census, for he implies that the birth took place 'in the days of Herod King of Judaea' (i. 5), i.e. in the days of Herod the Great who died 4 B.C., or a little time after his death, about the beginning of our era; with this would agree the date which he gives when the Lord was thirty years old, namely, A.D. 28-29. (Compare iii. 23 with iii. 1 and see the special note on iii. 1, p. 48.)

The census of A.D. 6-7 is recorded by Josephus (*Ant.* xvii. 13. 5; xviii. 1. 1); it took place under Quirinius, governor of Syria, and Coponius, procurator of Judaea; further, it was on the occasion of Palestine coming under direct Roman government on deposition of Archelaus, i.e. in 6 or 7. Josephus

---

[1] For this and the question of the census in general see Braunert, 'Der römische Provinzialcensus und der Schätzungsbericht des Lukas-Evangeliums', in *Historia*, Band vi (April 1957), Heft 2, p. 192. [2] P. 20.

describes it as an innovation, and says that resentment at it led to a rising of the Zeaiots under Judas of Galilee, the event referred to in Acts v. 37. It is hard to imagine that a census before this, while Herod was ruling as an ally of the Romans, has been lost to history. Herod, it is true, was not in high favour with the Romans, and might have failed to prevent them committing such an act of provocation as the taking of a census; but, if it took place, there would have been resistance to it of which Josephus would surely have known.

Ramsay's solution was to take Quirinius' 'governorship' as referring to a time when he held the office of *legatus* in Syria on a previous occasion. Ramsay believed that an inscription which he found in Antioch of Pisidia enabled him to date this legateship in the years 11 or 10 to 8 or 7 B.C. Tertullian (*Adv. Marc.* iv. 19) places the census of the nativity under Sentius Saturninus, i.e. 9–6 B.C. We should have to suppose that Quirinius and Saturninus were in office at the same time, but with different spheres of action. If Quirinius held a census in Syria at this earlier date it would still have to be shown how it can have included Palestine, which at that time was governed separately by Archelaus. Luke may have *thought* that this was the case but, even so, there are serious objections to this solution: Quirinius was certainly in command of an expedition against a Cilician tribe before A.D. 6, namely in 1 B.C., when on the staff of Augustus' grandson, Caius; but his status was not at this time that of governor, and the inscription found at Pisidian Antioch describes him as *Duumvir* or honorary Mayor of the city.

We may alternatively suppose that Luke made a mistake about the name of the governor: thus the census at which Joseph and Mary were registered would be that of 8–6 B.C., under Saturninus, as claimed by Tertullian, who must have been very confident of his accuracy to contradict an evangelist. But it must be admitted that there is no further evidence for a census at this earlier time: Josephus calls the census of A.D. 6 or 7 an innovation, and if the census were really that of 8–6 B.C., by the fifteenth year of Tiberius Jesus would be more than thirty years sold, which is the age given at iii. 23.

These difficulties have led to suggestions about the Greek of the following verse. The natural translation is 'This was the first census, made while Quirinius was governor of Syria'. Lagrange would translate: 'This census was previous to that which took place while Quirinius was governor of Syria'. This cannot be justified even if we accept the reading of the definite article before 'census', which is not well supported.

We can find no certain solution to this problem, and we may guess that either Luke or his source has introduced the census into the story to ensure the birth of Jesus taking place at Bethlehem. Another explanation is possible: Braunert, in the article in *Historia* referred to, would save Luke's historical reputation by assigning the 'error' to his source: it was not really an error, but a deliberate attempt to associate the Lord's birth with the rise of the Zealot movement. The argument may be presented as follows: an ancient tradition appears to have connected the origin of the Zealot movement with the census of A.D. 6–7 when the leader was Judas. In this connexion Josephus calls him Judas of Gamala in Gaulanitis or Judas the Galilaean; but Josephus tells us also of unrest following the death of Herod the Great in 4 B.C. which was at least as great as that provoked by the census of ten years later. Then, too, a Judas was leader; here Josephus calls him Judas son of Hezekiah (*Ant.* xvii. 10. 5), but it is possible that it was the same Judas who was the inspiration of the unrest on both occasions and that the earlier of these was the real birth of the Zealot movement. The association of the rise of the Zealots with the census was natural enough, since Judas became prominent then and lost his life in his patriotic attempt; the association of both with the birth of the Lord might well be due to a group who admired both Zealots and Jesus.

There can be little doubt that in the days of the Lord's ministry some Zealots were attracted to him (Luke vi. 15; Acts i. 13; cf. Luke ii. 11; xvi. 16; xxii. 37; xxiii. 19; and notes on these passages). These combined intense patriotism with belief in Jesus as Messiah (cf. Acts i. 6). It is exactly these twin convictions which characterize the Infancy Narratives, not least the older of the two traditions which we have found there, and which seems to be connected with other material in the gospel (see p. 32). It is this source which associates the birth of Jesus with the census of A.D. 6–7 to which a persistent tradition looked back as the birth also of the Zealot movement.

This theory is speculative, but does include a number of facts, including an explanation for Luke's 'double' chronology, the consistent scheme based on i. 5; iii. 1; iii. 23, and the rival date based on ii. 1-2. It should be noticed that the date given by the consistent scheme agrees with the tradition in Matt. ii. 1 ('in the days of Herod the King', cf. Luke i. 5).

xvii. CHRONOLOGY, AND IDENTIFICATION OF OFFICIALS

(iii. 1-2)

In iii. 1-2 Luke gives a sixfold indication of the date when 'the word of God came to John': 'the fifteenth year of Tiberius Caesar' is A.D. 28-29 if we reckon from the death of Augustus in 14; but if we reckon from the year of the association of Tiberius with Augustus as joint ruler (end of 11 or beginning of 12) we obtain the date 26–27.

Pontius Pilate was procurator of Judaea 26–36. Herod Antipas reigned 4 B.C.–A.D. 39. Philip his brother reigned 4 B.C.–A.D. 33 or 34.'In the priesthood of Annas and Caiaphas' is an inaccurate expression. Annas, more properly Hannas, ceased to be high priest in A.D. 15 and Caiaphas was high priest 18–36. The former was evidently known by the title 'high priest', which he bore *emeritus*, a not uncommon practice. The word for 'high priest' is in the singular, suggesting that Annas had the influence of a colleague on Caiaphas. In Acts iv. 6 he appears as even *the* high priest, no doubt a mistake due to his high prestige.

The date indicated may then be either A.D. 26–27 or 28–29.

A further problem is the identity of 'Lysanias, tetrarch of Abilene'. In 40 B.C. a Lysanias succeeded his father Ptolemaeus as lord of a principality with its capital at Chalcis. This Lysanias was put to death by Marcus Antonius in 36 B.C. at the request of Cleopatra, to whom the principality fell (Jos. *Ant.* xiv. 7. 4; xiv. 13. 3; xv. 4. 1). Coins exist with the inscription 'Lysanias tetrarch and high priest', but since the Lysanias so far mentioned was called 'king of the Ituraeans' by Dio Cassius (xlix. 32) and Porphyrius, it is doubtful whether they should be referred to him.

Details of this Lysanias and the subsequent history of his principality of Chalcis are given in full by Schürer (*Geschichte des jüdischen Volkes* (Leipzig, 1890), i, pp. 593 ff.). After the death of Lysanias this story is obscure, but is mainly a history of the division of his territory into four parts, with two of which we are concerned:

(1) Territory 'hired', i.e. held on payment of tribute by Zenodorus (Jos. *Ant.* xv. 10. 1). Coins are known, dating Zenodorus' rule to 32, 30, and 25 B.C. After the death of Herod the great part of the former territory of Zenodorus (who died in 20 B.C.) passed to Philip. This explains the reference to Philip as tetrarch of Ituraea.

(2) Territory round Abila of Lebanon, the second of the four divisions mentioned by Schürer, situated between Chalcis and Damascus, Abila being the modern Suk. This territory may be the 'tetrarchy of Lysanias' mentioned by Josephus in some further references, viz. *Ant.* xviii. 6. 10; xix. 5. 1; xx. 7. 1; *B.J.* ii. 11. 5; ii. 12. 8. These passages show that a tetrarchy of Abila belonged to a certain Lysanias before A.D. 37.

It seems necessary, therefore, to suppose that Josephus tells us of two men bearing the name Lysanias, the first having reigned over a considerable territory with its capital at Chalcis, and including Abila, but not called Abilene. This Lysanias was, as we have seen, put to death as early as 36 B.C.

The second Lysanias, ruling over territory round Abila of Lebanon, may well be the tetrarch meant by Luke at iii. 1. This Lysanias seems to have reigned until A.D. 53, since in that year the same territory was added by Claudius to the Kingdom of Agrippa II, Josephus remarking (*Ant.* xx. 7) that this territory had been the tetrarchy of Lysanias.

The inscription *C.I.G.* 4523, mentioning the names of Zenodorus and Lysanias, proves the existence of more than one Lysanias in the family to which 'Lysanias the tetrarch' belonged, since it names 'Lysanias the tetrarch' and another Lysanias.

Another inscription, *C.I.G.* 4521, refers to reigning emperors, in the plural, during the tetrarchy of Lysanias. This presumably reflects the joint rulership of Augustus and Tiberius, and dates the inscription to a time at least as late as A.D. 11. The Lysanias the tetrarch mentioned in it, therefore, may well be the second Lysanias to whom Josephus refers, and whom we take to be the ruler intended by Luke.

It remains an unsolved question why Luke mentions these apparently unimportant regions and princes, omitting, for example, the name of the ruler of Damascus. A possible answer, which can only be partial, is that suggested by Koh (*The Writings of St. Luke*, pp. 9 ff.)—that the gospel was intended to circulate—of course not exclusively—in these regions, the dates given being those which their peoples would understand. Only the emperor's year is exactly indicated and no solution is altogether satisfactory.

xviii. THE REJECTION AT NAZARETH

(iv. 14–30)

At the point where this passage begins Luke is emerging from a Q passage (iv. 3-13) into a block of Marcan narrative. At another junction of Mark and Q (Luke vi. 12-19; cf. Mark iii. 7-19) Luke allows himself considerable freedom in rearrangement and manner of presentation, involving some free writing, and we shall find that the same is true here. Our passage must be considered in connexion with Luke's omission of Mark's version of the rejection at Nazareth (Mark vi. 1-6). It might be urged that the present passage comes from a non-Marcan source which Luke preferred to Mark: the fact that Luke had already narrated this incident would account quite simply for his omission when he came to it at Mark vi. 1-6.

The matter is not so simple: the incident in its present form is awkwardly placed. In verse 23 Jesus refers to events in Capernaum, a place not hitherto mentioned in the narrative. The town makes its first appearance in verse 31a where it receives a typically Lucan 'apologetic' phrase ('a city of Galilee'), as though mentioned here for the first time. Moreover, this reference to previous great deeds can refer in Luke only to the tour summarized in iv. 14-15, which rather swiftly account for Jesus' reputation; apart from the lack of specific reference to Capernaum in these verses, they also fail to mention deeds of healing, narrating only teaching in synagogues. They correspond to Mark i. 14-15 which narrate a form of preaching by Jesus in these earliest days which suggests continuation of the work of John the Baptist. In his version Luke has concentrated attention on the admiration which Jesus' teaching aroused.

Verses 14-15 then appear to be due to Luke's freely rewriting Mark i. 14-15, a conclusion which an analysis of the vocabulary will support.

It seems reasonable then to conclude that Luke wrote his version of the rejection at Nazareth as a substitute for Mark vi. 1-6, which he omitted. This is consistent with his dislike of the incident in Mark iii. 31-35 when Jesus appeared to reject his family (cf. Luke viii. 19-21). Besides his desire to avoid representing Jesus as estranged from his family Luke has evidently some further motive which leads him to omit reference to Jesus' brothers and sisters. Again, the general impression which Luke wished to convey seems to be one of a triumphant visit (22) which he has combined with a tradition of rejection as narrated by Mark, which indeed he emphasizes (28-29). The passage will then illustrate Luke's way of dealing with a fact which at first sight seems to detract from the cause which he pleads: he throws a strong light upon it in order to show up its real significance. This is his way with the glorious but embarrassing fact that Jesus entered Jerusalem as a king (xix. 37 ff.). So here Luke boldly describes nothing less than the rejection of Jesus the Messiah by his own people: his own account of the birth and his present purpose make mention of the Lord's brothers and sisters at the best superfluous, at the worst à hindrance.

Luke then has the task of making Jesus' audience admire him but also take offence at him; this is done by narrating their admiration mingled with annoyance that the object of it should be someone whom they had known from boyhood (22). Moreover, the explanation of that at which they marvel is easily hinted, and that with some effect by writing, 'Is not this the son of Joseph?' instead of 'Is not this the carpenter, the son of Mary?'—a hint very obvious to the reader of the first chapter of the gospel.

We have seen that the verses which divide the narrative of the rejection from that of the Temptations (iv. 13-15) are Lucan in style and vocabulary, though verse 14 takes its subject-matter from Mark, showing that Luke has not laid Mark aside here altogether. We may therefore take iv. 16-30 closely with the preceding and so provide a clue to the order of the temptations in Luke: the hint of the angelic protection which is brought near the end of that narrative may be connected with the fact that Jesus escapes with mysterious lack of effort when threatened at iv. 29. Again, Luke had omitted the last half of Deut. viii. 3b (iv. 4; cf. Matt. iv. 4), 'but by every word that comes out of the mouth of God', but the phrase seems to be in his mind when he writes that the audience at Nazareth all marvelled 'at the words of grace coming out of his mouth' (22).

The main framework of the story is as in Mark: (1) Jesus teaches; (2) the people are astonished; (3) the people recall that they have known him since boyhood; (4) they are offended at him; (5) Jesus remarks on the fate of a prophet in his own native place. All these elements are present in Luke but the order is (1), (2), (3), (5), (4). The reason for this is clear: Luke's treatment of Mark elsewhere would lead us to expect that he would omit 'and they were offended at him'. Luke would have his readers believe rather that the prophet rejects the people, so Jesus makes his remark about a prophet's fate in his own country without provocation from the people and follows it with two examples of prophets who rejected their own people in favour of a foreigner. Then the people on hearing this cast him out. Analysis of the phrases will show that as far as verse 24 the outline is Marcan: for example, although Luke had begun with the careful definition of Nazareth as the place 'where he was brought up', under Mark's influence he writes 'in his native place' in verse 24. Again, as already hinted, Luke's account gives no justification for Jesus' strictures on his fellow-townsmen in verses 25-27.

It is not too much to say that Luke, in his desire to combine the narrative of a triumphant visit with a rejection, has given us an impossible story, but his motive is clear enough: that the author of Acts believed that the Gospel was sent to the Jews and on their rejection of it to the Gentiles hardly needs argument. To Stephen's speech may be added, for example, Acts xiii, 46: xviii. 6, xxvi. 20, 23; xxviii. 28. It is therefore not surprising that this theme should appear at the outset of the work of Jesus.

What is the origin of the non-Marcan element in this passage? Between συναγωγήν in verse 16 and verse 22 is a passage peculiar to Luke of 79 words, 26 of which are a quotation from

Deutero-Isaiah, which latter raises an important matter: Luke is on the whole very faithful to the LXX in his OT quotations (cf. e.g. the exact quotation at xx. 42-43 of Ps. cx. 1 and of Zech. xii. 3 at xxi. 24). It is therefore surprising to find that a passage introduced specifically as a quotation is in fact composite, made up of Is. lxi. 1, lviii. 6, lxi. 2 (first four words). In the quotation from Is. lxi. 1 A Θ fam 1 vg syr. pesh. Iren and others include the clause, 'to heal the broken in heart' and this may manifestly in these authorities have come in from the LXX after Luke had completed his gospel. Moreover, in Is. lxi. 2 Luke writes κηρύξαι for the καλέσαι of the LXX, thus both here and in Is. lxi. 1 according with the Hebrew, *liqero'*. A composite quotation is not in itself remarkable but in the context we are led to object that there is no passage in the OT where there 'is written' such a passage. We are therefore free to believe that Luke is here using a document which had already combined the passages. Alternatively Luke may well be aware of a tradition as yet oral which recited these passages as having been spoken by Jesus at this point. This would account also for his inclusion of the very offensive 'Physician, heal thyself!' of verse 23 (see note *ad loc.*) which in view of Jesus' own remark, as already argued, being unprovoked, must surely have existed in some tradition according to which the words were actually spoken *to* Jesus. Nothing else will account for Luke's inclusion of such words.

The remaining passage of the section we are considering, verses 25-30, comprises for more than half its length a striking saying or doublet, parallelism between the two halves of which ('There were many widows ... There were many lepers ...'), like the balance of phrases within each, is obvious and precise. To this formal attraction may be added the force and interest of the matter, and the internal consistency of their argument which contrasts them strongly with verses 23-24. These verses seem to owe their position here to Luke's desire to press home at the outset the fact that rejection was reciprocal, and his failure to make the people sound as if they had provoked the Lord makes the connexion between them and the rest of the incident very feeble. Whatever the origin of the passage, it bears the stamp of Lucan vocabulary, and we have here some evidence of his

5

attention to the LXX in the form Sidonia, which is found only here and in 1 Kings xvii. 9, to which Luke is here referring.[1] Nevertheless, this later part of the non-Marcan material in this passage joins easily with the earlier, verses 16b-22a, and it may indeed be that Luke has used a separate tradition now represented by verses 16-22a, 23a, 25-30, on which he has impressed his own vocabulary and style, but which may be entitled to be considered among the non-Marcan material of his gospel.

xix. JESUS AND PETER: THE CALL AND POST-RESURRECTION APPEARANCE

(v. 1-11 and xxiv. 34)

Luke's rejection of Mark i. 16-20 is not difficult to explain: it is too summary an account of the call of the first disciples to accord with the important rôle in the scheme of salvation which Luke assigns to them. Moreover, there are signs elsewhere of his high evaluation of the rôle and story of Peter (viii. 45; ix. 32; xii. 41; xxii. 8; xxii. 31; xxii. 61; and xxiv, 34, which will be discussed presently). The Apostle, though assuredly a fallible character, is according to the tradition of all four gospels the spokesman of all the disciples; Luke does not palliate in his account the faults of the apostle which are part of the tradition, but characteristically concentrates on them as much light as possible, so that they may be seen in proportion to Peter's character as a whole, and especially in relation to Jesus' influence upon him. There is therefore an obvious apologetic motive for Luke v. 1-11: if Gentiles and others on the fringe of the church, when reading or being informed about the rise of Christianity, objected to the failings of the most famous of the disciples, the answer lies in Peter's words in v. 8 taken with the Lord's reply in v. 10.

But we may urge another reason also for the narrative in Luke v. 1-11, which will appear as we examine the facts: in the first place, two traditions appear to be mingled, that of Mark i. 16-20 and that of John xxi. 1-14. Luke may be said to be the only evangelist thus to mingle Galilean and Jerusalem traditions, a fact perhaps illustrated to some extent by the distribu-

[1] See Sparks, *JTS*, xliv (1943), p. 133.

tion of the name Simon in his gospel (xxii. 31 and xxiv. 34). Secondly, the position of the passage is strange: Luke has already introduced 'Simon' to the reader (iv. 38), clearly following Mark, according to whom, at that point in the narrative, Simon was already a disciple. Again in verse 8 the Apostle is called without explanation Simon Peter,[1] but elsewhere in the gospel the name Peter is not used before it is bestowed by the Lord at vi. 14. An indication of the mingling of the two traditions is that as far as 'launch out into the deep' in verse 4 the impression is that Jesus and Simon are the only two in the boat, and that there are no nets in it (verse 2). But after this, plural verbs are used of other people than, and excluding, Jesus in the boat, and nets are let down, although it is true that the plural is not used consistently (cf. Peter's words, 'I will let down the nets' in verse 5). Again, the last words of verse 10 and the first of verse 11 suggest that one tradition related the individual call of Simon, while the other was of the call of the first four disciples together. There can be little doubt that the second tradition is that of Mark i. 16-20, and that Andrew drops out of the narrative in Luke v. 1-11 in order to enhance the particular and individual character of the call of Simon, the chief disciple, which is of course the subject of the other and non-Marcan tradition. The following elements appear to derive from Mark: Luke v. 2, 'but the fishermen . . . their nets' (cf. Mark i. 19); Luke v. 3 (cf. Mark iv. 1); Luke v. 10, beginning of verse to 'Zebedee' (cf. Mark i. 20), a clause awkwardly added to the main object already expressed, verse 11 bringing back abruptly once more the plural after a sudden return to Simon in verse 10 (cf. Mark i. 20). Here, too, the vocabulary is Marcan (ἀφέντες, Luke preferring the verb καταλείπειν).

Much of the vocabulary, on the other hand, is Lucan: to take one or two examples of many which might be quoted, ἐπιστάτα (only in Luke in the NT and always addressed to Jesus), and πλήθειν (common in Luke-Acts).

It is interesting that ἀποβαίνειν is used in this literal sense only here and in John xxi. 9. Finally, we should notice the curious phrase in verse 8, προσέπεσεν τοῖς γόνασιν Ἰησοῦ for which D reads προσέπεσεν αὐτοῦ τοῖς πόσιν, the word πόσιν

[1] Peter is omitted by D, W, fam. 13, Old Latin MSS., and syr. sin.

being supported by fam 1, 579, e, and the Syriac. The difficulty was evidently felt early; the solution may be that we should not translate 'fell at Jesus' knees' (which does not make good sense) but 'fell on his knees before Jesus' (taking 'Ιησοῦ as dative), the Greek representing the Semitic *qara'* *'al-birqayim* with *liphene*, *le* or *lenegedh* of the person honoured (cf. Is. xlv. 23; 2 Kings i. 13). Cf. for the dative προσέπεσεν αὐτῷ in Luke viii. 28. The presence of this Semitic phrase along with a number of rare words, not all of which are due to the subject, suggests that the non-Marcan tradition, which seems to underlie John xxi. 1-14, existed either in Aramaic or in 'translation Greek' close to the Aramaic original, while the Lucan vocabulary, spread throughout the passage, reveals that the author has rewritten the whole but without the thoroughness which he uses elsewhere.

What was Luke's motive in thus giving prominence to the call of Peter? In answering this question we may at the same time suggest the answer to another of equal interest: why does Luke, who alone of the synoptics affords a mention of the Lord's appearance to Peter after his Resurrection, make this mention so meagre (xxiv. 34)? Cullmann[1] has drawn attention to the fact that the Pseudo-Clementine writings show that in Jewish-Christian circles Paul's position as an apostle was contested on the ground that it was founded only upon a vision, and that the same work places in the mouth of Peter himself words categorically denying value to any kind of vision. If this attitude to the authority conferred by visions is old enough to have been known to Luke, we may claim that he dealt in Acts with the difficulty as it affected Paul, by representing him as granted apostolic authority by the Jerusalem apostles and in other ways; while to meet the difficulty concerning Peter's authority, which would have arisen if it had been founded upon a post-resurrection appearance of the Lord, another course was open, since it was part of the tradition that Peter had been a disciple from the first. This was to transfer the account of the appearance to a time in the early ministry of the Lord, and instead of choosing, as Matthew did, the occasion of the Confession of Jesus' Messiahship, to bring forward the occasion to the very moment of the calling of the Apostles, and to make Peter chief Apostle

[1] *Peter, Disciple, Apostle, and Martyr*, p. 62.

by virtue of being called first, and to the accompaniment of an appropriate miracle. John xxi preserves the tradition for us, in how primitive a form it is not our present purpose to inquire; Luke, perhaps in any case reluctant to use a tradition of an appearance in Galilee, when he came to narrate Resurrection appearances, had already used the story about Peter, and was therefore reduced to the brief statement of xxiv. 34.

XX. JESUS, THE CHILD, AND THE CHILDREN
(ix. 46-48 and xviii. 15-17)

In Mark ix. 33-35 the dispute about greatness, with the Lord's final word upon it, is easily separable from the incident of the child which follows (verses 36-37), although Mark has himself connected the two passages.

Matthew (xviii. 1-5), as well as Luke, has taken the two together by removing the Lord's final word on greatness to a position near the end of the child incident, and has in his customary manner filled out the child incident with material which brings out the meaning of his source. Thus he writes (xviii. 3-4) '. . . if you do not turn and become as children, you will not enter the kingdom of the heavens. Who then humbles himself like this child, he is the greatest in the kingdom of the heavens.' Thus Matthew leaves us in no doubt as to his view of the significance of the child; and he has warrant for this interpretation, for it is apparently that given in the famous passage about the Lord and the children at Mark x. 13-16, for there Mark reports Jesus as saying, 'I tell you truly, whoever does not accept the kingdom of God as a child shall not enter into it' (verse 15).

In this latter case Matthew (xix. 13-15) omits these words, but we have just seen (from Matt. xviii. 3-4) that this is certainly not because he disagrees with this interpretation, and therefore may well be because he has already used it. Luke, in his parallel to Mark x. 13-16, follows Mark closely (Luke xviii. 15-17) except in omitting, characteristically, Mark x. 16 with its description of the Lord taking the children into his arms. He repeats verbatim (verse 17) the saying in Mark x. 15 quoted at the end of the last paragraph. We have seen that Matthew interprets these words as they are usually interpreted to-day, namely, 'whoever does not accept the kingdom of God in a childlike manner . . .', and this interpretation was taken a stage further in the Fourth Gospel, in which Nicodemus is warned of the absolute necessity of being born again (John iii. 3, 5). This may well be the meaning intended by all three synoptics at Mark x. 13-16 and parallels, but it does not necessarily follow that this interpretation is correct for Luke ix. 46-48; here Luke has a curious alteration of Mark ix. 37 (Luke ix. 48), writing 'Whoever accepts this child in my name, accepts me; and whoever accepts me accepts him that sent me; for he who is junior among you all, he is the great one'. Part of this ('whoever accepts me accepts him that sent me') is paralleled in the non-Marcan Matt. x. 40, Luke also having a non-Marcan saying of similar meaning at x. 16; the last part is apparently parallel in meaning to Mark ix. 35, and if it were certainly Luke's parallel to that Marcan verse, it would be clear that Luke, like Matthew, has merely brought out the meaning of Mark in slightly different words. But the parallel may be apparent only: the clause at the end of the verse, from ὁ γὰρ μικρότερος to the end, recalls Luke vii. 28 = Matt. xi. 11, part of Luke's non-Marcan material, and it may be that here, as elsewhere, Luke allows such material to influence his presentation of Mark. We have therefore to interpret Luke vii. 28. The usual interpretation of this passage, viz. that the least (Gk. lit. 'less' but 'least' would assume a known use of the comparative for the superlative) in the kingdom of God is greater than John, is difficult; it acquiesces in a breaking-off of the Lord's words about John to make a general statement about the kingdom, and in the supposition that John is not in the kingdom at all, a very difficult doctrine too often glossed over when interpreting this passage, taking too literally Luke xvi. 16 and in a way not borne out by the parallel Matt. xi. 12. The thought is rather parallel to that of John i. 30: Jesus is claiming that though John's junior—both in years and in service of the kingdom—*he* (not some undefined person) is greater in that kingdom than John.

This interpretation of vii. 28 makes it possible to understand ix. 48 more clearly: Jesus used the child as a symbol of himself because he was conscious both of being 'the great one' and yet of being in some sense a 'junior'; vii. 28 suggests that this was in relation to John the Baptist, the pioneer of the movement which Jesus made his own. If the whole passage Luke ix. 46-48 be read from this point of view, it appears that Luke has taken the dispute of the Apostles as an occasion for arguing the pre-eminence of Jesus over John the Baptist, slurring over the fact that in his source the dispute was as to pre-eminence among the Apostles themselves, and thus once more showing his carefulness for their reputation.

xxi. THE LUCAN TEXT OF THE LORD'S PRAYER

(xi. 2-4)

Streeter[1] argued that the reading, 'May thy Holy Spirit come upon us and cleanse us' of 162 700 Gregory of Nyssa, Maximus of Turin, and perhaps also Marcion, was original, and that the differences between Luke xi. 2-4 and Matt. vi. 9-13, added to the fact that in Matthew the prayer occurs in a block of M, and in Luke in the middle of a block of L, indicated that this was not a Q passage. On the other hand, it is not certain that all the first eight verses of Matt. vi. are M; and in any case Q is not far away (Matt. v. 48) and in Luke is nearer still (xi. 9).

On the other points made by Streeter, Kilpatrick has shown[2] that the phrases in Matt. vi. 9-13 which have no parallel in Luke are explicable as editorial additions. If we read in Luke xi. 2-4 at the end of verse 2 'May thy kingdom come', we can reconstruct the core of the Lord's Prayer without either Matthaean or Lucan additions as follows (using Luke's language where there is a slight but insignificant difference): 'Father, may thy name be kept holy; may thy kingdom come; our bread for the morrow give us each day; and forgive us our sins, for we ourselves forgive everyone that is in debt to us; and do not bring us into temptation'.

Such a reconstruction would reveal a prayer of point and substance, common to Matthew and Luke: it could be safely assigned to Q, if we assume this common written source. Apart from any discussion of Q, we may admit that Streeter may well

---

[1] *Four Gospels*, pp. 276-277.
[2] *The Origins of the Gospel according to St. Matthew*, p. 21.

have been mistaken in his attempt to establish a Lord's Prayer in two versions independent of one another and of the authors who used them; but this should not obscure the fact that the reading 'May thy Holy Spirit come upon us and cleanse us' may be original.

This is a view with perhaps few supporters. Thus, for example, Metzger[1] writes, 'Although Blass, Harnack and Streeter were inclined to regard the petition for the Holy Spirit as original in Luke, it is altogether likely that the variant form is a liturgical adaptation of the original form of the Lord's Prayer used perhaps when celebrating the rite of baptism or of the laying-on of hands. Furthermore, the cleansing descent of the Holy Spirit is so definitely a Christian, ecclesiastical concept that one cannot understand why, if it were original in the prayer, it should have been supplanted in the overwhelming majority of witnesses by a concept originally much more Jewish in its piety ("thy kingdom come").' Whether or not the concept is in fact less Jewish than the familiar 'thy kingdom come' will be considered presently. As for its being supplanted, we may urge that this is part of the process by which the Matthaean version has completely ousted the Lucan in general Christian usage.

A view opposite to Metzger's has recently been expressed by Lampe,[2] who thinks that it 'seems likely', though controversial, that the petition 'May thy Holy Spirit come upon us and cleanse us' is part of St. Luke's own version of the Lord's Prayer. We may therefore venture to state the case for the authenticity of Gregory's reading.

In the first place, the words are Lucan: in verse 13 Luke writes 'he will give (the) Holy Spirit' where Matthew (vii. 11) has 'he will give good things': in view of Matthew's notorious 'spiritualizing' tendency it is unlikely that the alteration is on his side here (cf. e.g. Matt. v. 3). For καθαρίζω of a spiritual or metaphorical purification cf. Acts x. 15, xi. 9, and especially xv. 9 where the gift of the Holy Spirit is associated with a purification of the hearts of those who receive it. Here, indeed, there

---

[1] *Twentieth Century Encyclopedia of Religion*, ii (Grand Rapids, Mich., 1955), p. 673.

[2] 'On the Holy Spirit in the Writings of St. Luke', in *Studies in the Gospels* (ed. Nineham), p. 170.

may be an echo of the Lucan version of the Lord's Prayer, in the words, 'the Holy Spirit', 'having cleansed', and 'tempt'. (See the whole passage Acts xv. 8-10.)

Secondly, the support from tradition for the reading is far from negligible: for example, Gregory makes clear from the passage in *De Or. Dom.* iii[1] that the text of Luke as he knew it read this variant, in contrast, as he says, to Matthew's 'May thy kingdom come'. History bears powerful witness to the fact that the Matthaean version has entirely supplanted the Lucan in liturgical or private use: it may well be that this process was already active in the early centuries when the text of the NT was fluid.[2] In this connexion it should be observed that Matthew, whose interpolation of 'Thy will be done' has already been noted, chose 'Thy kingdom come' as one of a number of possible petitions in this part of the prayer. It is true that the reading of 700, etc., may have been due to liturgical modification. Gregory was no doubt taught from the liturgy; but in view of his evident ignorance of any other text for Luke whatever, and the ending of the passage at xi. 13, it remains at least possible that modification has been in the other direction.

The text of Gregory may then be what Luke wrote. More general considerations will support this view. Luke's eschatological framework includes a Christ who reigns in heaven, and on earth through his vicegerents the Apostles, sending to them the Holy Spirit who empowers them to reign with the same effectiveness which he would have if actually present. Thus Pentecost fulfils John the Baptist's prophecy of the coming baptism by one who would baptize with (holy) spirit and fire (Luke iii. 16), an event thus probably answering at any rate for Luke the ancient question, 'Why were the Apostles not baptized?' Although Luke does not equate Pentecost with the Parousia (as is well shown by Acts i. 11), the coming of the spirit to the Apostles is an essential stage for the coming of the kingdom, its importance being summed up neatly and clearly in Acts i. 8.

On the other hand, Luke's eschatology does not substitute the coming of the Holy Spirit for the coming of the kingdom: rather is the Holy Spirit the power by whose means the Apostles

---

[1] Migne, *P.G.*, 44, 1157 C. [2] Cf. Kilpatrick, *op. cit.* pp. 76 ff.

will make the kingdom fully 'come'. If, then, Gregory's text is to be taken as what Luke wrote, we must explore the possibility that Luke did not impress his own language and theology on a Lord's Prayer known to him in a variable form, but that he was taught the form of it known to Gregory. In this case it would follow that the Lord's Prayer was one of the influences which formed Luke's conception of the Holy Spirit rather than that his form of the Lord's Prayer has been formed by that conception. This is quite possible: to argue that 'Lucan theology' accounts for the presence of a certain passage, the use of a certain passage, the use of a particular vocabulary, or a characteristic way of presenting an incident, is not to preclude the influence of a source or sources. Liturgy may well have provided Luke with the canticles of the first two chapters, but they are full of 'Lucan theology': it is indeed to much of the non-Marcan material, perhaps to a definable strand in it, that much of his understanding of the Gospel is owed. Lucan theology may often be the theology of his sources.

If Luke was taught the Lord's Prayer, it was certainly a Lord's Prayer found in contemporary liturgy, our knowledge of which is necessarily very scanty; and it is admittedly difficult to find evidence among liturgies which will bear weight in a discussion involving some part of the text of the gospels, but there are certain indications which may properly be mentioned. Chase long ago pointed out[1] a number of passages from the New Testament which seemed to have affinities with the petition which we are considering, viz. Mark i. 10 and parallels (where Mark has εἰς αὐτόν and both Luke and Matthew have ἐπ' αὐτόν); Luke i. 35; iv. 18 (the last a quotation from Is. lxi. 1); John i. 33; Acts viii. 15; x. 44; xv. 8 f. (which has already been noticed); xix. 6; 1 Th. iv. 8; Gal. iv. 6; Rom. viii. 15; Tit. iii. 5; 1 Peter iv. 14 (cf. Is. xi. 2); and he added *Ep. Clem.* xlvi and *Barn.* i. We may perhaps add Jas. i. 17 as a passage containing an allusion to the same idea. A petition like 'May thy Holy Spirit come upon us and cleanse us' may therefore have been in constant use in the early days of the church's history. The references in Acts all refer to a coming of the Holy Spirit recognizable by some outward sign, while those in 1 Th. iv. 8; Gal.

[1] *The Lord's Prayer in the Early Church,* Texts and Studies, 1891.

iv. 6; Rom. viii. 15 are of a coming of the Holy Spirit into, or into the hearts of, believers. The same idea is clearly present in 1 Cor. iii. 16; 2 Cor. i. 22; Rom. viii. 9 ff.; 2 Tim. i. 14 (also given by Chase), where the indwelling of the Holy Spirit is taught. In Tit. iii. 5; 1 Pet. iv. 14; *Ep. Clem.* xlvi; *Barn.* i the preposition ἐπί is again employed, and this is in the main the Old Testament conception, as the dependence of 1 Pet. iv. 14 on Is. xi. 2 and of Luke iv. 18 on Is. lxi. 1 illustrates. The coming of the Holy Spirit on others than the Lord in these New Testament passages may be the result of prayer with the imposition of hands, is once the result of preaching the Word, and once simply of the imposition of hands; and it should be carefully noted that Gal. iv. 6 and Rom. viii. 15, if they refer to recital of the Lord's Prayer, make the reception of the Spirit the cause, not the result, of this recital. Eph. v. 26, if a reference to this recital of the Lord's Prayer after baptism, seems to preserve the same order. This would accord with Easton's suggestion[1] that the 'white stone' of Rev. ii. 17, referred to in the *Apostolic Tradition* of Hippolytus (xxiii. 14), is the Lord's Prayer taught by the bishop privately to the baptized after their initiation; and is therefore no evidence for the Lord's Prayer in the Lucan form being known to either St. Paul or to Hippolytus.

So far, our inquiry would not support any theory which went further than to say that the petition under discussion may have been widely used in the early church and imported by Luke into his version of the Lord's Prayer. It is therefore necessary to consider such further evidence as is provided by the early liturgy if we are to show substantial reason for believing that Luke knew the Lord's Prayer in the form which we are considering.

Dix argues[2] that liturgical practice has affected the New Testament text of the form of the words said over the Bread: when the Fraction was invested with symbolic significance— that of the 'breaking' of the Lord's Body on the cross—the phrase 'is broken for you' found its way into 1 Cor. xi. 24 and 'broken in pieces' into the reading of D* at this point. We have indeed to remember that in the earliest years of the church

---

[1] *The Apostolic Tradition of Hippolytus*, p. 95, in a note on xxiii. 14.
[2] *The Shape of the Liturgy*, pp. 132-133.

liturgical practice existed without direct warrant from those scriptures which were in fact at first the deposit rather than the causes of that practice, although they swiftly became authorities once they had been written. In the case of eucharistic procedure St. Paul refers to a tradition which he himself received, and when writing to the Corinthians about it, significantly says that it is 'from the Lord' (1 Cor. xi. 23).

To go further and conjecture what liturgical usage for which we have any evidence might give the clause we are considering the authority of eucharistic practice may seem hazardous and even to invite ridicule; but the words suggest the theology which lies behind the *epiklesis*, and at the same time behind baptism into the name of the Lord. Once more, Chase[1] has collected together much valuable material. In the previous clause of the prayer (Luke xi. 2) D reads ἁγιασθήτω ὄνομά σου ἐφ' ἡμᾶς.[2] The clue to interpreting this apparently obscure phrase (a task necessary without claiming that it is the authentic reading) lies in, e.g., Jer. vii. 12 and Deut. xii. 11; xiv. 23; xvi. 2, 6, 11;[3] in these last the Hebrew 'to cause my name to dwell there' is represented in the LXX by 'for my name to be invoked there'. Clearly the understanding is that the invocation of the name is a calling to one of God himself, but this is concealed for reasons of reverence. Chase argues that the 'upon us' in this clause 'is connected with an adaptation of the Lord's Prayer for use at baptism', and quotes Acts xxii. 16; Jas. ii. 7; 2 Th. i. 12. It is therefore a possibility that the Lord's Prayer with the phrase 'May thy name be hallowed upon us' was used before baptism, being a petition that God's holy presence[4] might dwell in the catechumens; while without the words 'upon us' those who had just received their initiation[5] might very properly use the phrase in the form with which we are familiar, meaning, 'May we, in whom thy name dwells, be kept holy, and thus be worthy dwelling-places of thyself'.

It seems natural to interpret 'May thy Holy Spirit come upon us and cleanse us' similarly as adapting the prayer for use by

---

[1] *Op. cit.* p. 31. [2] 'May thy name be hallowed upon us.'
[3] See further Chase, p. 34.
[4] For the Holy Spirit as the presence of God see below.
[5] See above, on the *Ap. Trad.* p. 63.

catechumens immediately before baptism. Thus they would pray for the same experience vouchsafed to Gentiles described in Acts xv. 8-10, and it would be possible on this evidence to regard 'Thy kingdom come' as appropriate to Jewish, and 'May thy Holy Spirit come upon us and cleanse us' as appropriate to Gentile use of the prayer. On the other hand, Luke's conception of the Holy Spirit and his coming is not Hellenistic but Jewish, continuous with the Old Testament and a perfectly logical development of the ideas in a long Judaistic tradition. Thus the phrase may be described as an invocation (or *epiklesis*) if not technically one used in the liturgy for invocation of the Holy Spirit upon the eucharistic elements; but it must be confessed that evidence that the Lord's Prayer could have been used in the eucharist in such a way as to effect consecration, partly by means of an *epiklesis* contained in it, is disappointingly meagre: Pope Gregory the Great's Epistle to John of Syracuse (*Ep.* ix. 12) provides the only hint known to us that the Lord's Prayer was used by the apostles in consecrating. If we turn to early liturgies, we find that Dix is doubtful whether the *Apostolic Tradition* contained an *epiklesis* and indeed believed that '*outside Syria* the use of the Eucharistic *epiklesis* of the Spirit cannot anywhere be traced back further than *c.* A.D. 375. In Syria the earliest certain evidence goes back to *c.* A.D. 330, though there are some traces of the theology it embodies to be found in Syrian documents of the third century.'[1] Indeed, to try to find some connexion between the Lucan version of the Lord's Prayer and the *epiklesis* may seem little more than a vain expedient of one wishing to assert that the *epiklesis* was an essential part of every primitive eucharistic prayer, against those who regard it as a Greek invention of the fourth century.[2] But, as Dix implies, we can see the growth of the Jewish Thanksgiving, in which such prominence was given to the glorifying of God's name, to the petition which is a forerunner of the *epiklesis* in the Prayer of Oblation of Bishop Sarapion.

It is therefore worth while considering the evidence of the Liturgy of SS. Addai and Mari,[3] with its ancient Semitic

---

[1] *The Treatise on the Apostolic Tradition*, p. 79.
[2] See Dix, *The Shape of the Liturgy*, p. 182.
[3] Dix, *op. cit.* pp. 179 ff. and E. C. Ratcliff in *JTS*, xxx (1929), pp. 23 ff.

characteristics, in the search for affinities with the phrase under examination. Ratcliff would exclude the *epiklesis* as a later insertion to bring this liturgy more into line with Greek Syrian liturgies, but Dix argues strongly that it is primitive.[1] The form of the *epiklesis* here ('And may there come, O my Lord, Thy Holy Spirit and rest upon this oblation of Thy servants, and bless and hallow it that it be to us, O my Lord, for the pardon of offences', etc.)[2] may not appear to illumine the phrase 'May Thy Holy Spirit come upon us and cleanse us' in the Lord's Prayer; but Dix aptly quotes G. F. Moore to show that in Jewish literature the Holy Spirit signifies the presence of God. Similar indeed is the doctrine of the Holy Spirit implied by Luke, who, for example, makes Gabriel say to Mary, 'Holy Spirit shall come upon thee, and the power of the Highest shall overshadow thee' (i. 35). If, as Dix argues, in the Liturgy of SS. Addai and Mari the effective and powerful presence of the Son is signified by 'Thy Holy Spirit', in Luke it is rather the presence of 'The Lord' in the Old Testament sense, and the petition for the Holy Spirit in the Lord's Prayer is for the presence of God.

Evidence from the New Testament may be added: St. Paul regards an offering in a metaphor probably taken from the eucharist as 'sanctified by Holy Spirit',[3] while the author of the Epistle to the Hebrews says that the blood of Christ 'who through the eternal[4] spirit offered himself blameless to God, shall *cleanse* our consciences'. The passage introduces the Spirit into the conception of cleansing by the blood of Christ found also at 1 John i. 7 and 1 Pet. i. 15 ff.; this mystical cleansing by his blood can hardly fail to have a eucharistic reference: Christians are cleansed by Christ's blood because they are baptized into his death and Resurrection, and their partaking of the eucharist is a constant renewal and reminder of the mystery: it is the Holy Spirit who makes the feast more than a reminder and sacramentally effective.

There is, then, some evidence that as early as New Testament

---

[1] *Op. cit.* pp. 182-183.

[2] Dix, *op. cit.* p. 179. Srawley, *Early History of the Liturgy*, p. 118, believes that it may be right to retain the *epiklesis*, recalling as it does the form found in Hippolytus. [3] Rom. xv. 16.

[4] Heb. ix. 14. D* P vg and some Old Latin read 'holy', but this is no doubt unconscious assimilation to a familiar phrase.

times Christians thought of the eucharist as made effective for them by the presence of the Holy Spirit, that is, of God the Holy Spirit; and we may add that 1 Cor. xvi. 22 and *Didache*, x. 6, suggest that worshippers too must be holy as they approach the eucharist.

The argument is inconclusive but makes it a possibility that the Lord's Prayer in the text of Gregory at Luke xi. 2 was used at baptism and the eucharist. Since some of the evidence is culled from the New Testament, we have further at least the bare possibility that the origin of such an invocation of the Holy Spirit, even of the Lord's Prayer in the form containing such a clause, lay in the practice of the Lord himself. In this connexion the words in xi. 1 are significant: 'Lord, teach us to pray, as John also taught his disciples.'

The form of the request, against the background of the custom by which rabbis habitually taught a prayer to their immediate followers, makes evident that the disciple is here represented as asking to be taught a prayer such as he, no doubt previously a disciple of John the Baptist,[1] had been taught by his former master. To some these considerations will suggest the authenticity of the occasion and the prayer which follows; others will argue that the occasion has been contrived by Luke for the express purpose of authenticating a form of prayer for which he wished to claim dominical authority. In either case Luke is emphasizing his own belief that the form which he gives is authentic, perhaps even esoterically imparted.

One further speculation may not be out of place: in all the references in the synoptics to the Feeding of the Five Thousand (Mark vi. 30-44; Luke ix. 10-17; Matt. xiv. 13-21) the Lord 'took the five loaves and the two fish and looked up into heaven and blessed and broke the loaves . . .'; and at the Feeding of the Four Thousand (Mark viii. 1-10, Matt. xv. 32-39) he 'took the seven loaves (and fish—Matt.) and gave thanks and broke . . .'. It may be that the words with which the Lord 'blessed' or 'gave thanks' are not given because they would be known by all Jews, and that Gentile readers would readily understand that some

---

[1] See John i. 35 ff. for the tradition that Peter and Andrew had been John's followers. For the possibility that this was true also of Jesus himself see Goguel, *Jean-Baptiste*, ch. vii.

customary formula was used; but early Christian practice allowed extempore eucharistic prayer (cf. 1 Cor. xiv. 16-17 and especially *Didache*, x. 7) and the interpretation that these meals were eucharistic may be supported by the phrase 'and looked up into heaven' recurring in the *anaphorae* of St. Mark, St. James, and other liturgies. Thus so early a witness to the Greek version of the Liturgy of St. Mark as a sixth-century papyrus[1] gives the *anaphora* in which the words of institution are introduced by a typical *berakah* and the prayer is specifically made to the Father to whom Jesus looked and 'after giving thanks and blessing and sanctifying and breaking he gave. . . .'[2] The phrase in the Lord's Prayer, 'Our bread for the morrow give us each day', is convincing proof that the Lord joined to petitions for the honour of God petitions concerning the sustenance of human life, entirely in the Jewish tradition. The meal shared with the five thousand, therefore, may have given occasion for a 'giving of thanks' or 'blessing' in a form peculiar to the Lord. If this form included prayer for the hallowing of God's name and the coming of the Holy Spirit (i.e. God's presence) upon the company, it would certainly be appropriate to the occasion.

If, then, the text of Gregory at Luke xi. 2 is authentic, while the explanation may be that this is a form of the prayer which Luke learnt from contemporary liturgy, such an explanation is itself consistent with the view that this form may be derived from the Lord himself.

xxii. THE DAYS OF THE SON OF MAN

(xvii. 22)

Luke xvii. 22, 'He said to the disciples, "The days will come when you will long to see one of the days of the Son of Man and you will not see one . . ."', is a verse for which no satisfactory explanation has been given. Dodd, in a footnote on p. 83 of *The Parables of the Kingdom*, remarks that 'The Day of the Son of Man' corresponds to the Old Testament expression,

[1] No. 465 in the *Catalogue of Greek and Latin Papyri*, John Rylands Library, Manchester University.

[2] Cf. the Liturgy of St. James, the text (from *De Sacramentis*, Lib. IV) known to Ambrose, and the pre-Gregorian text, e.g. as given in E. Bishop, *Liturgica Historica*, p. 85.

'The Day of Jehovah', and that the term underlying Luke xvii. 24 and 26, as well as Matthew's 'the *parousia* of the Son of Man', is 'The Day of the Son of Man'; but it must be admitted that the actual phrase does not appear in the gospels. Manson (*The Sayings of Jesus*, p. 142) also compares 'the day of the Son of Man' with 'the day of the Lord' in the Old Testament, and thinks that 'Strictly speaking, therefore, it is not proper to speak of "the days of the Son of Man"'. He cites with approval the suggestion by Torrey, *The Four Gospels*, p. 312: 'The present text depends on a misunderstanding of the Aramaic adverb *lachda* meaning "very much" as the numeral "one" with the sign of the accusative. The true meaning is then "you will greatly desire to see the day of the Son of Man".'

This kind of explanation not only assumes a mistake on the part of Luke in translating Aramaic, but a mistake of the kind which allowed him to use a phrase which is, 'strictly speaking, not proper', as though Luke had no eschatology of his own in which such a phrase might mean something of importance. But Luke has a coherent eschatology, and the purpose of this note is to suggest that the true interpretation is that Luke contemplated not one but a number of appearances of the Lord. The passage which follows warns first against being deceived by apparent signs, for in his day the Son of Man will shine like lightning (xvii. 24). This 'lightning when it lightens' is reminiscent of the description which Luke gives of the transfigured Lord (ix. 29) in place of the Marcan phrases (Mark ix. 3), Luke there writing 'his clothing became flashing (or lightning) white'. It is the glory which shone round the shepherds at the Nativity (ii. 9), which was also to blind Paul on the road to Damascus (Acts ix. 3, xxii. 11, xxvi. 13). It is true that Luke in this verse, xvii. 24, writes the singular, according to the RV ('in his day'), but in verse 26 he writes '... and as it was in the days of Noah, so will it be in the days of the Son of Man', and it is to be noted that the omission of ἐν τῇ ἡμέρᾳ αὐτοῦ[1] in verse 24 by so many authorities as B D e a b c i and the Sahidic is not necessarily due to homoioteleuton after ἀνθρώπου. The omission makes excellent sense and it may be that these authorities preserve the original, so easily assimilated

[1] 'in his day.'

to later interpretations, Matthew writing in his parallel passage (xxiv. 37) '. . . so will be the parousia of the Son of Man', as also at xxiv. 27 and 39. These later interpretations may indeed be nearer the intention of the original which Luke is using here (it is a 'Q' passage), but there is reason to believe that Luke has stamped his own form of eschatology on material itself envisaging only one day of the Son of Man, and that this was the original implication of xvii. 30-37; but just as at xxi. 20 he turns the cryptic Mark xiii. 14 into a prophecy of the siege of Jerusalem, so in xvii. 30 he turns 'so will it be on the day of the Son of Man' into 'so will it be on the day when the Son of Man is revealed', apparently referring to the same event as is prophesied at xxi. 27, which in Luke presages the deliverance of God's people after the destruction of Jerusalem by the Gentiles, not the final Judgment, as is clear from his pointed omission of Mark xiii. 27 and his substitution of xxi. 28, which is peculiar to Luke; it is this same destruction of Jerusalem which Luke makes xvii. 30-37 describe, giving to verse 37 a significance which the parallel Matt. xxiv. 28 (appearing in the context of Mark xiii) is far from possessing.

What other days are 'Days of the Son of Man'? For Luke, certainly the Transfiguration: it is one of the days of the Son of Man such as the disciples in the grim days ahead will long to see. Another is prophesied as the presage of the kingdom. Another of course is the final appearance; and, in addition to these, both Stephen and Paul experienced such a day, and Luke xvii. 22 shows that Luke thinks of Jesus as foreseeing these in the time of his earthly ministry. Can we add even more to these instances? If not without hesitation, yet there remains an obvious passage which illustrates several of the points which we have mentioned. This is Acts i. 11. The condensed style would preclude any description of glory in verse 3, but it is probably right to regard the 'forty days' as in any case falling outside the category of an appearance in glory, because Christ has not yet been exalted.

If not yet exalted, Jesus at this time speaks of matters connected with the kingdom of God, and after promising the disciples that they will receive power to be his witnesses, 'a cloud received him out of their sight', surely the same cloud which enshrined his glory at the Transfiguration. There is another link between the Transfiguration and the Ascension, connecting both with the Resurrection: this link is provided by the 'two men' 'in shining clothes' (xxiv. 4) where the word translated 'shining' is literally 'flashing' or 'lightning'. Before this, at the Transfiguration, 'two men were talking to him, who were Moses and Elijah' (ix. 30). This rather odd way of identifying the two figures is explained when we recognize that Luke is claiming that the source of the women's information and fright at the tomb was not a young man (Mark xvi. 5) nor an angel (Matt. xxviii. 2 ff.) but Moses and Elijah, linked at all their occurrences by his καὶ ἰδοὺ δύο ἄνδρες[1] (or ἄνδρες δύο) (ix. 30, xxiv. 4, Acts i. 10), but identified only at Luke ix. 30, where indeed the Marcan tradition made it obligatory. This identification is the more natural in that Moses and Elijah speak at the Transfiguration of the exodus which Jesus was to fulfil at Jerusalem: they therefore themselves reappear at the two triumphant and decisive stages of that exodus.

The Transfiguration is unique in being a day of the Son of Man occurring before he has entered into his glory, and it is significant that Luke links it so closely with a prophecy of the suffering by which he will enter into it. The Resurrection and Ascension may be regarded as days of the entering into glory, while Peter at Acts iii. 19-21 looks forward to days when the words of the 'two men' at the Ascension will be fulfilled, but in the meantime heaven must receive the Lord until the times of the restoration of all, the noun 'restoration' being derived from the verb for 'restore' in the apostles' question in Acts i. 6, and in the meantime repentance will bring 'seasons of refreshment from the presence of the Lord'. This restoration of all cannot refer to the *parousia*: the phrase would hardly suit a scene imagined to be one of judgment of all and the destruction of some; Peter is addressing the λαός (iii. 12) and insists that to them first the offer of Blessing—consequent on turning from their wickedness—is made (iii. 25-26). He is looking forward to the restoration of Israel, to the same event about which, according to Luke, the Lord prophesies in Luke xxi. 27. If, then, Luke intended by 'Days of the Son of Man' a number of glorious

[1] 'and see!—Two men.'

71

days, we can at least show that both the gospel and Acts give us a list of them—the Transfiguration, the Resurrection and Ascension taken together, the appearances to Stephen and Paul, the restoration of Jerusalem and Israel, and the final consummation.

xxiii. THE INSTITUTION OF THE EUCHARIST: DEFENCE AND
INTERPRETATION OF THE SHORTER TEXT

(xxii. 17-20)

This passage has been much discussed, presenting as it does a textual problem combined with a matter of great doctrinal interest.

The longer text as found in the Textus Receptus is read by the great majority of Greek MSS. and of the versions, with only minor differences; but the order of events narrated was later felt to be strange, especially by the Syriac Church; the Peshitta therefore omits verses 17-18, but in the following verses agrees with the majority of witnesses. When we turn to the earlier history of the text we find that the shorter version is given by D a ff² i l which omit 19b-20. Kilpatrick has shown that in C too a shorter text has been supplemented from the vg in 19b-20; and writes 'we may conclude that, in addition to the MSS which now omit xxii. 19b-20, probably an archetype of C and possibly of r² had the same omission. This conclusion agrees with the opinion that the words were absent from the earlier forms of the Old Latin and were first added in the fourth century.'[1]

The Curetonian Syriac has the shorter text in a different order, verses 19, 17, 18, 21 (omitting 'given for you' in verse 19).

The Sinaitic Syriac follows this order but, while it omits verse 20, has verse 19 intact. The only other significant differences in this authority are the addition of 'after supper' at the beginning of verse 17 and of 'this is my blood, the new covenant' at its end.

The order in the Old Syriac may easily be explained by the desire to bring the Bread and the Cup into the traditional order as found in Mark and 1 Cor. xi. 23-25; on this interpretation

---

[1] *JTS*, xlvii (1946), pp. 49 ff.

the Old Syriac accommodates the shorter text to the tradition of events in the longer text.

There are also literary signs that 19b-20 are an addition to the text: 'And the cup in the same way after supper' follows in 1 Cor. xi. 25 quite naturally after the verb 'took' in verse 23, but in our passage the main verb in verse 19 (which alone can provide a verb to govern 'cup') is 'broke and gave'. We cannot press the argument that εἰς τὴν ἐμὴν ἀνάμνησιν is a scribal addition here merely because the phrase is rare and paralleled at 1 Cor. xi. 24 f.,[1] but to the points already made may be added that Luke has at Acts x. 4 an alternative phrase in εἰς μνημόσυνον (cf. Mark xiv. 9, Matt. xxvi. 13) and the use of ἐμήν as an attributive adjective is not Lucan.[2] Kilpatrick accepts the view of W. L. Knox[3] that 'while the earliest narrative in the New Testament, 1 Cor. xi. 23, describes the Last Supper in a way which makes it clear that the eucharist is a commemoration of that incident and implies quite clearly the repetition of the words of institution, the Marcan narrative implies nothing of the kind except to the initiated reader, while the Fourth Gospel has dissociated the eucharist from the Last Supper completely'. He further suggests that on the basis of this interpretation we can omit Luke xxii. 19b-20 and put the Lucan account 'midway between Mark and John'. This is certainly consistent with Luke's position on several other theological matters.

In order to preserve the secret core of the rite from the uninitiated, Luke's account ended with deliberate abruptness at τὸ σῶμά μου (19a), 'a cue which the faithful would know how to supplement'.

The shorter text is therefore to be taken as authentic, even against the weight of manuscript evidence, with the aid of the explanation that it was subsequently filled out by a later copyist, who preferred a full account of the Last Supper to the maintenance of secrecy about the actual Christian rite, no doubt when this secrecy was no longer urgent.

It is remarkable that Jeremias, in arguing for the longer text,

[1] Although the argument of Benoit (*JTS*, xlix, No. 195-6, pp. 145 ff.) that *Luke* may have borrowed the phrase from 1 Cor. is precarious, since Luke's knowledge of the Pauline epistles is very doubtful.

[2] Kilpatrick, *op. cit.*

[3] In *Some Hellenistic Elements in Primitive Christianity* (1944).

believing that at the beginning of the second century verses 19b-20 were erased in the interests of secrecy, yet regards the language of these verses as non-Lucan, Luke having presented here 'not a literary composition from Mark and Paul' but 'a "third variation" of the liturgical formula of the Lord's Supper'.[1]

The case for the genuineness of the shorter text need not rest only upon the view that the account of the institution of the eucharist was cut deliberately short. If Luke decided to present the story in this way, he perhaps had also more positive reasons than the desire to preserve the arcanum of the rite: the action of eating bread was familiar, but the words with which Luke stops here are momentous. The bread which the Lord identifies with his Body was customarily given various symbolic interpretations: it was the bread of affliction in Egypt (Ex. i. 14) and of escape from the destruction of the firstborn (Ex. xii. 27), of the haste to escape from bondage (Ex. xii. 39); Philo adds the idea that the unleavened bread stands for imperfect nature and awakens in men hope for the gifts of nature. Again, as bread of affliction it shows that achievement is only through trouble and self-sacrifice. Thus Jesus may be interpreted as meaning, 'This is the bread of my affliction whereby you are brought out of bondage'.

Luke gives the words even more meaning by proceeding at once to the prophecy of the betrayal: as the disciples partake of the bread which the Lord has blessed and immediately after hearing the significant words, 'This is my Body', they hear him add, 'But behold the hand of him who is delivering me up'—for sacrifice—'is with me on the table'.

Again, if Luke was preserving the secrecy of the rite, his purpose was clearly remote from that which modern readers might anachronistically ascribe to him, that is, to give an account of the institution of the eucharist. He is governed rather by the idea of the kingdom and its association with the supper—both the banquet to come and the present supper which foreshadows it: he links the actions and sayings in the upper room with the kingdom which he expects. It is not a covenant which the Lord inaugurates, but a kingdom. No doubt all three synoptics had

[1] *Die Abendmahlsworte Jesu*, p. 78.

in mind Ex. xxiv. 8 ('the blood of the covenant which the Lord made') and Jer. xxxi. 31 ff., in which phrases linking closely 'covenant' (διαθήκη) and its verb (διατίθεσθαι) occur and recur (cf. Acts iii. 25). But while Mark and Matthew link the noun with the outpouring of the blood, Luke's shorter text links the verb with the kingdom: 'and I assign to you as my father assigned to me a kingdom' (verse 29).

We can then interpret the shorter text with perfect loyalty to Luke's main themes; and the subsequent appearance of the longer text is readily explicable by the desire to harmonize the passage with tradition.[1]

[1] Kilpatrick (*op. cit.* p. 53) suggests the possible history of the text.

NOTE ON THE TRANSLATION

THE translation follows for the most part the text printed in Huck's *Synopsis of the First Three Gospels*; where the reading accepted is that of Nestle's text or that of some ancient authority or authorities not adopted by either Huck or Nestle, the reading translated is noticed in the commentary.

The translation should be taken in close conjunction with the commentary: it is offered not as a rival to any of the modern translations now current, but as an attempt to represent the Greek in a manner faithful to the original which renders it more apt for comment rather than for reading aloud. In itself it will have little value for an English audience desiring to be left unaware of the difficulties of translating the original New Testament; it is for those who prefer to be shown those difficulties in order that they may be explained.

THE GOSPEL ACCORDING
TO ST. LUKE

i. 1-4. PROLOGUE

Since many have undertaken to compose a narrative of 1
the events fulfilled among us, according to the tradition of 2
those who from the first were eyewitnesses and ministers
of the word, I have decided that I too, having given minute 3
attention to everything from the beginning, would write
for you in order, noble Theophilus, so that you may know 4
the actual truth of the reports which you have heard.

undertaken. Since Luke includes himself (verse 3) the 1
Greek verb is not derogatory.

among us. I.e. among all who have been followers of the
Lord from the very beginning, from the baptism of John (Acts
i. 22).

eyewitnesses and ministers of the word. The narrative 2
set out to be according to the information handed on by eyewitnesses and ministers not necessarily of the Lord, but of the
word. Luke, who is now undertaking the same task as the
'many', will use information from those who have seen and
themselves assisted in the whole course and spread of the word.
Ministers retains the reference to a liturgical context. Cf. Luke
iv. 20, and the application of this title to Paul in Acts xxvi. 16.
The **word** means more to Luke than teaching. It is the spoken
word but it is able to cause and almost itself to be an event or
series of events. Cf. iv. 32, 36 with Mark i. 22, 27 and Luke
xxiv. 19; Acts viii. 4; xi. 1; xii. 24; xiii. 48; xix. 20, etc. This
sense is in accordance with the OT use of *dabar*, the word of
God, in, e.g., 1 Sam. ix. 27; 1 Kings xii. 22; Hos. i. 1; Jer. ii. 31,
etc. This appears to be the meaning of *logos* here, iv. 32, 36

showing that it may carry this full sense without the addition of 'of God'.

3 **Theophilus** cannot be identified, but there is no reason to doubt that the person to whom Luke addressed his work was as real as Lucretius' Memmius or Vergil's Maecenas.

4 **the actual truth.** Cadbury (*BC* ii. pp. 489-501) gives instances from papyri of the use of τὸ ἀσφαλές to mean 'the actual truth'. ἀσφάλεια no doubt bears the same meaning, and its position at the end of the sentence gives it emphasis. Luke sets out to give a true account of the matter behind the **reports** (λόγων in the plural not bearing a special sense here). Theophilus is then most probably an influential non-Christian.

have heard. For this rendering rather than 'in which you have been instructed' cf. Acts xviii. 25; xxi. 21; xxi. 24.

i. 5-25. THE PROMISE OF THE BIRTH OF JOHN THE BAPTIST

5 There was in the days of Herod king of Judaea a certain priest named Zacharias of the course of Abia, and he had a wife of the daughters of Aaron, and her name was 6 Elizabeth. They were both righteous before God, walking in all the commandments and ordinances of the Lord 7 blamelessly. And they had no child, because Elizabeth 8 was barren, and both were advanced in age. Now it happened that in the execution of his priestly office before 9 God in the turn of his course it fell to him according to the custom of the priestly office to enter into the Temple 10 of the Lord to burn incense, and the crowd of people were praying outside at the time of the incense-offering. And 11 an angel of the Lord appeared to him standing at the 12 right side of the altar of incense-offering. And Zacharias 13 was disturbed at seeing him, and fear fell upon him. And the angel said to him, 'Fear not, Zacharias, for your petition has been heard, and your wife Elizabeth will bear 14 you a son, and you shall call his name John; and you shall have joy and gladness, and many shall rejoice at his birth.

For he shall be great before the Lord, and wine and strong 15
drink he shall not drink, and he shall be filled with the
Holy Spirit even from his mother's womb, and he shall 16
turn many of the sons of Israel to the Lord their God; and 17
he will go before him in the spirit and power of Elijah,
to turn the hearts of fathers to the children and the disobedient by the wisdom of the righteous, to make ready
for the Lord a people prepared.' And Zacharias said to the 18
angel, 'In what way shall I know this? For I am an old
man and my wife is advanced in her age.' And in answer 19
the angel said to him: 'I am Gabriel, who stands before
God, and I was sent to speak to you, and to give you these
good tidings; and behold you will be silent and unable to 20
speak until the day when these things happen, because
you did not believe my words, which will be fulfilled in
their season.'

And the people were waiting for Zacharias, and were 21
surprised at his being so long in the temple; and when he 22
went out he was unable to speak to them, and they understood that he had seen a vision in the temple. He kept
nodding to them and remained dumb. And it happened 23
that when the days of his service were completed, he
went away to his own home. After these days Elizabeth 24
his wife conceived, and hid herself five months, saying,
'Thus has the Lord dealt with me in the days when he 25
looked upon my disgrace among men to take it away.'

in the days of Herod. Luke shows his art in this opening of 5
the main narrative, changing his style from classical to septuagintal Greek, which he uses for solemn passages. There is a
general likeness to the opening of the book of Ruth.

Herod the Great reigned over Palestine from 37 to 4 B.C.

Judaea has here this wider sense as at iv. 44; vi. 17; vii. 17;
xxiii. 5; Acts x. 37. Herod the Great is not mentioned again in
the gospel.

Zacharias. The name occurs several times among Levites;
cf. 1 Ch. ix. 21; xv. 18, 20, 24; xxiv. 25; xxvi. 2.

course. ἐφημερία, the word used by the LXX at 1 Ch. xxiii.
6. The LXX also uses διαίρεσις (e.g. 1 Ch. xxiv. 1) and Moffatt

translates 'division'. A 'course' or 'division' was on duty for more than one day. Cf. verse 23.

Abia or Abijah. Cf. 1 Ch. xxiv. 10.

6   **walking ... blamelessly.** The whole verse is septuagintal in style, cf., e.g., 1 Sam. viii. 3, 5; 1 Kings iii. 14; Dan. ix. 10 (Theodotion's version).

7   **they had no child.** Cf. Gen. xi. 30 and 1 Sam. i. 2. SB (ii. 71) quote R. Levi (*c.* A.D. 300) to the effect that everywhere in the Scripture where it says 'she had not' it was afterwards given her. This is true of Sarah and Hannah (Gen. xxi. 1 and 1 Sam. ii. 21). Jeremiah applies the thought to Zion, saying that no one cares for her, and prophesies her restoration and that her children shall be many (Jer. xxx. 17-20). Cf. Is. liv. 1; lix. 20.

9   **to burn incense.** A description of morning worship is given in Ecclus. l. 11 ff., in which the musicians and people are all mentioned in their due order. For musicians see also 1 Ch. xv. 16.

10   **the crowd of people.** Cf. Ecclus. l. 17.

11   **an angel.** See special note on angels, p. 43.

13   **John.** On the name and on John the Baptist in general (i. 15, 17, 24, 76, 80; iii. 16; vii. 18) see special note, p. 41.

14   **gladness.** The noun occurs elsewhere in the NT only at verse 44 and Acts ii. 46, Heb. i. 9 (a quotation from the LXX) and Jude 24. Luke uses the verb at verse 47 and x. 21. (Cf. Acts ii. 26, xvi. 34.) The contexts in Lucan writings suggest a gladness at divine events.

15   **strong drink.** See special note, p. 41.

17   **the spirit and power of Elijah.** Here and in verse 76 Luke associates John the Baptist with Elijah in contrast to his usual treatment. See special note, p. 41.

Luke is drawing upon Mal. iv. 5-6 (English version—the Hebrew is at Mal. iii. 23-24 and the LXX at iv. 4-5). For a similar saying see Ecclus. xlviii. 10. The passage in Ecclus. and the LXX of Mal. iv. 5 give a form of the saying apparently meaning that the hearts of fathers shall become childlike. Cf. Mark x. 13-15 (Matt. xix. 13-15; Luke xviii. 15-17); Matt. xviii. 3, 10; 1 Cor. iv. 15. If this is the meaning, much the same sense is given by the parallel clause, **and the disobedient by the wisdom of the righteous.**

to make ready for the Lord ... Cf. verse 76; and iii. 4 and parallels, where Is. xl. 3 is quoted, and the Q passage vii. 27 (cf. Matt. xi. 10).

Gabriel. See special note, p. 43.   19

good tidings. The noun *euangelion* does not occur in the Lucan writings but Luke shares with Paul the great majority of the occurrences in the NT of the verb εὐαγγελίζεσθαι. In the LXX it is specially connected with good tidings (2 Sam. i. 20; 1 Ch. x. 9; Is. xl. 9; lii. 7; lx. 6; lxi. 1), often with tidings of deliverance (e.g. Is. xl. 9). Luke quotes Is. lxi. 1 at iv. 18, the only example of his use of the verb with the dative alone, without any direct object. His general use of the verb is pliant and expressive, sometimes the object being persons who receive the good tidings, sometimes the subject-matter of the good tidings (e.g. the kingdom, Jesus, peace, the Lord, etc.). There are only two absolute uses of the verb, that is, without direct or indirect object, viz. Luke ix. 6 and Acts xiv. 7.

in their season. The 'fulfilling' or 'completing' of days and   20 times is a favourite theme with Luke; e.g. in verse 23 below Zacharias fulfils or completes his days of service (Greek *leitourgiae*; cf. the English 'liturgy'); and the noun 'days' occurs three times in the short space of verses 23-25. Cf. i. 57; ii. 6, 21, 22; iv. 21; ix. 51; xii. 56; xix. 44; xxi. 24; xxii. 53; Acts i. 3, 6, 7; iii. 20, 21; vii. 17, 45; xvii. 26, 30.

hid. See special note, p. 42.   24

thus has the Lord dealt with me. A septuagintal phrase. 25 Cf. Gen. xxxix. 19.

when he looked upon. A variant on the usual Lucan word for the divine solicitude, which is ἐπισκέπτεσθαι, a septuagintal rendering of the Hebrew *pāqad*. To 'look upon' means to 'take care for'. Cf., e.g., Ex. iv. 31 and Luke i. 68, 78; vii. 16; Acts xv. 14. For the whole phrase cf. Gen. xxx. 23.

i. 26-38. THE ANNUNCIATION

Now in the sixth month the angel Gabriel was sent from 26 **God to a city of Galilee whose name is Nazareth, to a** 27 **virgin betrothed to a man whose name was Joseph, of the**

house of David; and the name of the virgin was Mary.
28 And he entered her room and said, 'Rejoice, highly fav-
29 oured! The Lord is with thee.' But she was disturbed at
this saying, and began to ponder what this greeting might
30 be. And the angel said to her, 'Fear not, Mary; for you
31 have found favour with God. And behold, you shall conceive in your womb and shall bear a son, and shall call
32 his name Jesus. He shall be great and shall be called the
son of the Most High, and the Lord God shall give to him
33 the throne of David his father, and he shall reign over the
house of Jacob for all the ages, and of his kingdom there
34 shall be no end.' And Mary said to the angel: 'How shall
this be, since I have no husband?' And in answer the
35 angel said to her: 'The Holy Spirit shall come upon you
and the power of the Most High shall overshadow you;
wherefore that which is born shall be called holy, son of
36 God. And look, your kinswoman, Elizabeth, she too has
conceived a son in her old age, and this is the sixth month
37 with her who is called barren; for with God nothing shall
38 be impossible.' And Mary said, 'Behold the handmaid of
the Lord! May it be for me according to your word.' And
the angel departed from her.

On the whole passage i. 26-ii. 51 see the special note on the
Infancy Narratives, p. 20. Some fuller details, mainly linguistic,
are noticed in the commentary.

28   **Rejoice.** This is probably correct rather than to render χαῖρε
by some word of greeting; for the only other uses by Luke of
the verb where the sense is that of a greeting are in letters
(Acts xv. 23; xxiii. 26). The LXX background is to be found at
Zech. ix. 9, the kingship of Jesus being a theme of which Luke
never loses sight. Cf. the rejoicing of the disciples, xix. 37, where
Luke alone uses this verb.

highly favoured. It is impossible to preserve in translation
the assonance of the Greek, which must surely be intentional,
and is typical of late Judaistic writing. The verb χαριτόω is rare
and a Semitic equivalent is hard to find. In the NT it occurs
only at Eph. i. 6 and in the rest of scripture only at Ecclus.
xviii. 17, where the Hebrew original is not preserved.

you shall conceive. For the inspiration of this passage there 31
is no need to look further than Is. vii. 14 where the LXX reads
in all variants a future tense. It may well be that from the
παρθένος of the LXX at Is. vii. 14 the story of Mary's virginal
conception arose. That passages of Isaiah are in the background
is strongly suggested by the reminiscence of Is. ix. 6 f. in
verses 32-33.

Jesus. For Luke's silence on the etymology of the name cf.
ii. 21 and contrast Matt. i. 21. But see note on i. 47 below.

Son of the Most High. A title of the Davidic Messiah. Cf. 32
the promise that he shall receive **the throne of David his
father** and for the association of a scion of the Davidic dynasty
with sonship of God, cf. 2 Sam. vii. 14; Ps. lxxxix. 26-27; Is. ix.
6-7 (all post-exilic). The other passage in the OT in which the
'son of God' is the anointed king is Ps. ii. 7 (cf. Luke iii. 22).

he shall reign over the house of Jacob. The verse recalls 33
Mic. iv. 7, another prophecy of hope in time of affliction. 'The
house of Jacob' is a common phrase in the OT and occurs along
with 'house of Israel' in Micah. The patriotic strain is once
more apparent.

since I have no husband. See special note, p. 20.   34

shall come upon you. The Greek verb is used eight times 35
by Luke out of the total ten in the NT. The context often suggests coming with power or even violence (e.g. Luke xi. 22).

overshadow. All three synoptic gospels use the word of the
cloud at the Transfiguration (Mark ix. 7; Luke ix. 34; Matt.
xvii. 5). It is found elsewhere only at Acts v. 15. It is thus always
used of the divine power. The Greek word represents a rare
Hebrew verb, but one common in Aramaic: in the Targum it is
used of the cloud of the Lord and of the Lord overshadowing
to give protection. Daube argues for a connection between 'overshadow' and 'spread one's wing over a person' where the latter
is a refined phrase for sexual intercourse as in Ruth iii. 9. The
other OT passage suggesting the same meaning is Ezek. xvi. 8.

holy, son of God. The Greek shows that the two predicates
are to be kept separate. They are titles of the Lord to be interpreted according to the Semitic background manifest throughout the passage. The epithet 'holy' is applied to Jesus rarely in
the NT, elsewhere only at Mark i. 24; Luke iv. 34; John vi. 69;

Acts iii. 14; iv. 27, 30; 1 John ii. 20; Rev. iii. 7; but the use is significant. It is as filled with the **holy** Spirit that Jesus is opposed by an **unclean** spirit in Mark i. 24 and Luke iv. 34, and there, as at John vi. 69, the title accorded him is 'the holy one of God'. 1 John ii. 20 and Rev. iii. 7 show further the connexion between the epithet 'holy' applied to the Lord and his divine origin. Thus also the title **son of God**, in this context which describes the manner of the birth of the Lord, recalls Is. vii. 14, where the promised son will be called Immanuel, i.e. 'God with us'; again, in Is. ix. 6 the son given, the child born, includes among his titles, 'Mighty God'.

37   **for with God nothing shall be impossible.** A reference to Gen. xviii. 14; Luke apparently recalls the general sense of the passage in Gen. xviii, where the promise is that the word will be fulfilled in due season, that is, after the usual time of gestation. This explains the reference to the time since Elizabeth's conception mentioned in the previous verse.

38   **Behold the handmaid of the Lord.** See special note, p. 20.

i. 39-80. MARY'S VISIT TO ELIZABETH AND THE BIRTH OF JOHN THE BAPTIST

39 **And Mary arose in those days and made her journey with**
40 **haste into the hill-country, to a city of Judah, and entered**
41 **into the house of Zacharias and greeted Elizabeth. And it happened that when Elizabeth heard Mary's greeting that the babe leapt in her womb, and Elizabeth was filled with**
42 **the Holy Spirit, and cried out with a loud voice and said,**
43 **'Blessed are you among women, and blessed is the fruit of your womb! And how has it happened to me that the**
44 **Mother of my Lord should come to me? For see—when the sound of your greeting reached my ears, the babe**
45 **leapt with joy in my womb; and blessed is she who has believed for there shall be fulfilment of the words spoken to her from the Lord.'**
46, 47   **And Mary said: 'My soul magnifies the Lord, and my**
48 **spirit has rejoiced in God my saviour; for he has looked**

upon the humility of his handmaid; for see—from hence-
forth all generations will bless me: for the mighty one 49
has done great things for me. And holy is his name, and 50
his compassion is for generations and generations on
them that fear him. He has wrought victory with his arm; 51
he has scattered the proud with their scheming heart. He
has brought down the mighty from their thrones, and 52
exalted the humble; the hungry he has filled with good 53
things and the rich he has sent away empty. He has rescued Israel his servant, mindful of his compassion, as he 54
spoke to our fathers, to Abraham and his seed, for ever.' 55
And Mary stayed about three months with her, and 56
returned to her home. Now the time was fulfilled for 57
Elizabeth to give birth, and she bore a son; and her neigh- 58
bours and kinsfolk heard that the Lord had showed great
compassion to her, and they rejoiced with her. And it 59
happened on the eighth day that they came to circumcise
the child, and they began to call him after his father's
name, Zacharias. And his mother in reply said, 'No! He 60
shall be called John.' And they said to her, 'There is no 61
one in your family called by that name'. And they nodded 62
to his father to ask what he wished him to be called. And
he asked for a tablet and wrote on it the words, 'John is 63
his name'. And they all marvelled. And his mouth and 64
tongue were immediately opened and spoke, blessing
God. And fear came upon all their neighbours, and these 65
events were reported throughout the hill-country of
Judaea, and all who heard considered in their hearts 66
saying, 'What then shall this child be? For indeed the
Lord is with him.'
And Zacharias his father was filled with the Holy Spirit 67
and prophesied saying: 'Blessed is the Lord God of Israel 68
for he has visited and redeemed his people; and has
raised a horn of salvation for us in the house of his servant 69
David, as he spoke through the mouth of his holy ones, 70
the prophets, from of old, salvation from our enemies and 71
from the hands of all that hate us, showing compassion 72
to our fathers, and remembering his holy covenant, the
oath which he swore to Abraham our father, to grant us 73

74 that, rescued from the hand of our enemies, we should
75 serve him without fear in holiness and righteousness
76 before him all our days. And you, child, will be called
   "Prophet of the Highest", for you will go before the Lord
77 to make ready his ways, to give knowledge of salvation
78 to his people by forgiveness of their sins, through the
   feelings of compassion of our God, whereby he who has
79 risen from on high shall look upon us, to appear to those
   sitting in darkness and in the shadow of death, to guide
   our feet into the way of peace.'
80   The child grew and became strong in spirit, and was in
   the deserts until the days of his showing to Israel.

39   **hill-country.** ἡ ὀρεινή is the name given in the lists of the
   toparchies by both Josephus and Pliny to the toparchy of Jerusalem (A. H. M. Jones, *Cities of the Eastern Roman Provinces*,
   p. 274).
       a city of Judah. The vagueness of the dwelling-place of
   Zacharias and Elizabeth (cf. verse 23) is in accordance with the
   style of Luke, who 'apologizes' for mentioning place-names
   though he frequently mentions them when he knows them.
41   **leapt.** The Greek word is used by Luke alone of NT writers
   (cf. verse 44 and vi. 23, and Gen. xxv. 22).
       filled with the Holy Spirit. See special note, p. 38.
42   **Blessed are you among women.** The poetical language
   (cf. Deut. xxviii. 3 ff.) and the balance of phrases suggest a
   fragment of liturgy. Cf. xi. 27.
43   **how has it happened.** The phrase, which is Semitic, means,
   how can I have been thought worthy of such an honour?
45   **she who has believed.** 'She' is Mary as the daughter of
   Zion, so that all who believe will enjoy the fulfilment of the
   Lord's promises. The thought is developed in this way at xi.
   27-28.
46   **Mary said.** For discussion of the variant reading Elizabeth
   for Mary, and of the position of the Magnificat in the narrative,
   see special note, pp. 20 f.
       The whole song recalls the Song of Hannah, 1 Sam. ii. 1-10,
   but cannot be compared to it in detail. Elsewhere in Luke's
   gospel quotation from the OT often occurs in material from

Mark or Q. Such quotations or those added by Luke himself are almost certainly from the LXX. (Cf. iii. 36; xx. 42, 43; xxi. 24; and quotations in the speeches in Acts, for which see *BC*, ii. 95-106.) In the majority of cases the passage follows the original closely, but in the Magnificat, as elsewhere in these early chapters, we meet reminiscences rather than quotations of the OT, and the literary affinity is with late Judaism rather than directly with the scriptures. See also on verses 48 and 55.

my soul . . . my spirit. A Hebrew idiom often writes 'my 47 soul (*nephesh*)' for 'I'. The English phrase 'my soul' is indeed misleading: the *nephesh* is an expression for the whole being, a living body, whose living principle is the *ruach*, breath or spirit.

has rejoiced. See on i. 14 and cf. Hab. iii. 18.

Saviour. The child to be born bears a name with this meaning, although Luke does not emphasize this. See on i. 31 above, ii. 11, and the special note on John the Baptist, p. 41.

has looked upon the humility of his handmaid. Cf. 48 1 Sam. i. 11. With the words **all generations** Luke may show independence of both Heb. and LXX of Gen. xxx. 13. See on verse 46 above and 55 below.

holy is his name. Cf. Ps. cxi. 9.   50

his compassion. Cf. Ps. ciii. 17.

he has wrought victory. Cf. Ps. lxxxix. 10.   51

scheming heart. Lit. 'in the intention of their heart'. διάνοια is normally used for the 'mind' (cf. x. 27) and is not derogatory in itself.

brought down the mighty. . . . Cf. Ecclus. x. 14; Ezek. 52 xxi. 26.

exalted the humble. That is, the nation of Israel. See on vi. 20.

hungry. Cf. Ps. cvii. 9; cxlvi. 7.   53

Israel his servant. The servant is here as perhaps nowhere 54 else in the NT explicitly applied to Israel. Cf. Is. xli. 8-9; xlii. 1; Ps. xc. 13, and see the discussion of the 'handmaid of the Lord' in the special note on the Infancy Narratives, p. 20.

Abraham . . . for ever. This verse is interesting as providing 55 some indication that Luke did not himself compose the Magnificat, but obtained it from a source: the name Abraham appears to come from Mic. vii. 20 where the thought is similar,. but the verse closes with a reference to 2 Sam. xxii. 51. See on verse 46.

There is indeed nothing to stamp the Magnificat as Christian in origin, and nothing in it especially appropriate to a birth.

56   That **Mary** stayed but a short time and then **returned to her own home** before the birth of Elizabeth's child has often been remarked as strange. Probably the oddness of this escaped Luke in his carrying out of the task of combining the narrative with the quite different source in chapter ii.

58   The construction of the Greek of **the Lord had showed great compassion on her** may be compared to the LXX, Gen. xix. 19; 1 Sam. xii. 24; Ps. xvii. 51. For the rejoicing party

59   cf. 2 Esd. ix. 45. For the giving of a **name** in connexion with circumcision cf. ii. 21. According to SB, ii. 107 there are no other passages which imply this until about the eighth century. Lagrange regards it as natural, on the ground that tribes which carry out circumcision later change the names of the child at the ceremony. Thus when circumcision was transferred to childhood naming would be similarly transferred.

62   **nodded.** Implying that Zacharias was also deaf, perhaps due to the unconscious assumption that a κωφός was deaf and dumb, though verse 20 says nothing of deafness.

63   **tablet.** No doubt, as Lagrange remarks, of wood covered with parchment.

64   **his mouth and tongue were ... opened** is a bold zeugma, more striking still in the Greek since the verb is in the singular. Variants witness to the surprise which it has caused, and Sahlin would explain by a Hebrew original, since if ἀνεῴχθη repre-

65   sents *niphchath*, the zeugma would not be so harsh. The **fear** which came upon them all is best understood by observing the uses of φόβος in Luke, showing how justifiably the words 'awe' and 'fear' may both be used. Cf., e.g., v. 26 and xxi. 26 for uses of the word with different senses for the modern mind. The second half of the verse emphasizes the claim that Luke has wide support for his narrative.

67   **And Zacharias was filled with the Holy Spirit.** See special note, p. 38.

68   For the opening phrases cf. Ps. xli. 13; cxi. 9.

visited. See on verse 25 above and cf. verse 78; vii. 16; and Acts xv. 14.

redeemed. Lit. 'made redemption for'. If the theory in the special note on the Infancy Narratives (pp. 20 ff.) is correct, that Anna was originally the singer of the Benedictus, we may note the link between redemption here and in ii. 38. Luke never forgets the theme of redemption, introducing it significantly into his version of the Little Apocalypse at xxi. 28.

a horn of salvation. From 2 Sam. xxii. 3 and Ps. xviii. 2, the 69 twin sources for this song. The expression is not found elsewhere. For salvation see on **saviour,** ii. 11.

as he spoke. The claim that the events of the gospel were 70 prophesied in the ancient scriptures reappears in other passages peculiar to Luke: in xxiv. 27 the risen Christ claims to have fulfilled all that was written in Moses and the prophets, in xxiv. 44 all in Moses and the prophets and the psalms. Cf. Acts iii. 18, 21; viii. 31-35. Here the emphasis is appropriately on the prophets, because Zacharias is now prophesying (verse 67). If the song was originally placed in the mouth of Anna (see p. 24), she would be regarded as similarly inspired.

salvation from our enemies. Cf. Ps. xviii. 17; cvi. 10; and 71 see on verse 74 below.

compassion to our fathers. Cf. Mic. vii. 20 and Pss. cv. 8; 72 cvi. 45. Further important passages for God's covenant promise are Gen. xvii. 7 and Lev. xxv. 42. See on next verse.

to Abraham. Cf. Gen. xvii. 7 and xxvi. 24. Again, Jer. xi. 5 73 refers to an oath sworn 'to your fathers'. Cf. Acts iii. 25.

from the hand of our enemies. Cf. verse 71. For a 74 prophecy of deliverance with similar language cf. Jer. xxx. 8. Expectation of restoration from the eighth-century prophets onwards necessarily included hope of deliverance from enemies and could hardly be distinguished from it in the popular mind.

Who are the enemies meant? The hymn clearly expresses the hopes of the nation and not a mere part of it, so that the enemies must be those of the nation. Thus, if the hymn dates from any time after 63 B.C. (at the latest), these enemies must be the Romans. We may compare xix. 43 and xxi. 20 where respectively the enemies and the besieging army are presumably

Roman; but at least in xix. 43 they are carrying out a punishment which Jerusalem has merited, and elsewhere in Luke-Acts the Romans are represented as far from hostile (vii. 1-10; xxiii. 4, 14 f., 20, 22; Acts xviii. 12-17; xix. 31; xxiii. 26-30; xxiv. 24-27; xxv. 25; xxvi. 31 f.; xxvii. 3, 43; xxviii. 7, 16, 30 f.).

Luke probably intends that by enemies we should understand any of whatever race who oppose the new movement; but it seems likely that the hymn arises from a patriotic source where the Messiah was still regarded as the champion of Israel against her political enemies.

76   **'Prophet of the Highest.'** See special note on the Infancy Narratives for the Messianic force of this title (p. 20).

to make ready his ways. Cf. Mal. iii. 1; Is. xl. 3. See on verse 17 above and the special note on John the Baptist, p. 41.

If the Benedictus is in its original setting, the **child** is of course John the Baptist; but we have seen (special note on the Infancy Narratives, p. 20) that the hymn is really a welcome to the Messiah, and that only here and in verse 17 is John associated by Luke with Elijah. If then, originally, the Messiah addressed in the hymn was thought of as coming to prepare a way for the Lord, we can understand the adjustments made by Luke in order to address the hymn to John the Baptist as coming to prepare a way for the Messiah.

77   **forgiveness of their sins.** The hymn takes on a profounder theology here. Jer. xxxi. 34 had promised that knowledge of God, given by a new covenant, not only new but of a new order, would be made possible by forgiveness of sins. For the connexion in Luke between the covenant and the kingdom cf. the language of xxii. 29 and see the special note on the shorter text of xxii. 17-20 (p. 72); and for the connexion between the kingdom and the forgiveness of sins cf. Acts v. 31.

78   **feelings of compassion.** Applied to God the phrase is very bold: the Greek word is rare in the LXX but is found in the Wisdom literature and other late Judaistic works.

Shall look upon is a literal translation of the verb translated 'visited' in verse 68. See note on verse 25.

He who has risen from on high. The Greek is difficult to
79 translate and interpret: the words **those sitting in darkness** (verse 79) suggest that Is. xlii. 7 may be in the author's mind,

but he is certainly influenced also by Is. ix. 1-2. This latter passage is quoted at Matt. iv. 16 in a version differing from the LXX and in some respects nearer to the Hebrew (see Dodd, *According to the Scriptures*, p. 80). Matthew uses the verb ἀνέτειλεν, which recalls Luke's ἀνατολή. Possibly both go back to the same version of Is. ix. 1-2, and the appearance of the Messiah is in both compared to the rising of the sun.

Another possible explanation is that ἀνατολή is the LXX word for the Heb. *tsemach*, 'sprout' or 'growth', usually translated 'branch', and used of a future ruler from the stock of Jesse in Jer. xxiii. 5; Zech. iii. 8; vi. 12, and thus becoming a title for the Messiah in later Judaism. The translation is designed to cover both interpretations.

way of peace. Cf. Is. lix. 8.

was in the deserts. It is strange that Luke, to whom this 80 verse may be confidently assigned, should leave the impression that the Baptist was in the wilderness from his earliest days, when his source has represented the relation and fellowship between the families of the Baptist and of Jesus as so close. There is no NT evidence for contact between John and Jesus in boyhood, or indeed before the Lord's baptism, in spite of testimony to the contrary by many masterpieces of art. (But see the special note on John the Baptist, p. 41.) The phrase may half indicate, half conceal that John was adopted by Essenes, according to the custom related by Josephus (*B.J.* ii. 8. 2, 120); or, whether or not the Qumran community is to be identified with Essenes, John may have been associated with them or some similar sect. The *Manual of Discipline* conceives of the purpose of such a community as 'to go to the wilderness to clear there the way of (the LORD)' and proceeds to quote Is. xl. 3 (*Man. Disc.* viii. 14). Cf. Luke iii. 2 ff.

Again, Josephus represents John's teaching on baptism as the crown of a life of ethical and ceremonial purity rather than as its initiation (*Ant.* xviii. 5. 2). This agrees with that of the *Manual* on baptism: the initiate undertakes to separate himself from 'all perverse men who walk in the way of wickedness'. Of these latter the *Manual* says, 'These may not enter into water to be permitted to touch the purity of the holy men for they will not be cleansed unless they have turned from their wickedness, for uncleanness clings to all transgressors of his word' (v. 13-14).

showing. Cf. 2 Macc. ii. 8, 'The Lord shall show these things and there shall be seen the glory of the Lord and the cloud'. John's showing is described by Luke at iii. 1-6; there verses 5-6 cite Is. xl. 3-5, Luke alone of the synoptics including Is. xl. 4-5, which ends with the words, 'and all flesh shall see the salvation of God'. If, then, we take John's 'showing' as his appearance, his being manifested, Luke intends this as the opening of the Christian revelation. The full 'glory of the Lord and the cloud' of 2 Macc. are seen first at the Transfiguration (ix. 28-36).

CHAPTER II

ii. 1-20. THE BIRTH OF JESUS

It happened in those days that a decree went out from 1
Caesar Augustus that a census should be made of the
whole empire. This was the first census, made while 2
Quirinius was governor of Syria; and all went to be 3
enrolled, each to his own city. Joseph too went up from 4
the city Nazareth into Judaea, to a city of David which is
called Bethlehem, because he was of the house and clan
of David, to be enrolled with Mary, who was betrothed to 5
him and who was with child. And it happened that while 6
they were there the days were fulfilled for her to give
birth, and she gave birth to her son, her firstborn, and she 7
swathed him and laid him in a feeding-trough, for there
was no room for them in the lodging-house.

And there were shepherds in that country, lying out in 8
the fields and keeping guard by night over their flocks;
and an angel of the Lord appeared to them and the glory 9
of the Lord shone round them, and they were struck with
great fear. And the angel said to them: 'Do not be afraid, 10
for see—I come to you with good tidings of great joy,
which will be so for all the people: there was born for you 11
to-day a saviour, who is Christ the Lord, in David's city.
And this will be your sign: you will find the babe swathed 12
and lying in a feeding-trough.' And suddenly there was 13
with the angel a multitude of the heavenly host praising
God and saying: 'Glory in the highest to God, and on 14
earth peace to men of his favour!'

And it happened that as soon as the angels had gone 15
away from them into heaven, the shepherds began to say
to one another: 'Come on, let us go as far as Bethlehem
and see the thing which has happened which the Lord
has made known to us!' And they went in haste and found 16

Mary and Joseph, and the babe lying in the feeding-
17 trough; and when they had seen him they made known
the saying which had been spoken to them about this
18 child; and all who heard were astonished at the things
19 said to them by the shepherds, but Mary kept all these
20 sayings close, pondering them in her heart. And the shepherds returned glorifying God for all the things which
they had heard and seen, which were as they had been
told.

1   **a census.** See special note, p. 44.
7   **her firstborn.** Cf. Matt. i. 25. That Mary subsequently bore
other children is clear from viii. 19 (cf. Mark vi. 3; Matt. xiii.
55), and the translation is a natural one; but the phrase may
also be taken as 'the firstborn'. In what is perhaps the oldest
decalogue in the OT the first demand is the sacrifice of the
firstborn (Ex. xxii. 29; cf. xxxiv. 19-20), and this is of course
illustrated in the story of Abraham and Isaac (Gen. xxii. 1-19).
The demand is omitted in Deut. xv. 19-23, but P requires the
'sanctification' of human firstborns (Ex. xiii. 2, 12; cf. Num.
xviii. 15, which expressly instructs that they are to be redeemed,
as Jesus was, Luke ii. 22-24). In the NT Jesus is *the* firstborn
(Rom. viii. 29; Col. i. 15, 18; Heb. i. 6—cf. xi. 28 and xii. 23;
—Rev. i. 5). He is offered to the Lord according to the Law's
injunctions, ii. 21 ff.

9   **the glory of the Lord.** The biblical *kabod* (glory) or later
Jewish *shekinah* (dwelling-place or presence), showing the presence of God like the cloud in the OT (cf. Ex. xiv. 19-24; xvi.
10; xxiv. 16; xxxiii. 9-10; xl. 34-35; Ezek. i. 28, and see the
Introduction on Luke's Theology, p. 34). Even in later passages
concerned with the coming of the Son of Man Luke never
speaks of clouds, but of a cloud, meaning the *shekinah*. (Cf.
Luke xxi. 27 with Mark xiii. 26 and Matt. xxiv. 30.)

shone round them. The shepherds were enveloped in the
shekinah and felt **great fear,** exactly like the disciples at the
Transfiguration (ix. 34; cf. Mark ix. 7; Matt. xvii. 5).

10   **all the people.** That is, of Israel.
11   **saviour.** In the OT God is saviour of his people from
material evils and from their enemies (e.g. Deut. xx. 4; Jos.

94

xxii. 22; Judg. iii. 9, etc.; 1 Sam. xiv. 23, 39; 2 Kings xiv. 27; Is. xxv. 9; xxxiii. 22, etc.). The name of Jesus connects him with God acting as saviour (i. 47) and the title was given him in the early tradition when the hope of deliverance from political domination and oppression was still part of the eschatological expectation (Phil. iii. 20; cf. 1 Th. i. 9-10). In Acts Luke calls Jesus saviour in a deeper religious sense, in the speech which he gives to 'Peter and the apostles' (v. 31) and in that given to Paul at Pisidian Antioch (xiii. 23). In Eph. v. 23 Christ is 'saviour of the body', i.e. of the church. Elsewhere in the NT often it is God who is saviour; but some other instances remain where the title is given to Jesus, viz. in the Johannine and later literature (the Pastoral Epistles and 2 Peter); there it derives from a christology in which the thought of the heavenly origin of Jesus Christ is prominent.

In the present passage the meaning is primitive and the emphasis is on the power of the Messiah to save Israel from her oppressors.

The word 'salvation' in the gospel similarly means a vindication of Israel (i. 69, 71, 77; xix. 9) but in Acts takes on a deeper meaning (iv. 12; xiii. 26; xvi. 17; xxvii. 34).

Christ the Lord. The conventional translation conceals the difficulty of conveying the meaning of Χριστὸς κύριος. A literal translation would be 'anointed Lord', taking Χριστός as an adjective; but in view of its well-established use as a title this is impossible. If the words are to be regarded as in apposition, the effect is none the less that of a double title, and had Luke wished to avoid this he could have written 'Christ and Lord' (cf. Acts ii. 36). It is hard to believe that the form of the phrase is due to corruption of so well-known a title as Χριστὸς κυρίου[1] (for similar phrases cf. ii. 26; ix. 20; xxiii. 35; Acts iv. 26, which quotes Ps. ii. 2), and it must therefore be regarded as intentional.

Χριστὸς κύριος occurs in the LXX of Lam. iv. 20 and in *Pss. Sol.* xvii. 36. In the former the original was *meschiach Yahweh*, the anointed of the Lord, and should have been rendered by Χριστὸς κυρίου. In the latter we have no Hebrew original but it can hardly have been other than that lying behind the LXX of Lam. iv. 20.

[1] I.e. 'Christ of the Lord'.

It seems that the phrase with the two nominatives in such close juxtaposition occurred in a Greek-speaking environment, on the lips of those who were scarcely conscious that κύριος stood for the sacred name Yahweh. Such an environment would make possible the LXX mistranslation of Lam. iv. 20, and from it Luke or his source has unthinkingly adopted the phrase; it is too much to say that it argues a real identification of the Messiah with Yahweh, but it is an illustration of the mental process which makes it possible for minds nurtured in monotheism to apply to a human personality scriptural passages which were originally addressed or referred to Yahweh.

13   **the heavenly host.** Cf. Dan. vii. 10. The shepherds are permitted to see for a few moments the hosts who do service to the Ancient of Days, and who accompany the Son of Man as judge and even act as judges themselves (xii. 8-9).

14   **Glory in the highest to God.** It is difficult to find any literary antecedent for this phrase, but a salient theme of the OT is the covenant by which God is rendered due service and worship, and Israel through God's mercy receives his peace. The enactment of the new covenant depends upon the coming of the king and his acceptance. Cf. i. 32-33; ii. 34, and especially xix. 38, where the crowds at Jesus' entry into Jerusalem welcome him as king and echo the angels' song of this passage.

peace. See Is. lii. 7 for an OT passage implying for late Judaism that the Messiah was to bring peace. Cf. Is. lvii. 19. For Luke's use of peace as a gift of God equivalent to the well-being of God's salvation cf. i. 79; x. 5, 6; xix. 42. Jesus in the midst of his welcome as the peaceful Messiah implies that he is really being rejected when he mourns that the city did not know what was for her peace (xix. 42, and perhaps xii. 51).

men of his favour. (Nothing could be further from the true meaning than that sometimes suggested, 'among men of good will'.) Cf. Is. xlii. 1-4, quoted at Matt. xii. 18-21 in a non-septuagintal form. This same passage—and in this same form —probably lies behind the voice heard by the Lord at his baptism (Mark i. 11, and especially Matt. iii. 17). The verb usually translated 'I am well-pleased with . . .' means 'I have shown favour to . . .' The word here translated 'favour' is the noun of the same root. The old synagogue regularly prayed for God's favour. See further *Pss. Sol.* viii. 39; *Test. Levi* xviii. 4-5. The people of God's favour or choice is closely associated with the servant of Is. xlii. 1-4; xliv. 1-4; xlix. 5; lii. 13-15; liii. 11.(Is. xliv. 1-4 makes the connexion particularly clear.) Jesus, the king of this people, is expressly identified with the servant at xxii. 37, where Is. liii. 12 is quoted; again, the people chosen are the 'little flock' to whom God has chosen as an act of favour to give the kingdom (x. 21 and xii. 32).

come on! The particle δή represents, as often in the LXX, 15 the Hebrew particle of entreaty, *n'a.* Cf. Acts xiii. 2; xv. 36.

Mary kept all these sayings. Cf. verse 51 below, and for 19 both the LXX of Gen. xxxvii. 11 where the same verb is used for Jacob's remembering Joseph's dream of coming greatness.

ii. 21-52. THE CIRCUMCISION AND THE PRESENTATION IN THE TEMPLE

And when eight days were fulfilled for his circumcision, 21 his name was called Jesus, as it was called by the angel before his conception in the womb. And when the days 22 of their purification were fulfilled according to the Law of Moses, they brought him to Jerusalem to present him to the Lord, as it is written in the Law of the Lord, 'every 23 male that opens the womb shall be called holy to the Lord', and to offer sacrifice according to the injunction 24 in the Law of the Lord, 'a pair of turtle-doves or two young pigeons'.

And see—there was a man in Jerusalem whose name 25 was Symeon, and this man was righteous and devout, waiting for the consolation of Israel, and the Holy Spirit was upon him; and it had been revealed to him by the 26 Holy Spirit that he would not see death until he had seen the Christ of the Lord; and he came in the spirit into the 27 Temple. And when his parents had brought in the child Jesus to do for him according to the custom of the Law, he took him into his arms and blessed God and said: 28

29 'Now you send away your servant, Lord, according to
30 your word in peace: because my eyes have seen your
31 salvation, which you have prepared in the presence of all
32 the peoples, a light for revelation to the nations and glory
33 of your people Israel.' And his father and mother were
34 marvelling at the things spoken about him. And Symeon
blessed them and said to Mary his mother: 'See—this
child is destined for the fall and rising again of many in
35 Israel and for a gainsaid sign, and through your own soul
shall a sword pass, that the schemes of many hearts may
be revealed.'
36   And there was a prophetess Anna, daughter of Phanuel,
of the tribe of Asher; she was much advanced in years,
having lived with a husband seven years from the time of
37 her maidenhood; she was a widow of eighty-four years,
who did not depart from the temple in her service of God
38 by prayer and fasting night and day. And appearing at
that very moment she gave praise to God and spoke of
him to all those who were looking for the redemption of
39 Jerusalem. And when they had completed everything
according to the Law of the Lord they turned back to
40 Galilee to their own city Nazareth. And the child grew
up and grew strong, filled with wisdom, and the grace of
God was upon him.

21-22   And when ... and when ... were fulfilled. The repetition is ugly. For the argument that verse 21 belongs to the
source mainly confined to chapter i and has been placed here
by Luke see the special note, pp. 20 ff.; but it must be admitted
that verse 21 is connected with the following verses by their
common OT background: Lev. xii. 3 enjoins circumcision on
the eighth day, while Lev. xii. 6 is quoted at the opening of
verse 22, and enjoins the offering of 'a pair of turtle-doves or
two young pigeons', as quoted in verse 24.
22   to present him to the Lord. In obedience to Ex. xiii. 2, 12.
Cf. Ex. xxii. 29; xxxiv. 19; Num. iii. 13; xviii. 15, and for the theological significance see the note on ii. 7 above. The rule applied
to the firstborn of the mother only, and only to a male child; it
did not apply to the first child of a father unless also the first-

born of the mother. See on 21-22 above.

waiting for the consolation of Israel. παράκλησις often in 25
the NT means 'warning' or 'exhortation' but here, as vi. 24;
Acts iv. 36; ix. 31; xv. 31, and sometimes in Paul and the
Epistle to the Hebrews, it means 'consolation', and derives
from the OT, being used by the LXX. The idea of the consolation of Israel in later Judaism is based on Is. xl. 1 f. It is to
be brought by the Messiah, and implies the redemption of
Jerusalem (verse 38 below), and it is for this that the faithful
are to look when the eschatological woes are at their worst (xxi.
28). Symeon's 'waiting' is a pious expectation. So, too, Joseph
of Arimathaea was 'waiting for the Kingdom of God' (xxiii.
51). The verb is used in describing the characteristic of a particular group in verse 38. Cf. Is. lxii. 6 ff.

the Holy Spirit. See the special note, pp. 38 ff., and note
the connexion between possession of Symeon by the Holy Spirit
and his prophesying.

Christ of the Lord. See on ii. 11 above.   26

in the spirit. See on verse 25 above. **his parents.** See on 27
verse 33 below.

blessed God and said. The Song of Symeon alludes with 28
masterly brevity to the main themes of these early chapters.
Symeon by his age and piety is the very personification of
ancient Israel, the servant of God. Upon the child in his arms
are focused God's messenger sent as a 'comfort' in the eyes
of all nations (verse 31; cf. Is. lii. 9, 10), God's plan and its
fulfilment, God's glory and its revelation (verse 32; cf. Is. xl. 5;
xlii. 6; xlix. 6; xlvi. 13).

you send away. The verb seems to carry a double meaning: 29
verse 26 suggests that God 'sends away' Symeon by his death,
and the LXX use of the word suggests that God 'sets free' his
servant (not only Symeon, but also Israel). See below on
verse 34.

your servant. The word and the song take up the Servant
theme of Deut.-Isaiah. For references see on verse 28 above.

Cf. Is. xl. 5.   30

all the peoples. Cf. Is. lii. 10, which makes it probable that 31
the nations of the world are meant; but even the plural of λαός
may mean Israel (cf. Acts iv. 25-27).

32   **a light for revelation to the nations.** The meaning is clear, though the Greek construction is difficult. ·We might have expected ἔθνεσι but perhaps the phrases of the LXX of Is. xlii. 6 and xlix. 6, which have the genitive, influence this passage. D omits ἐθνῶν, no doubt because of the grammatical difficulty.

33   **his father.** Cf. 'his parents' in verses 27, 41, 43. The implication in both passages that Joseph was the father of Jesus strengthens the impression that we have in this chapter a source distinct from that of chapter i. The reading, 'Joseph and his mother', is not well supported, and is an obvious attempt at correction.

34   **for the fall and rising again.** The OT provides the clue to the symbol lying unexpressed behind the language of this verse. It is the 'rock of stumbling' which in Is. viii. 14-15 causes the falling (though not the rising) of many, and in Ps. cxviii. 22 may be said to be spoken against. So, too, according to xx. 17-18, the head corner-stone which is essential to the construction of the building, may be used for thorough destruction. Whether a man rises or falls depends on his acceptance or rejection of the 'Stone', which is the Messiah.

This interpretation requires that those who fall and those who rise again should be different groups, those destined to rise again being those now in an oppressed state (cf. e.g. vi. 20 ff.; xvi. 25; Jas. v. 1). But it is possible that the many who are to fall and rise again are one and the same group of people, that is, the true Israel, passing through death and resurrection; they are 'dismissed' and 'set free', like Symeon in verse 29 above.

35   **through your own soul shall a sword pass.** Symeon, in the spirit and prophesying, sees Mary but thinks of Israel, whom she represents. The sword will pass through the land; Ezek. xiv. 17 is probably the inspiration of this passage as of *Or. Sib.* iii. 316, where, in the centre of an oracle prophesying woes and ultimate destruction to Egypt, the phrase occurs, 'for a sword shall go through the midst of thee'. Cf. 2 Sam. xii. 10.

The words from our verse need not be thought of as in parenthesis: if Mary 'is' Israel the sword passing through her soul passes through the land. The sword is the instrument of the conqueror: the crucifixion pierces the soul of Mary and divides the land, or people: those who acquiesced in it fall through their rejection of the Messiah, who is thus the cause of division. Cf. xii. 51.

schemes. An undertone of hostility is suggested; cf. verse 52 below and the 'thoughts' (represented by the Greek word translated 'schemes' here) which the Lord divines in v. 22; vi. 8; ix. 46, 47; xxiv. 38.

Anna. Introduced with such a wealth of biographical detail 36 that it seems likely that she was a historical person. Her prophetic behaviour and that of Symeon are a usual phenomenon in Judaism. But if Luke or his source has invented her, the model may be Judith (cf. Judith viii. 1-4; xi. 17).

gave praise to God. As something which was his due. The 38 verb is used only here in the NT, and belongs to the Greek of late Judaism; in 1 Esd. viii. 91 and Ps. lxxix. 13 it is used of praising God out of distress and in Dan. iv. 34 (LXX) and 3 Macc. vi. 33 after divine deliverance.

spoke of him. A strange anti-climax after the elaborate introduction of Anna. See the special note on the Infancy Narratives (pp. 20 ff.) for the suggestion that originally in Luke's source the Benedictus followed here.

the redemption of Jerusalem. See on verse 25 above. Is. lii. 9 also has Jerusalem instead of the more usual Zion. The reading 'Israel' is not well supported and is quite unnecessary.

grew strong. Θ and some Byzantine minuscules would add 40 'in the spirit' but this has almost certainly come in from i. 80; at this stage Jesus has not himself received the Spirit who has been operative in the people and circumstances surrounding his birth. Until his baptism (iii. 22) he is filled with wisdom. See the following note.

wisdom. A concept occurring chiefly in the later strata of the OT, where it may mean skill, shrewdness, or, as here, the wisdom so closely allied with morality that its character can be summarized by Prov. ix. 10 (for example) in the words, 'the beginning of wisdom is the fear of the Lord'. Prov. viii unites this sense indissolubly with that personified Wisdom or craftsmanship by which God created the world. It is thus a Jewish conception that the wise man is wise in the ways of the world and in the ways of God and men. In this sense the child Jesus grew in wisdom (cf. verse 52 below). For the association of spirit and wisdom see Acts vi. 3, 10; and Acts vii. 10 for that of spirit and grace.

grace. Or 'favour'. χάρις means 'favour' or 'high regard' (e.g. Acts ii. 47) or that which wins this attitude in others. 'Grace' is retained in the translation to link with the OT phrase 'to find grace in the sight of . . .' where the LXX uses the same word.

ii. 41-52. CHRIST AT TWELVE YEARS

41 Now his parents went every year to Jerusalem for the
42 feast of the Passover. And when he was twelve years old, on their going up according to the custom of the feast,
43 and on their returning when they had completed the days, the boy Jesus stayed behind in Jerusalem, and his
44 parents were unaware of it; but thinking that he was in the caravan they went a day's journey and looked
45 for him among their relatives and friends, and not having found him they went back to Jerusalem looking for him.
46 And it happened that after three days they found him sitting in the temple among the teachers, both listening
47 to them and questioning them. And all those who were listening to him were astonished at his intelligence and
48 his answers. And when they saw him they were stupefied and his mother said to him: 'Son, why have you behaved like this towards us? See—your father and I have been
49 looking for you in terrible distress.' And he said to them: 'But why were you looking for me? Did you not know
50 that I had to be busy with my Father's affairs?' And they
51 did not understand the word which he said to them. And he went down with them and came to Nazareth, and was obedient to them. And his mother kept all these sayings
52 close in her heart; and Jesus progressed in wisdom and stature and in favour with God and men.

42   **twelve years old.** There is rabbinic authority for saying that the first twelve years were allowed for a mild and lenient

observance of feasts and fasts, while from the age of puberty, taken to be thirteen, a strict observance was required.

Why were you looking for me? This passage clearly be- 49 longs to a tradition which knew nothing of the virginal conception. This is clear from the very fact of Jesus' asking these questions and from the failure of Joseph and Mary to understand them; it is clear also from the naïve mention of 'his parents' in verses 41 and 43 and from Mary's reference to Joseph as 'your father' in verse 48. Cf. verses 27 and 33. The boy's questions are profoundly revealing, and may betray an authentic source, the passage being free from any elaboration. Verse 48 shows that a close affection bound Joseph and Mary to Jesus and verse 44 that they allowed him much freedom. Yet only now does it become apparent to him that they are unaware of his personal and private intuitions, which he had hitherto unconsciously assumed they shared.

with my Father's affairs, or 'in my Father's house', which the usage of the LXX makes possible. Cf. Gen. xli. 51.

progressed. The verse perhaps recollects 1 Sam. ii. 21, 26, 52 but this verb is not used in the LXX there.

in wisdom. Cf. Prov. iii. 1-4 for an idea of moral education leading to favour with God and man. According to Wis. vii. 20 it was part of the wise man's secret to have sure knowledge of the 'violence of spirits' and the 'thoughts of men'. It is these 'thoughts' which the mature Jesus can divine. See on 'schemes', verse 35 above.

iii. 1-20. JOHN THE BAPTIST

1 In the fifteenth year of the reign of Tiberius Caesar, during Pontius Pilate's governorship of Judaea, Herod being tetrarch of Galilee, Philip his brother being tetrarch of Ituraea and the Trachonitis region, and Lysanias the 2 tetrarch of Abilene, in the high priesthood of Annas and Caiaphas, the word of God came to John the son of 3 Zacharias in the wilderness. And he went into the whole Jordan district preaching a baptism of repentance for the 4 remission of sins; as it is written in the book of the words of Isaiah the prophet: 'A voice of one crying in the wilderness: "Make ready the way of the Lord, make his paths 5 straight. Every ravine shall be filled up and every mountain and hill shall be brought down; the crooked shall 6 become straight and the rough paths smooth ways. And all flesh shall see the salvation of God."'

7 He said to the crowds who came out to be baptized by him, 'Offspring of vipers, who has warned you to escape 8 from the coming wrath? Bear fruit then worthy of repentance, and do not start saying among yourselves, "We have Abraham for a father"! For I tell you that God can 9 from these stones raise up children for Abraham. And already the axe is directed towards the root of the trees; and every tree not bearing good fruit is being cut down and thrown into the fire.'

10 And the crowds questioned him saying, 'Then what 11 shall we do?' He answered them: 'Let whoever has two cloaks share with him who has none, and let whoever has 12 food do the same.' The tax-gatherers also came to be baptized and said to him: 'Teacher, what shall we do?' 13 And he said to them, 'Do not exact more than is allotted 14 to you'. Soldiers, too, questioned him, saying, 'And what

shall we do?' And he said to them, 'Do not threaten or 36
accuse anyone falsely, and be content with your pay'.
And as the people were in expectation and were reasoning 15
in their hearts about John, whether he were the Christ,
John responded by saying to them all: 'I baptize you with 16
water but one mightier than I is coming, and I am not
worthy to untie his sandal-strap. He will baptize you with
the Holy Spirit and with fire. His winnowing-fan is in his 17
hand for the purging of his threshing-floor and for gathering together the corn into his barn; but the chaff he will
burn with unquenchable fire.' And so with these and 18
many other warnings he preached the gospel to the
people.

But Herod the tetrarch, convicted by him about Herodias 19
his brother's wife and about all the evil things which he,
Herod, had done, added this above all, that he consigned 20
John to a prison.

in the fifteenth year. Reckoning the reign of Tiberius from 1
the death of Augustus in A.D. 14 the date is A.D. 28-29. For a
discussion of the chronological problems of this verse see the
special note, p. 48.

governorship. D and Eusebius read ἐπιτροπεύοντος, an
equivalent of *procurante* (read by all the Latin MSS.), thus de-
signating Pontius Pilate's position, as *procurator*, exactly. He
held the office 26-36. As a Roman province Palestine was
governed by *procurators* until A.D. 66. From A.D. 70 it was
governed by *legati Augusti pro praetore*. Hence D's ἐπιτροπεύοντος may be the original reading, changed to ἡγεμονεύοντος
by the later copyists to accord with the conditions of their
own day.

A procurator was of equestrian rank and responsible to the
emperor; in this instance this meant responsibility to the legate
of Syria, at this time Quirinius, whom Luke strangely does
not mention here. (See ii. 1-2 and page 44.)

Herod. Antipas was governor (tetrarch) of Galilee and Peraea
4 B.C. to A.D. 39.

Philip held his office 4 B.C. to A.D. 33 or 34.

Lysanias. (See p. 48.) If we take this Lysanias to be the

second of the two mentioned by Josephus, the date falls between 36 B.C. and A.D. 53 and probably between 20 B.C. and
A.D. 53. The date indicated by this verse seems to be A.D. 28–29.

2   **Annas.** More properly Hannas, who ceased to be high
priest A.D. 15. Caiaphas was high priest 18–36. See special
note, p. 48.

   the word of God. The phrase is unique in the NT but
recalls 'the word of the Lord' in the LXX, of which Luke
is very conscious here: the method of dating recalls, e.g.,
Jer. i. 1-3; cf. Amos i. 1; Hos. i. 1; Mic. i. 1; and among
historical books, e.g. 2 Kings xiii. 1. The addition of the
father's name, Zacharias, is paralleled at Hos. i. 1 and Jer.
i. 1.

3   **preaching a baptism of repentance.** Here Luke begins to
use recognizable sources: there may be a Q version of the
Baptism, but Luke has taken the full phrase here from Mark i.
4, and brought it to the fore; comparison with Matt. iii. 1-2
suggests that if there was a Q version, it too mentioned early
the baptism of repentance. The prominence given to this character of John's baptism emphasizes a unity of purpose between
John and the Lord: in xxiv. 47 the task given to the Apostles
after the Resurrection is also 'to preach repentance for the
forgiveness of sins'; and, it is added, 'to all nations'. This last
point is emphasized by Luke. See on next verse.

4   **as it is written.** Luke alone of the synoptics prolongs the
Q citation from Is. xl. 3 to add verses 4 and 5 of the Isaiah
passage (Luke iii. 5-6), which close by prophesying that 'all
flesh' shall see God's salvation.

   his paths. All three synoptics write this for the LXX 'the
paths of our God', an interesting indication of the growing
tendency to blur the distinction between God and the Messiah.

6   **the salvation of God.** This is for Luke apparently equivalent
to the Messiah, or the Messiah and his kingdom. Cf. ii. 30
where also the reference is to Is. xl. 5, and the use of the word
salvation in i. 69, 71, 77; xix. 9, where salvation is closely connected with the personal presence of the Messiah. See also the
note on saviour, ii. 11.

7   **Offspring of vipers.** No doubt a genuine memory of John's
words. It is unlike Luke so to represent the people in anyone's

mouth, and he does not use the phrase again. Contrast Matthew (xii. 34 and xxiii. 33), who makes the Pharisees and Sadducees here, as often, the objects of denunciation.

wrath. The wrath of God is a common idea in the prophets and Psalms, and the phrases, the day of the wrath of the Lord, or, the day of his wrath, are found in, for example, Zeph. i. 15, 18; ii. 2.

Abraham. For Abraham in this sort of context cf. John viii. 8 33 ff., and for the thought in Paul, e.g. Rom. iv. 9-12; ix. 7; Gal. iii. 6 ff. It is possible that the warning here (apparently from Q) reflects an early Judaizing controversy. Luke shows sympathy both with this type of warning (cf. xvi. 29-31) and with the special plea of Jewish heritage (e.g. xiii. 16 and xix. 9), which seems to contradict it.

the axe. For the grim warning to the tree of the nation cf. 9 xiii. 6-9 and Mark xi. 12-14 (Matt. xxi. 18-19).

share. The emphasis on this duty and its urgency may reflect 11 an expectation of an imminent return of the Lord. Cf. the primitive communism of Acts ii. 44 ff. and iv. 32 ff.

soldiers. This is the correct translation and the word is used 14 in a very general sense; but if they are Jews serving an alien power, their case would be parallel to that of the tax-gatherers; both Plummer and Lagrange plausibly suggest that they were Jews recruited for assisting local tax-gatherers, since the form of their question seems to connect them with the previous questioners, who are tax-gatherers.

about John, whether he were the Christ. The passage 15 faces the question of John's greatness. See Introduction, p. 41. Acts i. 5; xi. 16; xviii. 24-xix. 7 show no doubt as to his inferiority to the Lord, just as the Infancy Narratives make his position both honourable and subordinate.

not worthy to untie his sandal-strap. The Talmud lists 16 together among the duties of a slave, carrying his master's things before him to the bath-house and taking off his shoes. Matt. iii. 11 mentions the one duty, Mark i. 7, John i. 27, and Luke-Acts (here and Acts xiii. 25) the other. Rabbi Joshua ben Levi held that a disciple should do for his teacher anything a slave would do—except take off his shoes. His date is c. A.D. 250 but the principle may be older. All but Matthew represent the

Baptist as willing to perform even a slave's task for the Lord (Daube, *The New Testament and Rabbinic Judaism*, p. 266).

with the Holy Spirit and with fire. See special note on the Holy Spirit, p. 38.

20   **prison.** Luke does not narrate the execution of John and has grouped together all that he wishes to say about John here at the beginning of his gospel. (Cf. Mark vi. 17-29; Matt. xiv. 3-12.)

iii. 21-38. THE BAPTISM AND GENEALOGY OF CHRIST

21 It happened when all the people were baptized and
22 when Jesus was baptized and was praying that the Holy Spirit came down in bodily form like a dove upon him, and there was a voice from heaven: 'Thou art my son, to-day I have begotten thee'.

23   And he was Jesus, beginning at the age of about thirty years, being the son, as was supposed, of Joseph, the son of
24 Eli, the son of Matthat, the son of Levi, the son of Melchi,
25 the son of Jannai, the son of Joseph, the son of Mattathias, the son of Amos, the son of Nahum, the son of Esli, the son
26 of Naggai, the son of Maath, the son of Mattathias, the son
27 of Semein, the son of Josech, the son of Joda, the son of Joanan, the son of Rhesa, the son of Zerubbabel, the son
28 of Salathiel, the son of Neri, the son of Melchi, the son of Addi, the son of Kosam, the son of Elmadam, the son of
29 Er, the son of Jesus, the son of Eliezer, the son of Jorim,
30 the son of Matthat, the son of Levi, the son of Symeon, the son of Judas, the son of Joseph, the son of Jonam, the son
31 of Eliakim, the son of Melea, the son of Menna, the son of
32 Mattatha, the son of Natham, the son of David, the son of Jesse, the son of Obed, the son of Boaz, the son of Sala, the
33 son of Nahshon, the son of Aminadab, the son of Admin, the son of Arni, the son of Esrom, the son of Perez, the son
34 of Judas, the son of Jacob, the son of Isaac, the son of
35 Abraham, the son of Terah, the son of Nachor, the son of Serouch, the son of Ragau, the son of Phalek, the son

of Eber, the son of Sala, the son of Kainam, the son of 36
Arphaxad, the son of Shem, the son of Noah, the son of
Lamech, the son of Methuselah, the son of Enoch, the son 37
of Jared, the son of Maleleel, the son of Kainam, the son 38
of Enos, the son of Seth, the son of Adam, the son of God.

was baptized and was praying. Jewish custom and doc- 21
trinal considerations lie behind the narratives of the Baptism
in all three synoptics: Mark (i. 10) and Matt. (iii. 16) retain the
'coming up' from the water which in the baptism of proselytes
to Judaism symbolized entry into the people of God, and in
John's baptism perhaps a new entry into the Promised Land
(Daube, *The New Testament and Rabbinic Judaism*, pp. 106 ff.).
It seems that Luke may have been aware of these facts, even if
Mark and Matthew were not so aware, but included the 'coming
up' while quite unconscious of its meaning. Matthew seems to
be aware indeed of the difficulty attending the notion that Jesus
needed to be baptized and includes the dialogue between him
and the Baptist which explains this (Matt. iii. 14-15). Luke's
treatment is different:

(1) He hurries over the actual baptism, with the suggestion
that Jesus was baptized along with the whole people: he did not
need it, but acted in solidarity with his nation. This hurrying
over the actual event in a subordinate clause, with the Lord's
baptism expressed in a genitive absolute, makes it possible to
suppose John to have had no part in it. Indeed, there is some
evidence that in NT times people baptized themselves: D and
some Old Latin MSS. read ἐνώπιον[1] for ὑπ' in Luke iii. 7, while
at 1 Cor. x. 2 P46 B K L P, Origen, and the Byzantine text read
the middle voice ἐβαπτίσαντο. Cf. Acts xxii. 16. Lietzmann (*Handbuch z. Neuen Testament: Cor. 1, 2*, p. 45) quotes 2 Kings v. 14;
Mark vii. 4; Acts xxii. 16, and shows that there is Jewish evidence for people baptizing themselves. But only Acts xxii. 16
is an instance of Christian baptism, and Mark i. 9 makes it quite
clear that according to the original tradition Jesus was baptized
by John.

(2) Instead of the 'coming up' Luke gives as the moment of
the vision the praying of Jesus (see on v. 16). He sees the Holy

---

[1] I.e. 'in the presence of'.

Spirit in the form of a dove while in communion with God.

22   **the Holy Spirit** has here his first contact with Jesus directly.
For Luke his miraculous birth did not then guarantee his character; so far Jesus had grown in wisdom, and the Spirit had been
active in the events which surrounded his birth (i. 35).

in bodily form. Words generally held to show that Luke
was insisting that the dove was an objective phenomenon, but
this would contrast with careful hints that he avoids such a naïve
conception in Acts ii. 1-2, and the Greek word may mean
'appearance' rather than 'form'.

like a dove. Several considerations show the appropriateness of a dove here: (1) The voice from heaven is an example of
the *bath-qôl* (see special note, p. 39) and in several passages of
the Midrash the *bath-qôl* is likened to the chirping of a bird
(Abrahams, *Studies in Pharisaism and the Gospels*, i. 47). (2) The
dove is an emblem of Israel in rabbinic literature, and this may
be as old as the book of Jonah, since 'Jonah' means 'dove' and
one likely interpretation of the book would see Jonah as an
allegory of Israel and her task. (The references Hos. vii. 11 and
xi. 11 are probably mere passing metaphors.) (3) Jewish commentators on Gen. i. 2 say the brooding of the Spirit is like that
of a bird. (4) Philo describes wisdom as a dove (see Allen in
I.C.C. on Matt. iii. 16). (5) The dove has an apparently sacro-
sanct character among the Jews, young pigeons being frequently
the victims at sacrifices where a meal was not involved (Lev.
v. 7; xii. 8; Luke ii. 24), and was sacred with Philistines and
Phoenicians. (See further *Enc. Bibl.* s.v. 'dove'.) In the simple
words, **upon him,** it is perhaps in this context not fanciful to see
a reference to Is. xlii. 1 from whence is derived the Marcan
version of the voice's utterance.

Thou art my son, to-day I have begotten thee. This is the
reading of D a b c ff 1 r; in Justin it is the sole reading (*Dialogue
with Trypho*, lxxxviii). Clement of Alexandria (see especially
Paed. i. 25), the Ebionite Gospel, and Origen give partial support. Augustine knew the reading but states that it is not found
'in the older Greek manuscripts' (*de cons. Ev.* ii. 14). It is found
also in the later fathers, Methodius and Hilary. It is adopted here
for these reasons: (1) It is a quotation from Ps. ii. 7. It has often
been argued that authorities who read it here do so because of

the appropriateness of this scriptural quotation; but this appropriateness may well have led Luke to write it, for he sees the Psalms as well as Moses and the prophets as authorities for the NT (xxiv. 44).

(2) As Creed says, 'there is no consciousness on the part of Justin or of Clement or of Methodius or of Augustine that the reading might be heretical in tendency'. Luke may similarly have had none of that consciousness of heretical tendency which troubled later ages and which may have led to assimilation of the text to that of the other synoptics.

(3) The quotation recurs in Acts xiii. 33 where it seems to refer to the Resurrection; and in Heb. it is used in a discussion of the titles of the Lord (Heb. i. 5; v. 5). These NT references should dispose of the notion that NT writers would regard the doctrine implied as heretical. Once more we must not look for formal consistency in Luke in his application of titles to the Lord.

And he was Jesus, beginning. The translation must be de- 23
fended, the Greek being difficult. καὶ αὐτός usually in Luke (v. i; v. 17; viii. 1; viii. 22; xvii. 11) follows a previous clause, 'and it happened', and should be translated 'that he . . .', the construction being Semitic; but in xix. 2 it must be translated as here. Both the words 'Jesus' and 'beginning' are difficult to translate syntactically, but the name cannot be rejected on any manuscript evidence though 'beginning' is omitted by some and is differently placed in others. It is worth noting that Luke omits all reference to the beginning at Galilee which seems to be part of the tradition (Mark i. 9; Matt. iii. 13; Matt. iv. 12-16) and this word may be a remnant of it. (Cf. xxiv. 47 and Acts x. 37-38, and see Dodd, *According to the Scriptures*, p. 81.) The point of 'and he was Jesus' is clear when we consider that it stands at the head of a genealogy, and it may have been thought that it was appropriate for him to be beginning at the age of thirty on his Messianic inheritance, as the son of David, who was the same age at his accession (2 Sam. v. 4).

Although **as was supposed** is differently placed in the MSS. there is no reason for suspecting its authenticity. It is quite inept to accuse Luke of inconsistency. He does indeed include a genealogy which makes claims for Jesus through his descent through Joseph, in a gospel which elsewhere claims that his conception was virginal and miraculous. But in company, for example, with Matthew, he is in effect claiming that whatever way is taken of testing Jesus' claim to lordship, the test will establish the claim. Formal inconsistency may indeed be alleged but it is clearly no barrier to the evangelists, who throughout the Synoptic tradition equate Jesus both with the pre-existent Son of Man and with the child born at Bethlehem or Nazareth. But Luke nevertheless often remembers the significance of the story of the virginal conception, as he does here. Cf. his alteration of Mark at iv. 22. It is difficult to assign to a source either the genealogy here or that in Matt. i. 1-16. Luke derives the Davidic descent through David's son Nathan, Matthew through Solomon; Luke also has more names than Matthew from the Exile onwards, and thus provides a more probable number of generations for this period. The arguments for a Q version are not strong and it is possible that Luke used first-hand information. (On the preservation by Jewish families of their genealogies see Plummer, pp. 101 ff.)

27   **Rhesa.** Plummer is almost certainly right in suspecting that this title (meaning Prince) was attached to Zerubbabel as the head of the tribe of Judah at the time of the return from exile and has been mistakenly made into a name. The word appears only in Luke. Another explanation might be based upon a corruption in the LXX text of 1 Chron. iii. 17, which comes between Jeconiah and Salathiel. The Heb. original is *Assir* and RV is probably right to translate 'Jeconiah the captive', but if this is correct the LXX shows that this was soon forgotten. In **Salathiel** and **Zerubbabel** the genealogies in Luke and Matthew coincide (cf. Matt. i. 12). Beginning with Terah the material is peculiar to Luke, whose source was either Gen. xi. 10 ff. or the Codex Alexandrinus version of 1 Chron. i. 17 ff.; in either case it was the LXX version, where alone (though not

36   in all MSS.) the name **Kainam** may be found in this list of the descendants of **Shem.**

1 Chron. i. 1-4 is clearly the source for the names, **Noah** to

37,38 **Adam.** The **Kainam** in this section occurs also in the Hebrew; the version of Adam's descendants follow the P version of Gen. v., which does not appear to know of the legend of Gen. iv. 1-16 in which Cain and Abel are the two senior sons of Adam.

CHAPTER IV

iv. 1-13. THE TEMPTATION

Jesus full of the Holy Spirit returned from the Jordan and 1
was led by the Spirit in the wilderness, being tempted for 2
forty days by the devil; and he ate nothing in those days, 3
and when they were accomplished he was hungry. And
the devil said to him: 'If you are the Son of God, tell this
stone to become bread'. And Jesus answered him, 'It is 4
written: "Man shall not live by bread alone".' And he 5
led him upwards and showed him all the kingdoms of the
world in a moment of time; and the devil said to him: 6
'I will give you all this power and all their glory because
it has been delivered to me and I give it to whomsoever I
wish. If therefore you will worship before me all shall be 7
yours.' Jesus in answer said to him, 'It is written: "You 8
shall worship the Lord your God and you shall serve him
alone"'. And he took him into Jerusalem and set him 9
upon the pinnacle of the temple, and said to him, 'If you
are the son of God, cast yourself down from here: for it is 10
written: "He will instruct his angels about you, to guard
you"; and "They will bear you on their hands so that you 11
do not catch your foot on a stone"'. And Jesus in answer 12
said to him: 'It is said: "You shall not put the Lord your
God to the test".' And when he had completed every 13
temptation the devil left him for a time.

If the source of the narrative is Q, Luke has added as usual
his own touches of style, one of which may be the order of the
temptations. Lagrange may be right in thinking that he was
influenced by the climactic effect obtained by placing the temptation to put God to the test last in the series; but if—as is far
from being certain—the order in Matthew is the original, Luke
may have adapted the order in his gospel to bring the reference

to angelic protection as near as possible to the narrative of the rejection at Nazareth, at the end of which Jesus escapes being cast headlong with no apparent effort (iv. 29-30).

1   **full of the Holy Spirit.** Luke alone of the evangelists uses the adjective of the verb, to be full, with the Spirit (cf. i. 15, 41, 67; Acts vi. 3, 5; vii. 55; xi. 24). Here as elsewhere he seems to be influenced by the material of his early chapters.

2   **forty days.** A double reference to Moses and Elijah: Moses fasted forty days and forty nights before receiving the Law (Ex. xxxiv. 28; cf. xxiv. 18) and Elijah was forty days and forty nights without food on his way to Horeb (1 Kings xix. 8).

the devil. A word which may be etymologically connected with the Greek διάβολος which the LXX uses to translate *satan*, which is usually interpreted as 'adversary', one who stands up against, i.e. to accuse another. Cf. Zech. iii. 1; Ps. cix. 6. For the later meaning, 'tempter', cf. 1 Chron. xxi. 1. In later Judaism, 'Satan is one who seeks to destroy the relation between God and man, especially that between God and Israel' (*TWNT*, ii. p. 75). In the NT he appears under many names, Satan, the accuser, the evil one, the tempter, and the ruler—or even the god—of this world (cf. verse 6; John xii. 31, xiv. 30; xvi. 11; 2 Cor. iv. 4; cf. Eph. ii. 2), a sphere to which Christ, as bringer of God's sovereignty, is diametrically opposed (cf. Luke x. 18). The Lord is here, therefore, tempted by one who is the adversary in a very real sense, the opponent not only of men but of God. The battle between the two kingdoms is the basis of the Passion. Cf. Luke xxii. 3, 31, 53.

3   **If you are the Son of God.** The insidious voice refers to the word heard by the Lord at his baptism, and the first temptation is, like the others, such as to befall one conscious of his special position. The unpromising nature of a dry **stone** is the very antithesis of a loaf which it resembles in size. Cf. Matt. vii. 9 ('Or what man is there among you whose son shall ask him for a loaf and he will give him a stone?') which is curiously without parallel in Luke. There is no need to rationalize the temptation by interpreting it as the impulse to sway men by economic power: it is simply a temptation to misuse, that is, use for himself alone the special powers he now believes he possesses. The Lord's quotation is from Deut. viii. 3.

in a moment of time. Part of the Lucan adaptation of this 5
temptation; and it is possible that we owe to him the very
specific statement that the whole of worldly power is in the
hands of the devil. The Lord's reply is from Deut. vi. 13.

into Jerusalem. The removal to Jerusalem and the standing 9
on a pinnacle of the temple of course take place 'in imagination'
like the contemplation of the kingdoms of the world in verse 5.

cast yourself down. A temptation such as could come only
to one who thought himself specially chosen by God for protection. It is to put God to the test so that ever afterwards one
would know, and no longer walk by faith. To interpret it as a
temptation to self-advertisement is to miss the point. That the
Lord should regard passages of a psalm applying to himself (cf.
Ps. xci. 11-12) is in accordance with the way in which the early
church used them. Cf. Luke xxiv. 44.

Jesus' reply to this temptation (from Deut. vi. 16) guarantees
the interpretation given of it above.

for a time. For the translation cf. Acts xiii. 11. Conzelmann 13
(*Die Mitte der Zeit*) claims that in Luke's thought this was the
time of salvation, when 'Satan was far away, the time free from
temptation', and that it lasted from this point until Satan's
entry into Judas at the beginning of the Passion (xxii. 3). xxii.
28, 31, 53 all refer to Satan's activity, and xxii. 35 refers to the
untroubled time before its resumption; xxii. 36 warns of this
resumption, which will affect Jesus' followers after the Passion.
Although this view involves a perhaps strained interpretation of
xxii. 38, it lends considerable force to the passages discussed,
and to the Lord's warning not to fall into temptation in xxii. 40.

iv. 14-44. REJECTION AT NAZARETH AND MINISTRY AT CAPERNAUM

And Jesus returned in the power of the Spirit to Galilee, 14
and a report about him went out throughout the surround-
ing district; and he taught in their synagogues, honoured 15
by all. And he came to Nazareth where he had been 16
brought up, and entered as his custom was on the sabbath

17 day into the synagogue, and stood up to read. And there was handed to him the book of the prophet Isaiah, and he opened the book and found the place where it was
18 written: 'The Spirit of the Lord is upon me, because he has anointed me to preach to the poor, he has sent me to proclaim deliverance to captives and sight to the blind,
19 to send away the wounded set free, to proclaim the acceptable year of the Lord'.
20 And he closed the book, gave it back to the attendant, and sat down. And the eyes of all in the synagogue were
21 fastened on him. And he began to say to them, 'To-day
22 this scripture has been fulfilled in your ears'. And all witnessed to him and marvelled at the words of grace coming out of his mouth, and they said, 'Is not this man
23 a son of Joseph?' And he said to them: 'No doubt you will quote this saying to me:"Physician, cure yourself! The things which we have heard about in Capernaum—do
24 them here in your own native place!"' And he said, 'Indeed I tell you that no prophet is acceptable in his own
25 native place. In truth I tell you, there were many widows in the days of Elijah in Israel, when the heaven was shut up three years and six months, when there was a great
26 famine over all the land, and to not one of them was
27 Elijah sent, but to Sarepta of Sidonia, to a widow. And there were many lepers in Israel in the time of Elisha the prophet, and not one of them was cleansed—but Naaman
28 the Syrian.' And all in the synagogue were filled with
29 anger on hearing this, and they rose and thrust him out of the city, and brought him to an edge of the hill on which
30 their city was built, to throw him down the precipice. But he passed through them and went his way.
31 And he went down to Capernaum, a city of Galilee, and
32 he taught them on the sabbath; and they were astonished at his teaching, because his word was with authority.
33 And in the synagogue there was a man who had a spirit of an unclean demon, and he cried out with a loud voice,
34 'Let be! What business have you with us, Jesus of Nazareth? Have you come to destroy us? I know who you are—
35 the holy one of God.' And Jesus rebuked it saying, 'Be

silenced and come out of him!' And the demon, after
throwing him down among them came out away from
him without harming him. And wonder came upon them 36
all and they spoke to one another saying, 'What is this
word, that with authority and power he gives orders to
unclean spirits and they come out?' And a story about 37
him went out to every place in the surrounding country.

Rising and leaving the synagogue he entered Simon's 38
house. Now Simon's mother-in-law was beset by a high
fever, and they asked him about her. And he stood over 39
her and rebuked the fever, and it left her; and she rose
immediately and ministered to them.

And as the sun was setting all who had those ill with 40
various diseases brought them to him; and he laid hands
on each one of them and healed them. Demons also went 41
out of many shrieking and saying, 'You are the son of
God!' And he rebuked them and would not allow them
to speak because they knew that he was the Christ.

When it was day he went out and made his way to a 42
lonely spot; and the crowds kept looking for him and
came up to him and held on to him to prevent him going
away from them. But he said to them, 'I must preach 43
about the kingdom of God in the other cities too, for that
is why I was sent'. And he preached in the synagogues 44
of Judaea.

returned in the power of the Spirit. Luke, in contrast to 14
Mark i. 14, makes no mention of John the Baptist here because
he has already told the story of John and completed it at iii. 20.
This enables him to represent all the more clearly the guiding
influence of Jesus as the Holy Spirit, rather than the need to
continue John's work.

a report about him went out. These two verses, 14-15, present a summary of fame as though the Lord had already done
great deeds as well as preached. Cf. iv. 23 and observe that the
rejection at Nazareth (iv. 16 ff.) is from the outset made the
vehicle of a proclamation of messianic fulfilment and achievement. In Conzelmann's interpretation of the gospel (see on
verse 13 above) the story of salvation may be divided into (1)

the period belonging to Israel, the time of the Law and the Prophets, (2) the time of Jesus, which fulfils these (iv. 21 and Acts x. 38), and (3) the church's time, fulfilling what was inaugurated in the time of Jesus. The times of Jesus and of the *early* church are definitely past. They are not to be regretted, for the present time has its own function in the endurance of oppression with a patience which will bring its reward soon. (Cf. xviii. 7-8; xxi. 28.)

Such an interpretation presents the matter from the point of view of those who are very conscious of living in this world, their hopes as yet unfulfilled. Consistently with it, but focusing attention rather upon Jesus himself, we may say that he fulfils the Law and the Prophets by his Messiahship, i.e. kingship, upon which he can enter fully only by the way of the cross. From this point in time, or, more strictly, from his Ascension, he reigns, and by the Holy Spirit directs and strengthens the activity of the church whose task it is to make his rule effective. This task she discharges in part by her own suffering as well as by the proclamation of the gospel (Acts xiv. 22).

16   **Nazareth.** For the whole story of the rejection see Introduction, pp. 50 ff.

where he had been brought up. Luke is at his most careful, but he departs from this accuracy in verses 23-24.

stood up to read. If Luke had said that he was invited to read, this would have been according to the normal custom by which the president of the synagogue invited certain persons during the previous week to read either the Law or the Prophets. The person invited need not be an elder or even senior; he was in due course called upon during the service. Acts xiii. 14-15 is instructive but gives no hint, any more than this passage, of the previous 'warning' invitation. The date of the introduction of the reading from the prophets is uncertain (see SB, iv, Pt. 1,

17   pp. 153 ff.). Since the 'book' was a roll a strict translation would be 'he unrolled', but this is not specially implied by the Greek.

the place where it was written. For a full discussion of the composite passage which in fact follows see Introduction, p. 52. Cf. Is. lxi. 1 and 2; lviii. 6.

18   **The Spirit of the Lord.** The passage is extremely apt as a

118

summary of Lucan understanding of the historical Jesus, the
source of his strength and the nature of his work. The post-
exilic original (Is. lxi. 1) claims the gift of prophecy, which does
not distinguish sharply between the proclamation and the
accomplishment of events prophesied.

the attendant. The *khazan*, the subordinate official who 20
actually called upon those who had been invited to read. That
the Lord sat down suggests that this was not meant to be a
formal sermon such as did sometimes follow the reading. Cf.
Acts xiii. 16.

in your ears. A strange figure for fulfilment of scripture, but 21
for the ears as organs of reception of important truth cf. i. 44;
ix. 44. The idea is Semitic: cf., e.g., Acts xxviii. 27 which quotes
Is. vi. 10.

witnessed to him. That is, testified to his special gift and 22
claim. Their mood here is quite contrary to that of verses 28 ff.,
and Luke's account suggests that the Lord's own words are responsible for this change. Cf. Acts vi. 15 for a similar testimony
from the opponents of Stephen.

words of grace. The phrase recalls the part of Deut. viii. 3
which according to the best text is omitted at Luke iv. 4,
although included in the quotation in Matt. iv. 4. Men may
receive, and live by, words of grace, indeed the very word
of God coming out of the mouth of Jesus himself (see on
iv. 32).

a son of Joseph. Luke has designedly altered the form of
the question in Mark (vi. 3) in order to sharpen the contrast between what the people thought was true of the Lord's parentage
and the facts which he has given. Cf. the 'as was supposed' of
iii. 23.

you will quote. Perhaps a future tense to be taken literally, 23
that is, a prophecy of what the people will later say when Jesus
actually has done the things which made his reputation in
Capernaum. So Conzelmann, who believes that viii. 20 is a fulfilment of this prophecy. Another, perhaps more likely, explanation is that Luke has thus not very successfully disguised
what in fact the people did say; verses 24-27 then make a telling
answer to them. It must be admitted that the narrative is not
satisfactorily unified. This is not surprising when we consider

how Luke has used the intractable material of a story of rejection to convey a proclamation of achievement.

24   **and he said.** The words reveal a resumption of the Marcan
source, for there has been no interruption or change of speaker.

No prophet is acceptable. Not even when he proclaims the
acceptable year of the Lord (verse 19).

For a discussion of verses 24-27 see Introduction, pp. 50 ff.

26   **a great famine.** The famine in the days of Elijah is narrated
in 1 Kings xvii-xviii and the time of its duration can be roughly
gauged by xvii. 1 and xviii. 1. The widow is mentioned in 1 Kings
xvii. 9 ff., and the story of Naaman in 2 Kings v.

29   **to throw him down.** Recalls the temptation in verse 9. Luke
makes clear without emphasis that the Lord in fact does all
that he might expect to be able to do if he were the Son of God,
although it would be wrong to have done it for the reasons
which suggested themselves to him at his temptations: bread is
multiplied if not actually made (ix. 10-17); he enters into his
glory (xxiv. 26), which is the destiny better than ruling the
whole world in the usual sense; and he here escapes a death by
being dashed against rock with apparently supernatural ease.

31   **He went down to Capernaum.** Here begins a Marcan
section (cf. Mark i. 21 ff.).

32   **his word.** The use of *logos* here is very interesting. It can be
used in a quite general sense in the synoptics, but note that here
Mark (i. 22) relates the astonishment of the onlookers at first of
all the teaching (*didache*), then at the act of commandment to
unclean spirits (i. 27), but Luke makes the onlookers marvel at
'this word' (verse 36) which is regarded as responsible both for
the *didache* and the miracle. *Logos* is evidently for Luke more
than *didache*: it is teaching which carries conviction passing over
into commandment demanding obedience. Cf. v. 1; vii. 7; and
xxiv. 19, and see on verse 22 above.

33   **an unclean demon.** Making the man not necessarily ill in
body but causing his behaviour to be filthy in person and
speech. (See *ET*, lxv. 4, p. 121.)

34   **Have you come to destroy us?** Not necessarily a question,
but if so a rhetorical one, since it is precisely this which Jesus
has come to do: his kingdom is at war with that of the demons.
What Is. xi. 4 prophesies and Paul sets in a time yet to come

even after the resurrection (1 Cor. xv. 25) the synoptics relate
as beginning during the Lord's earthly ministry. Cf. especially
Mark iii. 22-27; Luke xi. 14-23; Matt. xii. 22-30.

the holy one of God. The phrase (both here and in Mark),
as well as that which begins the cry of the demons, may designedly connect with Elijah and Elisha. Cf. 1 Kings xvii. 18
and 2 Kings iv. 9. But see also Ps. cvi. 16 where a very similar
phrase is used of Aaron.

rebuked the fever. The action is in harmony with the con- 39
ception of illnesses being due to demons, although demons are
responsible for much else also. The other synoptics relate the
manner of healing rather differently.

on each one of them. No doubt in intentional contrast 40
with Mark i. 34.

shrieking and saying. This, with the words uttered, is 41
Luke's addition. Cf. Mark iii. 11. Luke has no hesitation in
declaring at the outset that Jesus is recognized at least by those
powers over which he has been given dominance as both the
Son of God and the Christ. There is no room in his gospel for
hinting, as in Mark, a gradual realization of these truths.

preach about the kingdom or 'preach the gospel of the 43
kingdom': the words are the Lucan equivalent of a much less
definite saying in Mark, and illustrate Luke's determination to
bring the kingdom to the forefront.

was sent. The Greek is the verb from which the term
'apostle', itself a Lucan word, is derived, and the meaning is
'sent by God'.

Judaea. The reading of a strong batch of witnesses; it should 44
be retained, being unlikely to have been introduced by a scribe.
It reflects the indifference to exact geography of the gospel, and
clearly embraces what we should now call Palestine; Luke
abandons the Marcan topography (cf. Mark ii. 1 and Luke v.
17), and that which his narrative implies bears little relation to
the actual geography of his scenes.

CHAPTER V

v. 1-26. THE CALL OF PETER. HEALINGS OF A LEPER AND A PARALYTIC

1 It happened that when the crowd was pressing on him and listening to the word of God, he was himself standing
2 by the Lake of Gennesareth, and he saw two boats standing by the lake; the fishermen had gone out of them and
3 were mending their nets. He entered one of the boats, which belonged to Simon, and asked him to put out a little from the land, and he sat down and taught the
4 crowds from the boat. When he stopped speaking he said to Simon, 'Push out into the deep water, and let down
5 your nets for a catch'. And Simon in answer said, 'Master, we have worked hard throughout the night and caught
6 nothing; but at your word I will let down the nets'. And when they had done this they netted a great shoal of
7 fish, and their nets began to tear; and they beckoned to their partners in the other boat to come and help them, and they came and filled both the boats so that they
8 started to sink. On seeing this Simon Peter fell on his knees before Jesus saying, 'Leave me, for I am a sinner,
9 Lord!' For astonishment had gripped him and all those
10 with him at the catch of fish which they had taken, as also James and John the sons of Zebedee, who were partners with Simon. And Jesus said to Simon, 'Do not fear. From
11 now you shall be a catcher of men.' And they brought their boats up on the land, left everything and followed him.

12 And it happened when he was in one of their towns, there was a man full of leprosy! Seeing Jesus, he fell on his face and prayed him with words, 'Lord, if you will,
13 you can heal me!' And he stretched out his hand and touched him, saying, 'I will; be cleansed'. And immedi-
14 ately the leprosy left him. And he ordered him to tell

nobody but 'Go away and show yourself to the priest, and offer for your cleansing according to Moses' regulation, as testimony to them'. But the account of him spread 15 abroad all the more, and many crowds met to listen and to be healed of their illnesses. But he retired among the 16 desert places and prayed.

And it happened on one of the days that he was teach- 17 ing, and Pharisees and law-teachers were seated who had come from every village of Galilee and Judaea and Jerusalem; and the power of the Lord was there for him to heal. And see—men bringing on a couch a man who 18 was paralysed, and they tried to bring him in and set him before him; and finding no way to bring him in because 19 of the crowd, they climbed up the building and let him down through the tiles, along with the couch, right among them in front of Jesus. And when he saw their 20 faith he said, 'Man, your sins are forgiven'. And the 21 scribes and Pharisees began to raise questions saying, 'Who is this who speaks blasphemies? Who can forgive sins except God alone?' Jesus, aware of their questions, 22 answered and said to them: 'Why do you raise questions in your hearts? Which is easier, to say "Your sins are 23 forgiven" or to say, "Rise and walk"? But so that you 24 may know that the Son of Man has authority on earth to forgive sins'—he said to the paralysed man—'I tell you —rise, take up your couch and go to your house!' And 25 immediately he rose before them all, took up what he had been lying on, and went away to his house, glorifying God. And amazement held them all, and they glorified 26 God, and were filled with awe, saying, 'We have seen unexpected things to-day!'

The passage narrating the call of Peter (verses 1-11) is discussed in the Introduction, p. 54.

Gennesareth. Applied to the lake only here in the NT, 1 Mark vi. 53 and Matt. xiv. 34 using it of the land on the side of the lake (which usually bears the name of Galilee). The territory is called Chinnereth in the OT, but the connexion between the two names is far from obvious.

3   **Simon.** Introduced into the narrative at iv. 38, where he is apparently already a disciple.

8   **fell on his knees.** For this translation see the Introduction, p. 55.

10 **as also James and John.** See Mark i. 19 and the Introduction, p. 55, for the rough construction of the sentence.

With verse 12 Luke embarks on a Marcan section (until vi. 19).

12 **in one of their towns.** A Lucan touch: Luke knows that his source, Mark, places the incident in an undefined but probably rural setting, but seems always inclined to imagine that important events must happen in important places, that is, towns.

fell on his face. The leper makes an obeisance even more profound than in Mark (i. 40). This is again typical of Luke, who also characteristically omits the apparently harsh action of the Lord in Mark i. 43.

14 **Moses' regulation.** Lev. xiii-xiv, especially xiii. 49 and xiv. 1-2.

16 **and prayed.** This is one of seven occasions when Luke alone states that the Lord prayed. The others in a Marcan context are ix. 18, 28, 29; and in other contexts, iii. 21; vi. 12; xi. 1; xxiii. 46.

17 **Pharisees and law-teachers ... from ... Galilee and Judaea and Jerusalem.** Luke makes the occasion very impressive, having only the hint of 'scribes' in Mark ii. 6 for this large and important audience; the significance is great: as in Mark ii. 12 also, all the onlookers show astonishment and apparently great approval at the end of the incident (verse 26).

The power of the Lord. Another Lucan touch, remarkable for the ambiguous use of the word Lord; in the context it may be taken to refer to God, but there are some passages which make one think that the ambiguity is deliberate. Cf. the note on Christ the Lord (ii. 11) and cf. 1 Th. iv. 14 and 16, where, in view of the mention of God active at the *parousia* in verse 14, it is possible to interpret 'the Lord' of God in verses 16 and 17, but the context and the fact that Paul is the author would suggest that Jesus must be meant.

19 **tiles.** The picture of the man brought on a bed or couch and let down through a roof of tiles reveals Luke's indifference to realistic detail, although the outlines of the picture are very

clear: the roof pictured by Mark (ii. 4) is a covering of poles supporting a rough mass of reeds, easily removed.

Authority on earth to forgive sins. It is not easy to deter- 24 mine whether Jesus means that he as the Son of Man has this authority or that man as such has it; but in the event it is to him that the people ascribe the power to heal, and the more likely interpretation is that Luke thought that the phrase referred to Jesus himself. It is important to observe that no theory that all disease is due to sin is necessarily implied: what is implied is that a man cannot find healing from God without forgiveness preceding it (see *ET*, lxv, No. 4, p. 121).

amazement held them all. Including presumably the 26 Pharisees and law-teachers who had begun by opposing the Lord's claim. But if Luke means to imply that they were not always hostile, the impression is soon removed (see verse 30 below).

v. 27-39. THE CALL OF LEVI AND THE QUESTION ABOUT FASTING

And after that he went out and saw a tax-collector named 27 Levi sitting at the tax-office, and he said to him: 'Follow me'. And he left everything, rose, and followed him. And 28, 29 Levi held a great reception for him at his house; and there was a great crowd of tax-collectors and others who were sitting down with them. And the Pharisees and their 30 scribes murmured against his disciples, saying, 'Why do you eat and drink with tax-collectors and sinners?' And 31 Jesus answering said to them, 'It is not those who are in good health who have need of a physician but those who are ill. I did not come to call righteous but sinners to 32 repentance.' And they said to him, 'John's disciples fast 33 frequently and say prayers, and so also do those of the Pharisees, but yours eat and drink'. But Jesus said to 34 them, 'Can you make the bridegroom's friends fast while the bridegroom is with them? Days will come; and when 35 the bridegroom is taken from them, then in those days they will fast.'

36   And he spoke a parable to them: 'No one tears a patch from a new garment and adds it to an old garment; otherwise, both the new will be torn, and also the patch taken from the new will not harmonize with the old.

37   And no one pours new wine into old wineskins; otherwise the new wine will burst the skins, and both the wine itself will be spilt and also the skins will be destroyed.

38, 39   But new wine must be put into new wineskins. And no one when he has drunk the old wishes for the new; for he says, "The old is better".'

27   **Levi.** 'Levi, son of Alphaeus', is the name given in Mark ii. 14, but Luke omits 'son of Alphaeus', probably for brevity; but all three synoptics speak of James the son of Alphaeus in their lists of the twelve (see Luke vi. 14 ff.). Mark iii. 16 ff. is the source for this list and is followed by the others in almost every name. The list does not include Levi. Cf. Acts i. 13.

28   **followed.** To be more precise, 'began to follow'. The imperfect tense suggests that this was indeed the beginning of a new life for Levi.

29   **Levi held a great reception.** An elaboration of Mark ii. 14-15. There it seems, though it is not certain, that Jesus is the host. Mark ix. 33 shows that he owned or tenanted a house in Capernaum, perhaps along with the disciples, or some of them. Luke may prefer to represent Jesus as too poor to have a house of his own (cf. Luke ix. 58; Matt. viii. 20) but at xv. 1-2 he implies that the Lord was host to a large number.

30   **Their scribes.** Luke distinguishes them from those of the Sadducees; is this slight touch meant to indicate that the hostility of the Sadducees was aroused only over the question of the resurrection? Luke does not mention them until the famous question xx. 27, but in the early chapters of Acts they are in opposition.

32   **to repentance.** These words should be regarded as peculiar to Luke at this point: their occurrence in a minority of unimportant MSS. in Mark ii. 17, and Matt. ix. 13 may be dismissed as assimilation to Luke. That Jesus' mission was a call to repentance is suggested by Mark only at i. 15 and vi. 12. In the latter passage it is the disciples who are engaged upon a mission

on which Jesus has sent them, and in i. 15 it may be argued
that Jesus is for the time merely continuing the work of John
the Baptist, whose disciple he has hitherto been. (Cf. Goguel,
Jean-Baptiste (Paris, 1928), pp. 241 ff.) Thus for Mark Jesus'
call to repentance is only a preliminary to the real work of the
Lord's ministry. Matthew associates repentance with John the
Baptist (iii. 2), and with Jesus only at xi. 20-21 and xii. 41,
which are Q (cf. Luke x. 13 and xi. 32). It is left to Luke to
represent the call to repentance as an integral part of the fully
developed *kerygma* of Jesus. In addition to the two Q passages
just quoted, Luke draws a moral from the parable of the Lost
Sheep (xv. 7), which, in contrast to Matt. xviii. 14, emphasizes
the penitence of the returning sinner; and Luke adds the
Lost Coin, with a precisely similar moral (xv. 8-10), which is
the overwhelming importance of even one repentant sinner.
Further, at xvii. 3 (cf. Matt. xviii. 15), and much more obviously at xvii. 4 (cf. Matt. xviii. 21-22), Luke makes clear that forgiveness depends on repentance, even between man and man.
In the passages peculiar to his gospel we find a solemn adjura-
tion to repentance at xiii. 1-5; at xvi. 30 the object of 'Moses and
the prophets' is evidently to bring people to repentance; finally
at xxiv. 27 the whole consequence of Jesus' death and resurrection is to be 'repentance and forgiveness of sins'.

John's disciples. Their mention implies their persistence as 33
a body after John's arrest; this is supported by vii. 18 (cf. Matt.
xi. 2) and Acts xviii. 25.

frequently and say prayers. A Lucan addition; cf. xi. 1,
where again the fact that John taught his disciples prayer is
mentioned. Luke may then have had further information of his
own about John, the first chapter of his gospel showing the high
honour in which he held him. For this contrast between John
and the Lord cf. the Q passage vii. 34-35 (cf. Matt. xi. 19).
Luke omits Mark's reference to a current fast (Mark. ii. 18);
this might be taken to be implied but for the introduction of
the word 'frequently'.

the bridegroom's friends. Literally 'sons of the bride- 34
chamber', the ceremony of an oriental wedding being chiefly a
matter for the bridegroom and his relatives (cf. John ii. 1-10,
in which there is no mention of the bride).

35   **Days will come.** The translation is literal, but a similar use
·of the Greek καί, in the Hebraic manner, at xix. 43, may mean
that we should punctuate and translate as follows: 'But days
will come when the bridegroom will be taken from them. Then
in those days, etc. . . .' The saying ought not to be quoted as a
direction by the Lord to fast; it is no more than a prophecy that
in days to come the disciples will have their fill of fasting
through sorrow (cf. xvii. 22). Luke nowhere and, one may say,
the gospels nowhere, report our Lord as enjoining fasting. At
iv. 2 Luke even avoids the technical word 'fasted'. Cf. Matt.
iv. 2.

36   **a patch from a new garment.** Luke has missed the point
of the original in Mark ii. 21: the parable did not imply that
such a process was even thinkable, Mark reporting the saying
as 'a patch of uncarded cloth'. In Mark it is not a question of
the new not harmonizing with the old, but the tear being made
worse. In the original the saying seems to have hinted that the
new substance of the life and teaching which Jesus has brought
must be cast into new forms. Luke emphasizes a different point,
viz. that the new teaching will not match the old and that it will
not be accepted by those who have grown fond of the old. Thus
we may suppose that verse 39 has been added by Luke to draw
out what he took to be the meaning of the saying.

vi. 1-19. THE CORNFIELDS ON THE SABBATH. THE
MAN WITH THE WITHERED HAND. THE CALL-
ING OF THE TWELVE. HEALINGS

It happened on a sabbath that he was passing through the 1
cornfields, and his disciples were plucking and eating
the ears, rubbing them with their hands.

But some of the Pharisees said: 'Why are they doing 2
what is not lawful on sabbaths?' And Jesus in answer 3
said to them, 'And have you not read what David did,
when both he and those with him were hungry? How he 4
entered the House of God, took "bread set out, and ate
and gave to those with him, for whom it was not lawful
to eat—but only for the priests?"' And he said to them: 5
'The Son of Man is Lord of the sabbath'.

It happened on another sabbath that he entered a 6
synagogue and taught; and there was a man there whose
right hand was withered, and the scribes and Pharisees 7
were watching to see if he would heal on the sabbath, to
find an accusation against him; but he knew their schem- 8
ings and said to the man who had the withered hand,
'Arise and stand in the midst!' And he arose and stood.
And Jesus said to them, 'I demand of you—is it lawful 9
on the sabbath day to do good or to do evil, to save or
destroy life?' And he looked round on them all and 10
said to him, 'Stretch out your hand!' He did so, and
his hand was restored. They were filled with madness 11
and discussed with one another what they could do to
Jesus.

It happened in those days that he went out to a moun- 12
tain to pray, and he spent the night in prayer to God.
And when it was day he called his disciples to him, and 13
after choosing twelve from them, he also called these

14 'apostles': Simon, whom he also called Peter, and
   Andrew his brother, and James and John, and Philip and
15 Bartholomew, and Matthew and Thomas, and James the
16 son of Alphaeus, and Simon called the Zealot, and Judas the
   son of James, and Judas Iscariot, who became the traitor.
17 And he went down with them and stood on a level
   place, with a large crowd of his disciples, and a great
   multitude of the people from all Judaea and Jerusalem,
   and the sea-coast of Tyre and Sidon, who came to listen
18 to him and to be healed of their diseases; and those who
19 were troubled with unclean spirits were cured. And the
   whole crowd were trying to touch him, because power
   from him was going out and healing them all.

1   **on a sabbath.** Many authorities add the curious word
δευτεροπρώτῳ—perhaps best explained, as Lagrange suggests,
by supposing that a copyist qualified this sabbath as the first,
in comparison with that of verse 6 (both being the occasions of
controversy), and that another qualified it as the second by
comparison with iv. 31; and that subsequently the two words,
δευτέρῳ πρώτῳ, were written together. If the word, as its very
difficulty suggests, is authentic, SB's comment is interesting:
they suggest (1) 'First in the Second year' of a jubilee period,
such a period having begun in the autumn. (But this would
make the event of vi. 1 occur in the spring, although the corn
was ripe.) (2) 'First sabbath after the Second day of Passover'
according to the Pharisaic interpretation of Lev. xxiii. 15, after
which there were to be seven sabbaths. (3) According to another
interpretation of Lev. xxiii. 15, the 'Second sabbath after 15
Nisan', which was the beginning of 50 days between Passover
and Pentecost. It seems curious for Luke to have thus referred
to a system of dating which is not even hinted elsewhere in his
gospel; but if either (2) or (3) is right, we may notice that Lev.
xxiii. 14 forbids any kind of corn to be eaten at this time,
whether prepared in any way or eaten as fresh ears. If the
system of dating is simply that of events in the Lord's ministry,
and we translate the difficult word (with AV) 'the second sabbath after the first', the first is that of iv. 31, and Luke is dating
by the Marcan account; by his own full account iv. 16 would

be the first and this the third. Of course the reference to Lev.
xxiii. 14 is not necessary to explain the illegality of the disciples'
action, since it was regarded by the rabbis as threshing, win-
nowing, and preparing food.

rubbing. The Greek word occurs only here in the NT and
the only other references given in LS are Dioscorides (a medical
writer of the first century A.D.) and Nicander (2nd century
B.C.), who uses the middle voice. It would therefore be possible
to see in it an example of unconscious intrusion of medical
vocabulary. It is not noticed by Hobart in *The Medical Language of St. Luke.*

Jesus in answer. In Mark ii. 24 the question had been 3
addressed to Jesus but Luke has made the Pharisees complain
to the disciples, an example of the reverence with which he
treats the Lord, although the logic of the events is made slightly
less clear.

what David did. Narrated 1 Sam. xxi. 1-6. The Lord
chooses this example because rabbinic tradition held that
David's action took place on a sabbath. In 1 Sam. the high
priest is called Ahimelech, and the Abiathar of Mark ii. 26 is
his son (1 Sam. xxii. 20). Both Luke and Matthew omit the
reference to the high priest, but Mark's reference is not necessarily his mistake, since there is some evidence that the confusion began in the Greek text of the OT.

schemings. Cf. ii. 35 and v. 22.   8

And he looked round on them all. Luke's account obscures 10
completely the point of this, which is in Mark expectation of an
answer, the lack of which makes Jesus angry. Luke has robbed
the incident of drama in the interest of reverence for the Lord;
yet xiv. 1-5 shows that he can invest a short incident with
dramatic power when he wishes.

to pray. See on v. 16. It is typical of Luke to represent the 12
Lord as thus preparing for the choice of the twelve, for he gives
to all his disciples a high place in the Kingdom. (Cf. vi. 20.)

'apostles.' Luke ascribes the use of the term to Jesus him- 13
self, and uses it in five other passages of the gospel (ix. 10; xi.
49; xvii. 5; xxii. 14; xxiv. 10) and frequently in Acts. Mark and
Matthew each have the term only once (Mark vi. 30 and Matt.
x. 2). In Mark vi. 30 it is appropriately applied to the twelve

on their return from being sent out; for the word means 'a sent one'.

Luke may therefore be introducing here a term which became current during the period of the early church rather than during that of the Lord's ministry; but it is not impossible that Jesus used the term *shaliaḥ*, or rather the Aramaic form *sheluḥa'*, which has the same meaning as the Greek 'apostle' and in rabbinic literature denotes a messenger given full powers to represent his sender; these powers of the Apostles are specifically referred to in Matt. x. 40 and the principle that those whom Jesus sends are as himself is elaborated in Luke x. 16. Cf. Acts xxvi. 17 and 1 Cor. i. 17.

14 f.   **Simon.** He has already been 'called Peter' (v. 8, q.v.). The list is like that of Mark iii. 16 but Luke correctly translates when he calls the other Simon 'the Zealot', Mark merely transliterating the Aramaic *qan'ana'*. This is hardly a departure from Mark, but the omission of Thaddaeus from Mark iii. 18 and the substitution by Luke in verse 16 of Judas son of James cannot be dismissed simply on the ground that these two, Thaddaeus and Judas, may be identical. Luke seems to have had another tradition (though not necessarily a written one) which he followed here and at Acts i. 13.

15   **James, son of Alphaeus.** See on xxiv. 10.

17   **went down.** Luke sets the scene of the calling of the twelve on the mountain, as Mark also had; but Luke desires to recount not only the healings of Mark iii. 7-12, but also the sermon, which tradition evidently placed on a mountain (Matt. v. 1). Luke therefore brings the sick folk to a 'level place', which is a compromise between the sea-level, more suitable for the bringing of sick folk, and the mountain of the teaching; in order to do this, he has to alter the order of Mark iii, placing the healings after the call of the twelve.

Tyre and Sidon. The mention of these cities makes clear that the Lord is in the north country; so Mark iii. 7 f., but Luke has abandoned the Marcan topography (cf. iv. 44; v. 17; vi. 6), and the topography which he has invented here, placing the scene halfway down a mountain-side, forbids mention of the lake of Galilee implied in Mark iii. 9.

19   **power over him.** Cf. the scene at iv. 32 and v. 17.

132

And he lifted up his eyes on his disciples and said: 20

'Blessed are the poor, for yours is the kingdom of God.

'Blessed are those who are hungry now, because you 21
will be satisfied.

'Blessed are those who weep now, because you will
laugh.

'You are blessed when men hate you, and when they 22
shut you off from their company, and revile you, and cast
out your name as evil on account of the Son of Man.

'Rejoice in that day and dance: for see—your reward 23
in heaven is great; for their fathers acted in the same way
towards the prophets.

'But woe to you, the rich, because you have your com- 24
fort already. Woe to you who have been filled now, 25
because you will be hungry. Woe, you who laugh now,
because you will mourn and weep. Woe when all men 26
speak you fair: for their fathers acted in the same way
towards the false prophets.

'But I say to you my hearers: Love your enemies, do 27
good to those that hate you, bless those that curse you, 28
pray for those that insult you. To him that strikes you on 29
the cheek offer the other and do not prevent him who is
taking away your cloak from taking your tunic as well.
To everyone that asks of you give, and of him that takes 30
away what is yours do not ask it back.

'And as you wish that men should act towards you, so 31
act towards them. And if you love them that love you, 32
what grace are you showing? For the very sinners love
those that love them. For indeed if you do good to those 33
who do good to you, what grace are you showing? The
very sinners do the same. And if you lend to those from 34
whom you hope to receive something, what grace are
you showing? The very sinners lend to sinners to receive
like favours. But love your enemies and do good and 35
lend without looking for anything in return; and your
reward will be great, and you will be sons of the highest,

36 because he is kind to the graceless and evil. Be pitiful
because your father is pitiful.

37   'And do not judge, and you will not be judged; and do
not condemn and you will not be condemned. Forgive
38 and you will be forgiven. Give and it shall be given to
you. Fair measure, pressed down, shaken together, and
overflowing will they give into your bosom; for with the
measure that you measure it will be measured to you.'

39   And he spoke a parable to them: 'Can a blind man lead
40 a blind man? Will not both fall into the pit? A disciple
is not above his teacher; but everyone instructed will be
like his teacher.

41   'Why do you look at the speck in your brother's eye,
but the beam which is in your own eye you do not
42 notice? How can you say to your brother, "Brother, let
me take out the speck which is in your eye" when you
do not see the beam which is in your own eye? Hypocrite,
take the beam first out of your own eye, and then you will
see clearly to take out the speck which is in your brother's
eye.

43   'For there is no good tree yielding rotten fruit, nor
44 again a rotten tree yielding good fruit. For each tree is
recognized by its own fruit: for they do not gather figs
from thistles, nor from a thornbush do they pick a bunch
45 of grapes. The good man from the good treasure of his
heart brings out good, and the evil man out of evil brings
out evil; for from the surplus of the heart his mouth
46 speaks. Why do you address me, "Lord, Lord", and do
not what I say?

47   'Everyone who comes to me and listens to my words,
48 I will show you to whom he is like: he is like a man
building a house, who dug and went deep and laid a
foundation on rock; and when there was a flood the river
beat against that house, and it was not strong enough to
49 shake it, because it had been well built. But he who has
listened and not done is like a man who built his house
upon the earth without a foundation, against which the
river beat, and immediately it collapsed, and the fall of
that house was great.'

his disciples. It is a persistent part of the tradition that the 20
teaching gathered here was addressed to the disciples. Cf. Matt.
v. 1-2. Luke retains this tradition even though verse 19 shows
that according to his account crowds were present.

poor. It is also traditional that the disciples are poor, but not
merely because they were the Lord's disciples during his earthly
ministry: it was the destiny of the true Israel to be poor, that is,
despised and weak among the nations, in order to be exalted by
God. Here, as at iv. 18, Jesus fulfils the prophecy of Is. lxi. 1:
he has been 'anointed . . . to preach to the poor' and 'to proclaim deliverance'. This is the theme of the Magnificat (i. 46-55)
where (verse 54) Israel is called God's servant, recalling the
suffering servant of Deutero-Isaiah. See the section on the Infancy Narratives (pp. 20 ff.), and the commentary on i. 50, 52,
53, 54. Again, the 'poor man', the humble people who are
oppressed, but who await God's vindication, are an important
theme of the psalms. Cf., for example, Pss. ix. 12, 17-20; x; xii. 5;
xviii. 16-20; xxii. 24; xxxi; xxxvii; lxviii. 7-10; lxix. 32-33; lxx;
lxxii. 11-13; lxxxii; lxxxvi; cvii. 9, 41; cxiii. 7; cxlvi. 7; cxlvii,
2-6; cxlix; and see A. R. Johnson, *Sacral Kingship in Ancient
Israel*, pp. 70, 81-82, 110, 126.

you will be satisfied. Cf. i. 53 and note.   21

those who weep. This saying, the latter part of verse 21, is
paralleled generally by Matt. v. 4, but seems to be in a more
primitive form. Matthew may well have added 'in spirit' to the
beatitude which he has in Matt. v. 3, 'after righteousness' in
v. 6, and 'falsely' in v. 11.

laugh. The simple verb (here and in verse 25) does not occur
elsewhere in the NT.

The considerations arising out of this verse cumulatively suggest that Luke has the sayings in this passage in a form nearer
the original than that in which they appear in Matthew.

you are blessed. The comparative length of the last beatitude along with the change to direct address, may be paralleled
in Jewish liturgy and in the OT, e.g. Is. lxiii. 7 ff.; Ecclus. xlvii.
12 ff.; xlviii. 1 ff. See Daube, pp. 196 ff.

shut you off from their company. This certainly includes 22
'excommunication' from the synagogue, and no doubt much
more besides. (Cf. John ix. 22; xii. 42; xvi. 2.)

cast out your name as evil. Either saying evil about the disciples specifically by name, or using their names in a curse, or as a curse (SB, ii. 159). The saying may then owe something to the knowledge of curses from the Jewish synagogue to which Christians as a body were subject in the early days of the church. (Cf. Acts xxviii. 22; 1 Pet. iv. 14.) In any case, Luke's readers are assured that the present experience of Christians in the world was foreseen by their Lord.

on account of the Son of Man. The Son of Man is in origin a corporate personality: he may be a real individual but nevertheless includes his fellows within himself. If we compare verses 13 f. and 18 of Dan. vii. we see that the Son of Man may be equated with the 'saints (holy, devoted ones) of the most high'. This corporate sense is perhaps never entirely absent in the synoptic gospels: Jesus is the Son of Man but as such includes within his corporate personality all who belong to him.

23 **dance.** An attempt to find one word for the one word in Greek, which means literally 'leap'. See on i. 41.

the prophets. Their persecution could not be gainsaid by any who knew the stories of Jeremiah, Ezekiel, and Amos in the OT, while a strong tradition existed that Isaiah had suffered a martyr's death.

24 **Woe.** Not the pronunciation of a curse: it is rather witnessing to a fact plain for all to see or understand, which the speaker does not claim to bring about but of which he has clear insight. That these woes were part of the original document or oral tradition used by Luke here is suggested by parallelism between them and the beatitudes, which is even stronger if the clause 'and cast out your name as evil for the sake of the Son of Man' may be regarded as an addition to the original; if so, it seems to be part of the traditional saying as known to both Matthew and Luke, for each has something of the kind, though differing as to its form.

25 **you who have been filled now.** The thought is akin to that of Jer. xxxi. 10 ff., in which ransomed Jacob will come to the good things of the Lord, and they will not hunger any more (cf. verse 21; John vi. 35; Rev. vii. 16). Jer. xxxi. 14 says, 'My people will be filled with my good things' where the word filled is the same as this verse 25. Cf. i. 53.

false prophets. See, e.g., Jer. xiv. 13 ff.; xxiii. 9 ff., 27-28; 26
Ezek. xxii. 23 ff., and for the people's satisfaction with false
prophets, Jer. v. 31. In these verses there is little or no sense of
an imminent general judgment: the kingdom 'is' the disciples';
and the reversal of lots by which the rich will lack and the poor
gain comfort in the kingdom need not come by any catastrophic
means. Other passages show a more elaborate eschatology (see
Introduction, p. 35).

Love your enemies. This injunction will not appeal to those 27
with no loyalty to anything beyond the immediate. Moral
systems may be divided into two classes. In the first, typical of
Greek speculation, the good is identified with something known
in human experience, to which another name than the good can
be given, such as pleasure or happiness. In the second the good
is indefinable and transcendent. For Judaism and Christianity,
whose ethics belong to this latter class, it is founded upon the
prophetic consciousness and is what God ordains. Thus the key
to this whole passage lies in verse 35, where the radical injunction to love enemies is repeated, and the reward, that 'you
will be sons of the highest', is offered as the explanation of so
difficult a commandment; God is kind to all without distinction
of their worth, and his 'sons' have the privilege of being like
him. All that comes between these two ends of the commandment is elaboration in rabbinic style, and discussion of the
merits or otherwise in this or that case of offering 'the other' 29
'to him that strikes you on the cheek', is to miss the essential
matter of the teaching. Rom. xii. 14; 1 Cor. iv. 12; 1 Pet. ii. 23,
all show that this ethic was early regarded as essential to the
Christian life, but the language of Rom. xii. 18 shows that Paul
at least did not expect it to produce universal peace.

do not ask it back. Matt. v. 42 has instead of this injunction 30
the bidding to be ever willing to lend.

as you wish. The 'Golden Rule', recognizing the self- 31
regarding aspect of a man's ethical life, expresses in another way
the thought of Lev. xix. 18 ('thou shalt love thy neighbour as
thyself'), which is quoted at Matt. v. 43. See on x. 27.

grace. To find grace in the sight of anyone is a common 32
phrase in the OT, literally translated in the LXX. It begins by
meaning 'favour' and then comes to mean those qualities which

obtain or deserve favour. Thus the same word comes to be used to denote both the quality and the gift of God which gave it, the reward being paradoxically regarded as the same as the gift which deserved it. It is consequently very hard to preserve these shades of meaning in English, and the word translated 'favours' (verse 34) is merely the plural of the word translated 'grace' here.

35   **sons of the highest.** A good illustration of the Semitic use of the term 'son of' to mean 'disciple of', 'one having the same nature as'. See also on verse 27 above.

graceless. An attempt to meet the difficulties which the word presents (see above). Here the meaning is 'ungrateful', which almost preserves the play on the word.

37   **forgive.** The Greek verb suggests the remission of a debt. Cf. the language in the Lord's Prayer, Luke xi. 4; Matt. vi. 12.

38   **Give and it shall be given to you.** These words seem to serve as an introduction to the saying about good measure, so that the latter does not connect with the saying about judging, as it does in Matt. vii. 1-2.

will they give. The sense requires that the overflowing good measure will be the reward given not by men but by God, and he is the real subject of the verb 'give'. For a similar vague 'they' in the Greek see xii. 20, 48.

bosom. The full part of the garment above the girdle, which could serve as a pocket; see Is. lxv. 7 and Ps. lxxix. 12.

39   **a parable.** Serves to dissociate the following sayings from verses 37-38, and from here to the end of the next verse the connexion is rather loose. Matt. xv. 14 takes the saying about the blind leading the blind as directed against the Pharisees, which may be due merely to his strong tendency to magnify the hostility between the Lord and them.

40   **A disciple.** It is an intriguing problem to conjecture the probable original context of this saying. In Matt. x. 24-25 and John xv. 20 it is used to reinforce the warning that persecution, not having spared the master, is not likely to spare his followers, and at John xiii. 16 to emphasize the necessity of humility; but all these seem to be clearly secondary applications. Luke's use of it in a context which can hardly be original illustrates both the antiquity and the loss of the original connexion of the saying.

speck. The saying about the speck and the beam in the eye 41
is attached by Matthew to the saying about judging, where it is
obviously appropriate. That Luke was apparently reminded of
it by the 'blind leading the blind' suggests that he did not know
it in the context of judging. It is characteristic of him that he
dwells on the inward character of a disciple, and is thus led by
this saying to the saying about the good and rotten tree.

no good tree. This saying makes the same point as Matt. vii. 43
16 ff. (that a good disciple is known by his works), but the
addition of verse 45 shows that Luke was probably thinking
that the main point of the tree saying is that it is necessary to
be a 'tree' of a certain character in order to bring forth fruit of
that character; moreover his rendering lacks the forthright repetition of Matt. vii. 16 and 20 ('By their fruits you shall know
them').

heart. This verse is paralleled by Matt. xii. 35, but Luke 45
alone interprets the treasure as the heart, though this is no doubt
implied in the saying in the last half of the verse, also found at
Matt. xii. 34.

'Lord, Lord.' There seems no connexion between this say- 46
ing and the foregoing, since to call Jesus Lord, if it proceeded
from an overflow of the heart, would indicate a good heart, but
this saying reminds us that this is not enough: Luke has here
returned abruptly to the real point of the tree saying which
Matthew interpreted more naturally.

a foundation on rock. Recalling the language of Matt. xvi. 48
18: it is pertinent to observe that the foundation of good discipleship here is doing and not the mere calling of Jesus 'Lord'
(or even 'the Christ'?). The present passage may therefore be
good support for those who interpret Matt. xvi. 17-19 as a
warrant for founding the church on the rock, Peter, as the type
and representative of the working Apostle who not only recog-
nizes the lordship of Jesus but carries out the things which
he says, rather than on Peter whose authority and whose
successors' authority rests on his acknowledgment of Jesus'
lordship. Matt. xvi. 23 reminds the reader that Peter is
capable of betraying the very apostleship which has just
been commended.

vii. 1-17. THE CENTURION'S SERVANT. THE WIDOW OF NAIN AND HER SON

1 When he had completed all his sayings in the hearing
2 of the people, he entered Capernaum. Now a certain
centurion's servant was ill and about to die, and this
3 servant was precious to him. Having heard about Jesus
he sent to him elders of the Jews, asking him to come and
4 save his servant. They, when they came to Jesus, besought
him earnestly, saying, 'He to whom you would grant this
5 is worthy of it; for he loves our nation and has himself
6 built the synagogue for us'. And Jesus went with them,
but when he was not far from the house the centurion
sent friends to him to say, 'Do not trouble yourself, sir;
7 for I am not worthy for you to come under my roof. That
is why I did not think it right for me to come to you
myself. But speak with a word and let my boy be healed.
8 For I too am a man set under authority, having under
myself soldiers, and I say to this one, "Go!"—and he
goes; and to another "Come here!"—and he comes;
9 and to my servant, "Do this!"—and he does it'. And
when Jesus heard this he marvelled at him, and turning
to the crowd following him, he said, 'Not even in Israel
10 have I found such great faith'. And when they who had
been sent returned to the house they found the servant
well.
11 And it happened that on the next day he went into a
city called Nain, and there went with him his disciples
12 and a great crowd; when he approached the gate of the
city, there was just being brought out dead one who was
the only son of his mother, and she was a widow, and a
13 considerable crowd of the city was with her. And when
he saw her the Lord was moved with pity for her and said

to her: 'Don't cry'. And he approached and touched the 14
bier, and the bearers stood still, and he said, 'Young man,
to you I say—Rise!' And the dead man sat up and began 15
to speak, and he gave him to his mother. And awe seized 16
them all and they glorified God saying, 'A great prophet
has arisen among us', and, 'God has visited his people'.
And this story about him went out in the whole of Judaea 17
and all the surrounding country.

For the story of the centurion's servant cf. Matt. viii. 5-13.
Differences between the two accounts are noticed below.

he sent elders. This part of the story is peculiar to Luke. 3
On no other occasion in the gospels are elders called 'elders of
the Jews' and the full explanatory phrase suggests that Luke
had Gentile readers in mind. Other considerations suggest that
he was also just as mindful of Jewish readers, viz. the implication, confined to this passage in the whole NT, of a
friendly relation between elders and Jesus, the elders' appeal to his Jewish sympathies, and the compliment to Israel
implied in 'not even in Israel' in verse 9. The whole episode
serves to impress on any reader that a Roman could be
found who respected both the Jews in general and Jesus in
particular.

It is likely that Luke has himself invented the detail of the
sending of the elders, knowing that the synagogue had been
built at the instance of a centurion and using this as an opportunity to introduce into the days of Jesus' ministry a character
like Cornelius (Acts x). The construction of the story bears this
out: in verse 3 the centurion sends to ask Jesus to come but in
verse 6 (from Q) tells him that it is not necessary for him to
come. Luke has also added an apology for the centurion's not
coming to Jesus himself (7a), but it cannot be regarded as a very
satisfactory explanation from a man with so earnest a request
and so great respect for the Lord. The story in Matt. viii. 5-13
is free from these contradictions.

my boy. According to verses 2 and 3 the sick man was a 7
servant or slave, but our translation in this verse may cover the
use of παῖς here, which means either 'child' or 'servant'.
'Boy' is used for a servant in the East also in modern times.

11   **Nain.** The rising of the widow's son at Nain is peculiar to Luke. The septuagintal style, the reminiscence of 1 Kings xvii. 23 ('and he gave him to his mother'), and possibly the locality, connect the passage with iv. 25-30, which is based on the same part of 1 Kings. Nain is the modern hamlet Nein, two miles west of Endor and between it and Shunem, where Elisha raised the widow's son (2 Kings iv. 8-37). It is not mentioned elsewhere in the gospels.

12   **there was just being brought out.** Literally, 'and—see! There was being brought out . . .'

the only son of his mother. The dead young man prefigures the death of Jesus himself and Mary's bereavement. In connexion with this theme note that although Jesus is not Mary's only son, iv. 22 avoids mention of Jesus' brethren, in contrast to Mark vi. 3 and Matt. xiii. 55-56.

15   **and he gave him to his mother.** Cf. 1 Kings xvii. 23 and see above on verse 11. If Luke was thinking also of Jesus' own death and resurrection we may compare John xix. 26.

vii. 18-50. THE MESSAGE OF JOHN THE BAPTIST. THE WOMAN IN SIMON'S HOUSE

18   **And John's disciples reported to him about all these**
19   **things; and John called to him two of his disciples and sent them to the Lord to say: 'Are you the Coming One or**
20   **are we to look for another?' And when they came to him the men said, 'John the Baptist sent us to you to say: "Are**
21   **you the Coming One or are we to look for another?"' At that time he was healing many from diseases and scourges and evil spirits and to many blind he gave**
22   **sight; and he said in answer to them, 'Go and report to John what you have seen and heard: sight is restored to the blind, the lame walk, lepers are cleansed, and the deaf hear; the dead are raised, the poor have the gospel**
23   **preached to them. And blessed is whoever does not stumble at me.'**
24   **And when John's messengers had left, he began to say**

to the crowds about John: 'What did you go out into the wilderness to look at? A reed being shaken by the wind? But what did you go out to see? A man dressed in luxu- 25 rious clothes? Well, those in gorgeous dress and luxury are in the palaces! But what did you go out to see? A 26 prophet? Yes, I tell you—and more than a prophet! This 27 is he about whom it has been written: "See—I send my messenger before your face, who will prepare your way before you". I tell you—a greater than John among those 28 born of women there is not. But his junior is in the king-dom of God greater than he.' And all the people listening 29 and the tax-collectors acknowledged God's justice, hav-ing been baptized with John's baptism. But the Pharisees 30 and lawyers set at nought God's counsel for themselves, not having been baptized by him. 'To whom then shall I 31 liken the men of this generation, and to whom are they like? They are like children sitting in the market-place 32 and calling to one another with the words: "We have piped to you and you did not dance. We have mourned and you did not weep." For John the Baptist came neither 33 eating bread nor drinking wine, and you say, "He has a demon". The Son of Man has come eating and drinking, 34 and you say, "See—a man who is a glutton and a winedrinker, a friend of tax-collectors and sinners!" —And wisdom's justice has been declared by all her 35 children.'

One of the Pharisees invited him to dine with him; and 36 he entered the Pharisee's house and reclined. And see— 37 there was a woman who was a sinner in the city, and having learnt that he was reclining in the Pharisee's house, and having brought an alabaster container of myrrh, and taken up her stand behind him at his feet, 38 weeping, began with her tears to wet his feet, and wiped them dry with the hair of her head, and covered his feet with kisses and anointed them with the myrrh.

And on seeing this the Pharisee who had invited him 39 said to himself, 'If this were a prophet, he would know who it is and what sort of woman it is who is clinging to him—that she is a sinner'. And in answer Jesus said to 40

him, 'Simon, I have something to say to you'. The other
41 said, 'Say on, teacher'. 'A creditor had two debtors: one
42 owed five hundred denarii, the other fifty. As they could
not repay, he made a gift to both of the debt. Which of
43 them will love him most?' Simon answered, 'I suppose
the one to whom he gave the greater sum'. And he said
44 to him, 'You have judged rightly'. And turning towards
the woman, he said to Simon: 'You see this woman? I
entered your house; you gave me no water for my feet.
She has with her tears wet my feet and with her own hair
45 wiped them dry. You gave me no kiss; but she from the
time I came in has not ceased to cover my feet with
46 kisses. You did not anoint my head with oil but she has
47 anointed my feet with myrrh. For this reason I tell you,
her sins—her many sins—are forgiven, because she loved
48 greatly; he to whom little is forgiven loves little.' And he
49 said to her, 'Your sins are forgiven'. And those who were
reclining with him began to say to themselves, 'Who is
50 this, who forgives sins?' But he said to the woman, 'Your
faith has saved you. Go in peace.'

18   **John's disciples.** See special note on John the Baptist,
pp. 41 ff., where the point is made that the Fourth Gospel may
be held to reveal that there was a dispute between John's disciples and Jesus, although that gospel is very firm in sub-
ordinating John to Jesus and suppresses the baptism. John is
the earthly witness *par excellence* to Jesus (John i. 7, 15, 19, 29,
30, 32, 34; iii. 26 ff.; v. 33). By contrast our present passage
(Q) represents a much earlier stage—perhaps the earliest written
stage—of thinking on the subject, and shows John doing no
more than entertaining the possibility that Jesus is the Coming
One (that is, he who was popularly identified with Elijah).
Jesus invites John to go further and accept him as the Messiah,
and identifies John before the people with the 'messenger' or
Elijah. This is of course inconsistent with Luke's own final
view, according to which John is the herald of the Lord, who
is himself the fulfilment of the 'Elijah' expectation. Cf. i. 76
and note; iii. 16 and note. It should be noticed that in the
synoptics John is never reported as accepting Jesus as Messiah

or even as the Coming One, and that even the Fourth Gospel is not altogether consistent on this point.

sight is restored to the blind. . . . The signs of the Mes- 22 sianic age in this sentence and the others, to the end of the verse, are foreshadowed in, e.g., Is. xxix. 18-19; xxxv. 5; lxi. 1. The last probably provides the reference to the poor having the gospel preached to them; Luke has already used this passage from Deutero-Isaiah at iv. 18.

my messenger. According to the later tradition the Mes- 27 senger goes before the Lord's face (Mal. iii. 1) and is identified with the angel who went before the face of his people as they journeyed out of Egypt into Canaan (Ex. xxiii. 20).

his junior. The usual interpretation of this passage is that 28 the least in the kingdom of God is greater than John; but it is unlikely that the Lord would regard John as outside the kingdom. See special note, p. 58.

And all the people listening. This and the following verse 29 seem to make a rather abrupt intrusion into the Lord's words, and it is just possible that they may be interpreted as part of what he is saying: 'All the people, having listened (*sc.* to John) acknowledged God's justice, by being baptized by him. . . .' But it is more likely that they are a comment by Luke himself. (Cf. xx. 1-8 and parallels.)

lawyers. See on x. 25.　　　　　　　　　　　　　　　　30

God's counsel. See on xxii. 22.

the men of this generation. This passage becomes clear if 31 we suppose that the men include both John and Jesus on the one hand and their contemporaries on the other: it is Jesus who has 'piped' and failed to make his contemporaries 'dance', and John who has 'mourned' and failed to make them 'weep'. The Lord seems to have overheard children complaining to their playmates that they cannot rouse them to any kind of game. Whether this complaint was in itself some sort of game must remain a conjecture, but it should be noticed that if we take the Lord's words as they stand, the complaint must be part of the game to which he refers.

Klostermann thinks that **wisdom's children** are the tax- 35 collectors and sinners who have accepted both John and Jesus; but, although verses 29 f. suggest this, the phrase would more naturally apply to John the Baptist and the Lord. The wisdom is that of Prov. viii; Ecclus. xxiv; Wis. vi. 22-ix. 18 (cf. esp. Wis. vii. 27). Its presence in men of very different gifts is still that of the same wisdom; further, the methods of men so differently gifted are their own justification, since they spring from the same divine source. See also on ii. 52.

37   **woman who was a sinner.** No more than a general similarity can be claimed between this passage and Mark xiv. 3-9 (cf. Matt. xxvi. 6-13). On the other hand, between verses 37 and 38 of this passage and John xii. 1-3 there is some similarity, extending to the action of the women though not to the actual wording of the evangelists. This similarity between Luke and John is greater than that between Luke and Mark here (see J. N. Sanders on 'Those whom Jesus loved' in *NTS*, vol. 1, no. 1 (September 1954), pp. 29 ff., esp. 36 ff.). But there seems little doubt that here are combined two traditions: one, the story of the action of the woman, with the criticism of Simon, and with an ending supplied by the Lord's words 'You see this woman? . . .', i.e. verses 37-40 (first seven words), and 44 (from 'you see') to 47. The second comprised the opening words of verse 44 (omitting 'he said to Simon'), verses 48 and 49, followed by the conversation with Simon recorded in verses 40-43, and ending in 50. If Luke found them already combined but changed the order, this will account for the less than logical connexion between the argument that he to whom most is forgiven will love most and the statement that the woman's sins are forgiven because she loved greatly. It will also account for the curious opening of verse 44 in which the Lord turns to the woman but addresses Simon. On the other hand, the analogy of v. 1-11 where Luke appears to have combined two traditions with little regard for logical sequence (see Introduction, p. 54) may suggest that once again he has been the agent who combined the material available. The source of most of it must remain unknown to us, although two affinities are clear: one is of course that with Mark xiv. 3-9, where we find the same subject and the name Simon (whom Luke begins by calling 'a Pharisee'); and the other is with the story represented also by John xii. 1-3. It is worth noticing that the tradition as known to Luke did not identify the woman with Mary the sister of

Lazarus, although the family of Lazarus and his two sisters are known to Luke and John alone of the evangelists (Luke x. 38-42; John xii. 1-11). The identification in the Fourth Gospel receives a curious insistence, being given in advance of the incident itself (John xi. 2). The popular identification of the woman who was a sinner with Mary Magdalene is without foundation: see below on viii. 3.

Go in peace. The apparent quotation from 1 Sam. i. 17 may 50 be purely accidental, but even so will illustrate Luke's septuagintal style.

CHAPTER VIII

viii. 1-21. THE MINISTERING WOMEN. PARABLES

1 And it happened on the following day that he made his way through town and village proclaiming and preaching the gospel of the kingdom of God, and the twelve with
2 him, and some women who had been cured of evil spirits and illnesses, Mary called Magdalene, from whom seven
3 demons had gone out, and Joanna the wife of Chuza Herod's steward, and Susanna and many others, who ministered to them from their possessions.

4 When a great crowd gathered and people from each
5 town also came to him, he said by parable: 'A sower went out to sow his seed, and as he sowed, some fell by the path, and was trodden down and the birds of heaven
6 ate it up. And another fell on rock, and when grown it
7 withered, because it had no moisture. And another fell in the middle of thistles, and the thistles grew up with it and
8 smothered it. And another fell on good soil, and when grown brought forth fruit an hundredfold.' Saying this he called out: 'He who has ears, hear well!'

9 Now his disciples asked him what this parable might
10 be. And he said, 'To you it has been granted to know the mysteries of the kingdom of God, but to the rest only in parables, that seeing they may not see and hearing they
11 may not understand. But this is the parable: the seed is
12 the word of God. Those by the path are those who have listened and then the devil comes and takes the word from their heart, that they may not believe and be saved.
13 Those on the rock are they who when they hear accept the word with joy, and these have no root, and they
14 believe for a time and in a time of trial fall away. And that which fell among the thistles—these are they who have listened, and are smothered as they go on their way

148

by anxieties and riches and pleasures of life, and perfect
no fruit. But that on the fair soil—these are they who 15
have listened with a fair and good heart, keep the word
and bring forth fruit by perseverance.

'No one when he has lit a lamp hides it in a basin or 16
puts it under a bed, but he puts it on a lampstand so that
those who come in may see the light. For there is nothing 17
hidden which will not become clear, nor concealed
which will not be known and come into clearness. Watch 18
then how you listen: for to him who has it shall be given,
and from him who has not shall be taken away what he
seems to have.'

There came to him his mother and his brothers, and 19
they could not reach him because of the crowd; and it 20
was reported to him: 'Your mother and brothers are
standing outside wanting to see you.' And he said in 21
answer to them, 'My mother and my brothers are these
who are listening to and doing the word of God'.

Verses 1-3, peculiar to Luke, form an introduction to the
next block of Marcan material. They yield ample evidence of
Luke's own hand in style and vocabulary, of which perhaps the
most characteristic and interesting is the phrase, 'preaching the
gospel of ("evangelizing") the kingdom of God' in verse 1. A
similar phrase is found at xvi. 16, Acts viii. 12, and at Luke iv.
43, where it is clearly an alteration of Mark.

he made his way. In Luke Jesus is always a sojourner. Cf. 1
ix. 57-58, and the connexion there between the journey and
the saying. There is no such introduction to the saying in Matt.
viii. 20. The Galilaean women connect the present period of
wandering with the Lord's first appearance, which was in
Galilee.

some women. The women from Galilee, later to be wit- 2
nesses of the Resurrection, are shown playing their part as
witnesses from the first alongside the Apostles. (Cf. Acts i. 14,
21.) They stand in the same relation to Mary the mother of
Jesus as the Apostles to the Lord's brethren. Mary and his
brethren desire to see him but find they have forfeited their
close relation to him (viii. 19-21; cf. xi. 27-28). Their place is

taken for this period, that of the Lord's earthly ministry, by the Galilean women and the Apostles respectively. After the Resurrection the two groups, family and disciples, are united (Acts i. 14) (Conzelmann).

Mary called Magdalene. Probably because she was of Magdala, a small place near the sea of Galilee, not mentioned otherwise in the NT (the reading at Matt. xv. 39 of the most trustworthy MSS. is Magadan); that she had had **seven demons** cast out means that she had suffered from seven different diseases, which may but does not necessarily include morbid mental states; there is nothing whatever in the phrase or in any other evidence to warrant the medieval identification of her with the 'sinner' of vii. 36-50, or with Mary the sister of Lazarus, nor to warrant the common assumption that it means that she had been a prostitute. According to Mark xv. 40-41 (cf. Matt. xxvii. 55-56) and xv. 47 (cf. Matt. xxvii. 61) and xvi. 1 (cf. Matt. xxviii. 1) she was one of the women who had followed the Lord from Galilee and was a witness of the crucifixion, burial, and the empty tomb. In the Fourth Gospel she is present at the Cross (xix. 25) and the sole first witness of the Resurrection (xx. 1-18).

3   She is introduced with **Joanna** again at Luke xxiv. 10, the latter not being mentioned elsewhere in the gospels; **Susanna** appears only here. **And many others** will account for different companions of Mary Magdalene mentioned by Mark in his list of the ministering women, who are no doubt those referred to again in Acts i. 14, and whom Luke mentions without giving their names in xxiii. 49, 55 f.; xxiv. 1; but he names three of them at xxiv. 10 f.

It would be interesting to know more of **Chuza, Herod's steward,** and Manaen, Herod's foster-brother (Acts xiii. 1), whose mention in such contexts encourages belief that Herod's fear of disaffection, which Josephus says prompted his execution of John the Baptist, made him the more readily acquiesce in the execution of Jesus, of whose popularity he would have close knowledge if his steward's wife was a follower. If Luke knew this of Antipas, it will explain both his omission of Mark vi. 17-29, as the wrong explanation of John's death, and also his reporting the incident of xxiii. 6-16.

a sower. But the parable is most pointed if it is thought of 5 as that of the four different kinds of soil. See below where the interpretation is discussed.

on the rock. This would seem to be a place where the seed 6 could not germinate at all; Mark's 'rocky ground' makes better sense, and we have here an instance of Luke's indifference to verisimilitude in detail (cf. details of v. 19).

an hundredfold. Mark iv. 8 has 'thirtyfold and sixtyfold 8 and hundredfold' (cf. Matt. xiii. 8). By his compression Luke has avoided any apparent affinity with gnosticism: the Naassene gnostics, according to Hippolytus (*Elenchus* v. 8), used the parable to serve their teaching; and it was a common gnostic notion that adherents after baptism advanced in knowledge and as such were said to 'increase' and 'bear fruit'. (For the latter expression cf. Irenaeus, *Adv. Haer.* i. 1. 3; 4: 4; 18: 1; 21: 5.) Luke has also avoided the 'increasing' of Mark iv. 8. (Cf. Luke xix. 13.)

Paul uses this gnostic terminology in Col. i. 6-11 in expressing his own opposition to gnostic teaching. 'Bearing fruit' and 'increasing' in the Christian life leads there also to 'perseverance' (cf. verse 15 below).

hear well! Taking ἀκούειν ἀκουέτω as a Semitism, the construction of an infinitive absolute with the same verb in a finite part being common in Hebrew, and conveying emphasis. The usage found in *koine* Greek may well be due to this Semitic influence. (Cf. Luke xxii. 15.) But the use in Greek of the infinitive rather than a participle is very rare.

his disciples asked him. Luke omits the Marcan 'in pri- 9 vate' and limits the question to the one parable of the soils. Contrast Mark iv. 10, and note that Matt. xiii. 10 reveals the real preoccupation of the evangelists, asking why the Lord speaks 'to them' in parables, and this question, though not put in Mark, is that which receives an answer in Mark iv. 11-12, as in verse 10 here, though Luke softens the answer in Mark a little. Creed (*ad loc.*) rightly points out that there is great difficulty in regarding the answer here as authentic, since in Mark iv. 33 it is suggested that parables were a means whereby the people could be made to understand. Again, the disciples' question seems contrived: can they really have failed to understand this parable?

10   **the mysteries of the kingdom of God.** The inner secrets which show the plan of God for the coming, the establishment, and the character of the kingdom. In fact these are taught partly by parables and partly directly; they concern God and his plan in time, the work and destiny of the Messiah, and the people who will belong to it, together with the manner of their entering it. The parable of the soils is teaching on this last element of the mysteries. God's people are always potentially his kingdom, and are often likened to a tree or plant, now threatened with being cut down and burnt (e.g. Luke iii. 9; xiii. 6-9), now shown its great possibilities (e.g. Luke xiii. 18-21). Here they are likened to the soil in which the kingdom can grow—or cannot grow.

To you it has been granted. For the privileges of the disciples see vi. 20-23; x. 23-24.

that seeing they may not see. See on verse 9 above. The phrase must not in any case be taken solely to express purpose: parables are not used *in order to* conceal the truth, but parables are used, and *the consequence is* that 'the rest' do not perceive the truth they are meant to convey. In classical Greek the distinction between the two meanings can be easily made; but *koine* Greek often uses the same construction for both.

11   **this is the parable.** We may indeed doubt whether it is. The interpretation is awkward in all three gospels, due to their failure to see that the distinction between the word and the mind receiving it must be kept in the parallel of seed, and soil receiving the seed. Luke seems to have a dim apprehension of the fact that it is really a parable of four different kinds of soil, for in verse 13 he avoids the confusion of soil with seed implicit in Mark's 'those sown on rocky ground' (Mark iv. 16); yet in this same verse he shows the same carelessness of detail as in verse 6.

14   **perfect no fruit.** The verb is not found elsewhere in the NT, and is rare in Greek, although the cognate adjective is common. The word appears to have quasi-medical connexions (cf. Hobart, p. 65), but is certainly not exclusively medical.

15   **with a fair and good heart.** Again Luke shows signs of

desiring to clear the confusion in Mark: he has grasped the fact
of the importance of the soil in which the seed is sown. Cf.
xi. 28. He introduces into the text a later conception of discipleship in crisis by his use of **perseverance,** not found elsewhere
in the gospels but a keyword in Paul (cf., e.g., Rom. v. 3-4). The
phrase should be understood with reference to **in time of trial**
(verse 13). Luke associates the teaching with the life of a
Christian receiving instruction in his own day.

　　No one when he has lit a lamp. Cf. xi. 33 (Q) which has 16
influenced the Lucan form of this saying, while at xi. 33 in turn
Marcan influence is shown. The next verse also has a Q counter-
part, which has caused Luke to alter the phrase in Mark iv. 22,
'except to be made clear' to 'which will not become clear', and
to add a short phrase of similar meaning at the end of the verse.
Luke has used Q to simplify Mark's version, which Black (pp.
57-58) regards as a curious expression; but is not Mark still
thinking of the fruitful seed which must remain hidden a long
time precisely in order that it may be manifested? If this is the
right interpretation of Mark, Luke has missed this point, just
as, with Matthew, he missed apparently the point of Mark iv.
26-29; both omit this passage which is a commentary on Mark's
form of the saying in Mark iv. 22.

　　to him who has. Again there is a Q version, at xix. 26.　　18
　　his mother and his brothers. The form in which Mark iii. 19
31-35 tells the story is not at all acceptable to Luke. If he had
already written the Infancy Narratives, he could not easily represent Jesus' mother as one of a party which had come to take
charge of him (Mark iii. 21, which Luke omits); he might also
naturally dislike the picture of Mark iii. 31, in which the Lord's
mother and brothers are shut off from communication with him
without the explanation being at once obvious; Luke therefore
gives this with the words, **because of the crowd.** Consistently
Luke omits the question of Mark iii. 33, which might seem
hostile. These considerations explain the change of position in
the narrative which Luke has made for this incident: Mark
places the Beelzebub controversy between the setting out of the
family and their arrival, and thus suggests that the Lord's own
family is divided against itself (cf. Mark iii. 25) and that his
own mother and brothers are guilty of the unforgivable sin

(Mark iii. 29-30, cf. verse 21). Luke avoids these imputations and makes the incident and saying suitable for addition to parables and similar sayings. viii. 4, followed by the narration of parables, suggests the presence of a crowd who would be a natural obstacle to any who wished to see Jesus, and in verse 21 the same point is made as at verse 15 (cf. xi. 28). But the words of the Lord in verse 21 are not simply for general application: the Lord's family are during this period on the fringe of his followers (verse 19) and join the company of full believers only after the Resurrection (see above on viii. 2).

20   The **brothers** of the Lord in the absence of any hint to the contrary must be understood to be brothers in the usual sense. They are named at Mark vi. 3, and the tradition of their hostility is preserved in John vii. 3, 5; but they are mentioned as a group, with Mary, the mother of Jesus, among the early believers in Acts i. 14. The brother who was presumably the elder, James, became the leader of the church in Jerusalem, and is mentioned first in Acts xii. 17 in this connexion. John xx. 17 suggests that the word 'brothers' was used by the Lord of his disciples (cf. Matt. xxiii. 8 and xxviii. 10) but see John ii. 12, where the disciples and brothers are distinguished.

viii. 22-56. THE STILLING OF THE STORM. THE GADARENE DEMONIAC. JAIRUS' DAUGHTER AND THE WOMAN WITH THE HAEMORRHAGE

22 **It happened on one of the days that he entered a boat, and so did his disciples, and he said to them, 'Let us cross over to the other side of the lake'. And they set sail.**
23 **And as they were sailing he fell asleep; and a storm of wind came down on the lake, and they began to fill with**
24 **water and were in danger. They went to him and woke him up saying, 'Master, master, we are lost!' But he awoke and rebuked the wind and the wave; and they**
25 **stopped, and there was calm. And he said to them, 'Where is your faith?' They were filled with awe and amazement, saying to one another, 'Then who is this,**

that he commands the winds and the water and they
obey him?'

And they sailed down to the country of the Gerasenes, 26
which is opposite Galilee. When he disembarked on the 27
land a man from the town met him, who had demons,
and for a long time he had put on no clothes, and would
not stay in a house, but among the tombs. On seeing Jesus 28
he shrieked out and prostrated himself before him, and
said with a loud voice, 'What have you to do with me,
Jesus, son of the most high God? I beg of you, do not
torture me!' For he was ordering the unclean spirit to 29
come out from the man; for many times it had seized
him, and he was well bound with chains and fetters to
hold him, and breaking through the bonds he was driven
by the demon into the desert places. Jesus asked him, 30
'What is your name?' And he said 'Legion!' For many
demons had entered him. And they besought him not to 31
order them to depart to the abyss; now there was a large 32
herd of swine feeding on the hillside, and they besought
him to let them enter into them, and he let them. And 33
the demons, coming out from the man, entered into the
swine, and the herd rushed down the cliff into the lake
and were drowned. The swineherds, seeing what hap- 34
pened, fled and reported it in the town and fields. So they 35
came out to see what had happened, and came to Jesus
and found sitting down the man from whom the demons
had gone out, clothed and sane, at Jesus' feet, and they
were afraid. And those who had seen it reported to them 36
how the demonized had been saved. And all the people 37
of the surrounding district of the Gerasenes asked him to
leave them, because they were seized with a great fear;
and he entered a boat and returned. And the man from 38
whom the demons had gone out prayed him that he
might be with him, but he dismissed him saying, 'Return 39
to your home and tell what God has done for you'. And
he went away proclaiming through the whole town what
Jesus had done for him.

And when Jesus returned the crowd welcomed him, 40
for they were all waiting for him. And see—there came 41

a man whose name was Jairus, and he was a ruler of the
synagogue, and he fell at Jesus' feet and besought him to
42 come into his house, because he had an only daughter, of
twelve years, and she was dying. And as he was going the
43 crowds began to press in on him; and a woman who had
had an haemorrhage for twelve years, who had spent her
whole living on physicians, and had not succeeded in
44 being healed by any, approached him from behind and
took hold of the hem of his cloak, and immediately the
45 flow of her blood stopped. And Jesus said, 'Who was it
who held on to me?' On all denying it, Peter said, 'The
46 crowds are hemming you in and crushing you'. But
Jesus said, 'Someone held me. For I felt power gone out
47 of me.' And the woman, seeing that she had not escaped
notice, came trembling, and prostrating herself before
him, told for what reason she had held on to him, before
all the people, and how she had been immediately
48 healed. And he said to her, 'Daughter, your faith has
49 saved you. Go in peace.' While he was still speaking
there comes someone from the synagogue-ruler's house
to say, 'Your daughter has died; don't trouble the master
50 any more'. But Jesus on hearing it, answered him, 'Do
not be afraid! Only believe, and she shall be saved.'
51 Having come to the house, he would not let anyone
come in with him except Peter and John and James and
52 the father of the child, and her mother. They were all
weeping and bewailing her; and he said, 'Do not weep.
53 She is not dead, but asleep.' And they laughed at him,
54 knowing that she had died. But he took her by the hand
55 and called her, saying, 'Get up, my child'. And her
spirit returned and she stood up immediately; and he
gave instructions for something to be given her to eat.
56 And her parents were amazed, but he told them not to
tell what had happened.

A block of Marcan material, Luke's alterations of which are
chiefly stylistic.
25   'Then who is this?' The disciples now presumably begin
to form that opinion which is eventually expressed by Peter at

ix. 20. In between these two points Mark but not Luke has a further reference to the disciples' opportunity to recognize the Lord's real status. (Mark vi. 52, in the block omitted by Luke.)

Gerasenes. The question of the original reading here and 26 in Mark v. 1 is difficult. It might appear from the evidence that 'Gergesenes' is the most likely original reading in Luke: Origen had a marked preference for it from his personal knowledge that there was a town Gergesa at the place demanded by the story (*Commentary on St. John*, vi. 41), but he is also influenced by his own mystical interpretations. Luke does indeed speak of the demoniac as belonging to a town, an idea which he retains in verse 39, where Mark records the spread of the report in the whole Decapolis. But 'Gerasenes' is the best attested reading, and may perhaps be retained also on the ground of being the most difficult, since Gerasa was two days' journey away from the edge of the lake.

do not torture me! Cf. iv. 34 and the note there.   28

Legion. Possession by many demons witnesses to many dis- 30 orders, or to a very severe disorder. To interpret as the loss of the unity of the man's personality may well be justified but is not the primary meaning. The analogy between the man and Israel (possessed by the Roman power with its legions, not therefore dwelling in her own home but with the dead) is striking but probably accidental. Luke does not consistently treat the man as possessed by more than one demon.

the abyss. Not elsewhere in the gospels, and in the NT 31 only at Rom. x. 7 and in the Apocalypse, where it is the abode respectively of the dead and of evil spirits; it is frequent in the LXX for the sea; there may be a connexion in Luke's mind between the depths of the 'sea' and that of the pit which is the abode of evil spirits which has determined the use of the word here. Then it should be noted that in spite of their plea the demons are consigned quite literally to the abyss.

tell what God has done for you. A command for a pagan, 39 for such these people (as keepers of swine) must be from a Jewish point of view. That he proclaimed what Jesus had done rather than what God had done was natural, but may be intended by both Mark and Luke to underline the fact that what Jesus does is the action of God.

42   **an only daughter.** A Lucan touch to heighten the feeling
of the story. In Mark v. 23 she is just 'my daughter'.

43   **had not succeeded in being healed.** Although Mark v. 26
adds 'but rather grew worse' the omission of this by Luke is
hardly evidence for his being a physician, for he makes plain
enough the uselessness of the physicians who had tried to heal
the woman, and a glance at a synopsis will show that he is
condensing considerably at this part of his gospel.

45   **Peter** becomes the spokesman in Luke for 'his disciples' in
Mark v. 31. Cf. Luke xxii. 8. The reverse process may be seen
where the story is discreditable to Peter at xxii. 46 (cf. Mark
xiv. 37).

49   **has died.** May imply that until now there has been a possibility of cure; more probably to emphasize that the child was
indeed dead. Thus Luke, although on the whole he is condensing Mark here, adds

53   **knowing that she had died** in verse 53 to Mark v. 39-40
in order to make the miracle certainly one of raising from the
dead.

54   **Get up, my child.** The call is of someone awaking the girl
from natural sleep. Luke omits the Aramaic given by Mark
(v. 41), but retains a Semitic vocative in ἡ παῖς.

55   **she stood up.** This unexpected detail (also in Mark v. 42)
suggests a story once attested by an eyewitness. No story in
the gospels shows the reserve of the writers better, or better
illustrates the candour with which they leave open the facts to
a naturalistic interpretation, while making clear the evangelists'
own complete conviction.

---

ix. 1-17. THE SENDING OUT OF THE TWELVE. HEROD. THE RETURN OF THE TWELVE. FEEDING OF THE FIVE THOUSAND

After calling together the twelve he gave them power 1 and authority over all demons and to cure diseases. And 2 he sent them to proclaim the kingdom of God and to heal, and he said to them: 3

'Take nothing for the journey, neither staff, nor purse, nor food, nor money, and do not have two tunics. And 4 into whatever house you enter, stay there, and go out from there. And as many as do not accept you—on going 5 out from that town, shake off the dust from your feet, as a witness against them.'

Going out they went through the villages preaching the 6 gospel and curing everywhere.

Now Herod the tetrarch heard about everything that 7 had happened, and was perplexed on account of it being said by some that John had risen from the dead, by some 8 that Elijah had appeared, by others that one of the old prophets had arisen; and Herod said, 'John I beheaded; 9 but who is this about whom I hear things of this kind?' And he was anxious to see him.

And the apostles returned and narrated to him what 10 they had done; and he took them aside and withdrew privately to a town called Bethsaida. But the crowds 11 learnt of it and followed him, and he welcomed them and spoke to them about the kingdom of God, and those who were in need of treatment he healed. Now the day began 12 to decline and the twelve approached and said to him, 'Dismiss the crowds so that they may go into the villages round about and into the fields and bivouac and find provisions, for here we are in a desert spot'. But he said to 13

159

them, 'Give them something to eat yourselves'. But they
said to him, 'We have no more than five loaves and two
fish—unless we are to go and buy things to eat for all this
14 people!' For there were about five thousand men. But he
said to his disciples, 'Make them recline in parties of
15 about fifty'. This they did and made them all recline.
16 And he took the five loaves and two fish, and looking up
into heaven he blessed them, and broke them up and
17 gave them to the disciples to set before the crowd. And
they ate and all were satisfied, and what they left was
taken up—twelve baskets of scraps.

1   **demons and . . . diseases.** In the Marcan account (vi. 6-13)
power is given over unclean spirits only, but in the sequel the
twelve cast out demons and healed many by anointing with oil.
Luke makes clear that the power given included that to heal
diseases, and adds curiously in the next verse that they were
sent both to preach and to heal.

2   **to proclaim the kingdom of God and to heal.** To proclaim the kingdom of God may be equivalent to the task of
preaching repentance in Mark vi. 12, for according to Luke this
preaching is almost the same as proclaiming the kingdom (cf.,
e.g., xxiv. 47); but the addition of 'to heal' after verse 1 suggests strongly that Luke has inserted here almost automatically
what was to him a formula of apostleship, even though it in
part duplicated what he had already written. Indeed, verse 2 is
a summary of what the risen Christ enjoined and what the
Apostles in the early chapters of Acts carried out. Luke thus
brings forward into the Lord's earthly ministry the bestowal
of authority originally received after the Resurrection; this is
authority given to the twelve, while at v. 10 the same sort of
authority is given to Peter, their leader.

3   **neither staff.** With these words Luke is supported by Matt.
x. 10 against Mark's 'except only a staff' (vi. 8). It is an
attractive explanation that Mark mistranslated an Aramaic *la*
or *wela* ('neither . . . nor') by reading it as *'illa* ('except').
This is rejected by Black (p. 158) on the ground that it does not
account for Mark's 'only', but if Mark did wrongly read (or
hear?) his source so that he translated *wela* by 'except', it

would be natural for him to add 'only'; but the explanation may simply be that Matthew and Luke were both correcting Mark.

Herod. He is said by Mark (vi. 16) to have himself expressed 7 the belief that Jesus was John the Baptist risen from the dead, and even, according to a considerable weight of MSS., to be the originator of this superstition (vi. 14).

Elijah. See on i. 17, 76; vii. 18, 27; and see Introduction, p. 41. 8

John I beheaded. This peremptory and emphatic statement 9 makes Herod Antipas sound contemptuous of such superstition as Mark ascribes to him (see on verse 7). Luke seems to be hinting his knowledge that Herod feared in Jesus a continuation of the popular movement which he thought to have suppressed by executing John the Baptist (Jos. *Ant.* xviii. 5. 2, and see the note on Luke vii. 18). He omits here Mark vi. 17-29 but at iii. 19-20 he accepts the Marcan tradition about the relation between Antipas and John. Luke seems therefore to accept the Josephus tradition without altogether abandoning Mark, and at xiii. 31 shows his knowledge that Antipas wished Jesus out of the way. Luke no doubt knew that this was for the same political reasons which had led to the execution of the Baptist, but he avoids emphasizing this blemish in his portrait of a politically harmless Christianity.

he was anxious to see him. For Antipas' curiosity cf. xxiii. 8. A comparison with Mark vi. 16 shows deliberate alteration and addition by Luke here. The reason for the addition of these words is theological: we have seen cause to believe Luke aware of the facts but unwilling to stress them. His additions here and at xxiii. 6-16 represent Antipas as wishing to 'see' Jesus, like his family at viii. 20. xxiii. 8 shows the motive (in an Antipas thus presented) as credulous curiosity. No one will 'see' Jesus until they accept him as one come in the name of the Lord (xiii. 35; cf. Matt. xxiii. 39).

The name **Bethsaida** may indicate that Luke's copy of Mark 10 contained Mark vi. 45. Luke prefers in any case to site events in or near towns rather than in relatively unidentifiable country, although his indifference to topography at many points suggests that desire to site an event accurately is not his main motive: it is rather to make the events grow in importance in the sight of his readers. This view is supported by verse 12, in which,

in order to make the plight of the crowds plausible Luke introduces through the mouth of the Apostles the fact that, a town
notwithstanding, they were 'in a desert spot'. The difficulty of
this has evidently been felt by more than one scribe, since the
variant readings suggest several different combinations by which
a town may be reconciled with a desert spot. It remains possible
that a tradition connected the event with the district near Bethsaida. Cf. the prominence of Philip of Bethsaida in John vi. 5:
Philip would know where the local shops might be found.

11   **welcomed them** rather than was moved with compassion
(Mark vi. 34), an idea obnoxious to Luke, who also omits the
Marcan reference to Num. xxvii. 17 (cf. 1 Kings xxii. 17) per-
haps because he thought that the crowds had a shepherd in
Jesus himself.

13   **Give them something to eat yourselves.** Cf. 2 Kings iv.
42-44, and for this command esp. verse 42. The Lord fulfils the
expectations attached to Elijah who was to come. Cf. also on
verse 17 below.

   two fish. Fish accompany loaves in early Christian catacomb
pictures of eucharistic elements.

16   **looking up into heaven.** These words are introduced into
the canon in the liturgy of St. Mark (sixth century) within the
context of the Words of Institution, which open with 'in the
night in which he gave himself up . . .'

17   **what they left.** Cf. 2 Kings iv. 44.

   twelve baskets. No doubt one gathered by each of the
Apostles, but with the further hint that the Lord has provided
enough for the future for all twelve tribes: it was part of the
expectation of the Messiah that in his day there would be a
miraculous abundance.

ix. 18-36. THE RECOGNITION OF THE LORD'S MES-
   SIAHSHIP AT CAESAREA PHILIPPI. CONDITIONS
   OF DISCIPLESHIP. THE TRANSFIGURATION

18 **And it happened that when he was praying in private
   his disciples joined him, and he asked them, 'Who do
19 the crowds say that I am?' And they said in answer,**

'John the Baptist, but others, Elijah, others again that
one of the ancient prophets has arisen'.

And he said to them, 'And you—who do you say that 20
I am?' Peter answering said, 'The Christ of God'. And he 21
with severe warning ordered them to say this to no one,
having told them that the Son of Man must suffer much 22
and be set at nought by the elders and high priests and
scribes and be put to death, and on the third day be
raised.

And he said to them all: 'If anyone wishes to come 23
after me, let him deny himself and take up his cross daily,
and follow me. For whoever wishes to save his life will 24
lose it; and whoever loses his life for my sake will save it.
For what advantage will a man have who has gained the 25
whole world but lost or forfeited himself? For whoever is 26
ashamed of me and my words, of him the Son of Man will
be ashamed, when he comes in his glory and that of his
father and of the holy angels. But I tell you truly, there are 27
some of those standing here who will not taste of death
until they see the kingdom of God.'

It happened about eight days after these words that he 28
took Peter and John and James with him and went up into
a mountain to pray. And while he was praying the appear- 29
ance of his face became different and his clothing became
flashing white. And suddenly two men were speaking 30
with him, who were Moses and Elijah, who appeared in 31
glory and spoke of his departure which he was about to
accomplish in Jerusalem. But Peter and those with him 32
were heavy with sleep, but after fully awaking they
saw his glory and the two men standing with him. And it 33
happened that as they were separating from him, Peter
said to Jesus, 'Master, it is good that we are here, and let
us make three tents, one for you and one for Moses and
one for Elijah'—not knowing what he was saying. While 34
he was saying this a cloud appeared and began to overshadow them; and they were afraid as they entered into
the cloud. And there came a voice out of the cloud saying, 35
'This is my son, the chosen: listen to him'. And at 36
the utterance of the voice Jesus was found alone. And

they kept silent and told no one in those days anything of what they had seen.

Whatever the reason or reasons which led Luke to omit Mark vi. 45-viii. 26, a considerable effect is gained by the consequent order of material in this chapter: Herod (verse 9) has asked the question, 'Who is this?' The feeding of the five thousand suggests an answer (cf. John vi. 14-15) and now Jesus asks what answers are being given to it. Peter gives one answer (verse 20) and finally God himself one even more awesome (verse 35).

18   **when he was praying.** Streeter argued that this phrase shows knowledge of Mark vi. 46 but Luke introduces prayer as an occupation of Jesus so freely (see on v. 16) that this is totally unwarranted.

joined him. Reading συνήντησαν which is read or implied by B 157 f (*occurrerunt*) and the Gothic version. Streeter accounted for Luke's omission of Mark vi. 45-viii. 26 by the theory that his copy of Mark was so mutilated that it broke off at αὐτὸς μόνος in Mark vi. 47 and that Luke was thereby led to think that a reunion of the Lord with his disciples after some considerable separation was necessary to continue the story at Mark viii. 27 with which Luke's supposed copy of Mark continued and with which this verse is parallel; Streeter thought that συνήντησαν implied such a reunion, but the verb could be used after the very temporary and local separation implied by the Lord withdrawing from his disciples to pray.

19   **John the Baptist.** See on verses 7 and 8 above.

20   **the Christ of God.** This claim has been implied—but only implied—already. See the note on John's disciples at vii. 18 ff., which is a Q passage. Jesus makes the claim there only by allusion. In Mark he makes it openly before the high priest (xiv. 61-62) but associates with it a saying which belongs not to the Messiah but to the Son of Man. In Luke a direct claim to Messiahship is avoided even there (see xxii. 67 ff.).

21   **severe warning.** The injunction to silence is common to the synoptics, but Matthew implies acceptance of the title (Mark viii. 30; Matt. xvi. 20).

22   **the Son of Man.** This title, confined in the synoptics to the

Lord's own utterances, is that by which he chooses to designate himself, in contrast to his reluctance to accept that of Messiah.

must suffer much and be set at nought. These words associate the Suffering Servant with the Son of Man (Is. liii. 3).

and on the third day be raised. (ἐγερθῆναι.) But D, the Old Latin, and Marcion may well preserve the original in their reading 'after three days rise' (ἀναστῆναι), like Mark ix. 31 except for a slight difference in word order. Mark always uses the phrase in this latter form (cf. viii. 31; x. 34). Elsewhere Luke writes 'on the third day' (xviii. 33; xxiv. 7). The phrases would be taken by the ancient world to mean the same, namely what in modern English would be expressed by 'on the second day afterwards' or 'two days afterwards'; but 'on the third day' is the liturgical formula, although it occurs in the Apostles' teaching in the NT only at 1 Cor. xv. 4. Cf. 1 Pet. iii. 22; Rom. viii. 34; Col. iii. 1; Eph. i. 20; Heb. i. 3, 13; Acts vii. 55, where the emphasis is on the exaltation rather than the historical Resurrection, for which see, for example, Acts ii. 31; v. 30; xiii. 30.

if anyone wishes to come after me. The Marcan form 23 of the saying slightly altered. At xiv. 27 (cf. Matt. x. 38) we have the Q form. In Mark viii. 34 and Matt. xvi. 24 the challenge to the Lord's contemporaries is still discernible, and the saying is easily interpreted as a summons to share his sufferings.

daily. By this word Luke addresses the challenge rather to his own contemporaries.

whoever wishes to save his life. However profound as 24 religious psychology, this saying, found also in Q (xvii. 33; cf. Matt. x. 39), may have had originally an application to the actual situation in which it was spoken: to reject the Messiah at this crisis might mean to escape death at the hands of the Romans but would mean destruction when the Son of Man came with the angels to carry out the judgment on behalf of God. Thus a man may gain the whole world but **forfeit,** that 25 is, be deprived for punishment of, **himself,** that is, his life.

The Son of Man. Not here identified absolutely with the 26 Lord himself; indeed the identification seems to be just avoided; a man's response to Jesus determines his fate before the Son of Man, but not expressly because they are one and the same.

But the identification, if thus avoided in the Marcan version of the saying (cf. Mark viii. 38), is clear enough in the Q version (cf. Luke xii. 9; Matt. x. 33).

in his glory and that of his father and of the holy angels. It seems a primitive christology which imagines that the Son will come in a glory which is, as it were, shed upon him partly by those angels above whom he is set; but the notion is natural to those thinking about the figure of apocalyptic, the Son of Man: the original Christian conception of the coming judgment is one which included God as active in it (cf. 1 Th. iv. 14) and according to which he would send his angels to gather his elect from the four corners of the earth (Mark xiii. 26 f.), founded on the Lord's own promise himself to gather his own from the four winds (Zech. ii. 6, LXX). The Son of Man is an addition to this scene and is associated with it in the later Jewish apocalyptic (cf. *Enoch* xlvi; lxxi). Mark viii. 38 also probably reads 'and of the holy angels' rather than 'and with the holy angels' (reading καί with P45 W syr. sin.). Luke has met the difficulty for the reverence of a later day by 'in his glory' and Matt. xvi. 27 by writing 'with his angels', a phrase which has no doubt been responsible for the accepted text in Mark (cf. also verse 32).

27   **until they see the kingdom of God.** This is the probable text: Luke avoids altogether the difficulties which Mark ix. 1 raises, since the identity of those who will so certainly see the kingdom is made clear in the following passage: they see it in the Transfiguration, consistently with Luke's view of the kingdom as in part a reality attainable in the present (cf. xvii. 21). But the kingdom of God, thus seen in the glory of his son, is different from the final judgment, which is the subject of verse 26.

28   **about eight days.** The curious dating helps to connect the Transfiguration closely with the prophecy in verse 27. Why Luke has altered Mark's six days (ix. 2) has baffled many commentators. It is possible that it is due to a recollection of the omitted Mark viii. 2 (another curious example of an expression of time in 'a nominative without construction of any kind' as Plummer describes Luke's syntax here). The three days in Mark viii. 2 added to the six of Mark ix. 2 would be represented by Luke as eight (cf. Mark viii. 31; Matt. xvi. 21; Luke ix. 22). Farrer has suggested that after eight days is the octave of the

Lord's first prophecy of resurrection (ix. 27) but why then does Luke write 'about eight days'?

John and James. The order reflects the tradition which brings Peter and John together in the early chapters of Acts; cf. Mark ix. 2.

became different. Luke avoids the apparent metamorphosis 29 of Mark ix. 2, too reminiscent of heathen deities for Luke's Hellenistic readers.

flashing white. The word is septuagintal. In Nahum iii. 3; Ezek. i. 4, 7; Dan. x. 6 (LXX) (the only OT occurrences) it is the brightness rather than the suddenness which is significant. This is important in interpreting xvii. 22-24.

two men. The at first sight odd way of introducing Moses 30 and Elijah is deliberate, enabling Luke to hint at the identification of the **two men** similarly present at the Resurrection (xxiv. 4) and at the Ascension (Acts i. 10).

glory accompanies a supernatural event at ii. 9 and at Acts 31 vii. 55; xxii. 11. The glory is that of the LORD whose cloud or *shekinah* presently appears (verse 34; cf. Mark ix. 7).

his departure. Or 'exodus' (to transliterate the Greek word). This connects Jesus with Moses; like his namesake Joshua in the OT he is Moses' successor, and as such accomplishes an exodus or deliverance.

accomplish. Or 'fulfil', a favourite word with Luke: Jesus will fulfil what Moses prefigured by leading the people out of Egypt. McArthur (*The Evolution of the Christian Year*, p. 97) quotes Gregory Nazianzen, *Or.* I, as claiming a close identification of the Christian experience at the Paschal celebration with the solemn dread and subsequent deliverance of the Exodus. Cf. Introduction, p. 72, on the institution of the Eucharist, especially on the words 'This is my Body'.

were heavy with sleep. Mark ix. 4-5 makes no suggestion 32 that the vision was at night but Luke may have regarded this as natural quite unconsciously. It is also possible that Luke sought a way of excusing Peter's random words, about which the tradition interestingly persists in apologizing.

saw his glory. But for a moment or two only, the glory with which God may invest his chosen, which in John i. 14 has become the glory always visible in the incarnate son.

33 **as they were separating from him.** The phrase enables
Luke to excuse Peter's words to a certain extent, since they
now sound like an attempt to delay the departure of Moses and
Elijah. It is difficult to find any influence which assisted Luke
in his modification of Mark here. Matt. xvii. 6 suggests the
influence of Tobit xii. 16-22 and it has been argued that the
same passage influenced Luke xxiv. 13-35, 44-47; but there is
no influence from Tobit in the present passage.

34 **a cloud.** The *shekinah*. See on xxi. 27.

35 **This is my son.** Cf. Matt. iii. 17 and the note on ii. 14 above.
the chosen. Cf. xxiii. 35. Ps. lxxxix. 20 may be said to find
its fulfilment in this passage; and Ps. cvi. 23, with its ideas of
Moses the chosen deliverer from wrath and the destruction of
God, is no less relevant; Luke clearly intended to represent
Jesus as the new chosen Moses. (The true reading is probably
ἐκλελεγμένος, P45 B S Old Latin syr. sin. sa bo.)

x. 37-50. THE EPILEPTIC BOY. SECOND PREDIC-
TION OF THE PASSION. DISPUTE ABOUT
GREATNESS. THE STRANGE EXORCIST

37 It happened on the following day that when they had
descended from the mountain a great crowd met him.
38 And suddenly a man from the crowd shouted, saying,
'Teacher, I do beg of you to look at my son, for he is my
39 only one, and see—a spirit seizes him and he suddenly
cries out and it tears him with foaming, and will hardly
40 leave him, bruising him. And I begged your disciples to
41 cast it out but they could not.' Jesus answered and said,
'Faithless and perverse generation, till when shall I be
42 with you and bear with you? Bring your son here.' While
he was still approaching the demon tore him and con-
vulsed him, but Jesus threatened the unclean spirit, and
43 healed the boy and gave him to his father. And all were
astonished at the majesty of God.
  While all were marvelling at all the things which he
44 was doing he said to his disciples, 'Set these words within

your ears; for the Son of Man is going to be handed over
into the hands of men'. But they did not understand this 45
saying, and it was hidden from them so that they did not
perceive it, and they were afraid to ask him about this
saying.

An argument came up among them about which should 46
be the greatest. But Jesus on knowing the argument in 47
their hearts, took a child and set him by his side and said
to them, 'Truly I tell you, whoever accepts this child in 48
my name accepts me, and whoever accepts me, accepts
him who sent me; for he who is naturally inferior among
you all, he is great.'

In answer John said, 'Master, we saw someone casting 49
out demons in your name, and we stopped him, because
he does not follow with us'. But Jesus said to him, 'Do not 50
stop him: for whoever is not against you is on your side'.

Luke condenses Mark ix. 14-29, and groups together the
statement about the boy's symptoms (from Mark ix. 18, 21, 22).
The condensation is caused by more than a desire for brevity,
since Luke spares the reputation of the disciples by omitting
Mark ix. 14-16, 28-29, and rejects the notion that the faith of
the father played any part by omitting the moving passage,
Mark ix. 21-24.

my only one. Luke is fond of adding this pathetic detail. 38
Cf. viii. 42; in vii. 12 it may be due to his source.

it tears him with foaming. Luke's description, like Mark's 39
(ix. 18), is graphic and easily recognizable as epilepsy, although
the evangelists differ not a little in detail.

faithless and perverse. Not even Luke's arrangement of 41
the material can disguise the fact that these words must be
about the disciples if not directly addressed to them. But **perverse**, which is omitted by a e Marc Tatian (venetus), is
probably an assimilation to Matt. xvii. 17; even the common
source, Mark ix. 19, has suffered the same fate in P45 W
fam 13.

healed the boy. As though this were a separate action from 42
the casting out of the demon, although the manner of it is not
stated.

43 **While all were marvelling.** In strong contrast to the retirement through Galilee narrated by Mark ix. 30, occupation with admiring crowds is the background for this second prediction of the passion, which in Luke lacks the prophecy of the Resurrection (Mark ix. 31; Matt. xvii. 23).

44 **within your ears.** For ears as recipients of divine truth see on iv. 21. Here the phrase is paralleled by Ex. xvii. 14.

45 **it was hidden from them.** Luke thus adds to the Marcan account (ix. 32) a reason for the obtuseness of the disciples; what they failed to understand was the necessity of suffering for the Son of Man. It was hidden from them until the Resurrection and even then they are slow to believe that the Lord's death and Resurrection were a foreseen necessity (xxiv. 6-7, 11, 25-26, 32, 44-46).

47 **took a child.** Luke omits, with Matthew (xviii. 2), the homely detail of Jesus taking the child in his arms, and by his words 'set him by his side' shows that he pictures an older child, who would better represent what he wishes to teach: for discussion of this and the whole passage, together with xviii. 15-17, see Introduction, p. 57.

48 **naturally inferior.** μικρότερος . . . ὑπάρχων. Perhaps 'naturally junior'. Cf. vii. 28 and Introduction, p. 57, where it is argued that the reference is concrete and to Jesus himself.

49 **In answer.** Luke does not use the word always with this meaning but sometimes to mean 'beginning to speak'. See iii. 15; but here there may be a sense of continuing the conversation, for the Lord has just spoken of those who accept him being identical with those who accept him who sent him. John instances one who, he thinks, did not accept Jesus, because he did not belong to the company of the disciples.

50 **not against you.** This saying is apparently contradicted by xi. 23 (= Matt. xii. 30); though this may be the reason for Luke's change of 'against you' from Mark's 'against us' (ix. 40), the contradiction remains, and is perhaps best explained by assuming that the sayings are from different points in Jesus' ministry: the present saying would be applicable during the earlier Galilean ministry and xi. 23 when he had 'set his face to go up to Jerusalem' (ix. 51).

ix. 51-62. THE JOURNEY UP TO JERUSALEM: SAMARITAN VILLAGES AND WOULD-BE DISCIPLES

It happened that in the fulfilment of the days of his 51
assumption he set his face to go to Jerusalem, and he sent 52
messengers before his face; and they went into a village
of Samaritans, to prepare for him. And they did not wel- 53
come him because he was manifestly going to Jerusalem.
On seeing this the disciples James and John said, 'Lord, 54
do you wish that we should call fire to come down from
heaven and destroy them?' But he turned and rebuked 55
them, and they went to another village. And as they were 56,57
going on their way someone said to him, 'I will follow
you wherever you go!' And Jesus said to him, 'The foxes 58
have earths and the birds of the heaven places to lodge,
but the Son of Man has nowhere to lay his head'. And he 59
said to another, 'Follow me'. But he said, 'Allow me first
to go and bury my father'. And he said to him, 'Let the 60
dead bury their own dead, but do you go away and spread
the news of the kingdom of God'. Yet another said, 'I 61
will follow you, Lord; but first allow me to take leave of
those who are in my home'. But Jesus said to him, 'No 62
one who has set his hand to the plough and looks behind
him is of use to the kingdom of God'.

The journey cannot be satisfactorily traced on a map: Jesus
travels through Samaria, steadfastly set for Jerusalem (ix. 51-
53). At xviii. 35-43 and xix. 1-10 he is indeed at Jericho but
before this he is in Galilee (xiii. 31-33) which really lies behind
him to the north. xvii. 11 reveals Luke's geographical ignorance
beyond hope of defence. Conzelmann is no doubt right: Luke
did not know Palestine, and the journey is less a departure to
new places than a new stage in the Lord's mission. Before he
has been conscious of his calling; now he is conscious of the
necessity of suffering. There is therefore no attempt to preserve the sense of actual travel. x. 1 and 17 suggest a stay in
one place until the seventy return and xiii. 22 stresses the
protraction of the journey.

51   **assumption.** The Greek word is that used of Elijah's being received into heaven in the LXX of 2 Kings ii. 9-11 and in 1 Macc. ii. 58, though in these cases the verb is used, the noun appearing only here in biblical literature. The comparison with Elijah is again manifest in verse 54, and may be intended by the choice of the verb in Acts i. 2 (contrast verse 9). For the constant attendance of Moses and Elijah on the Lord in the Lucan literature see on ix. 30.

 set his face. A phrase which in the LXX certainly implies decision and may (as at Jer. xliv. 12) imply determination. But **his face**, as in the following sentence, has no stronger meaning than 'himself', as commonly in rabbinic writing. For the LXX use cf. Ex. xxxiii. 14; Deut. iv. 37; 2 Sam. xvii. 11; the LXX's use of 'himself' in Deut. iv. 37 where the Hebrew would suggest the use of 'his face' shows the Semitic origin of the expression.

 The special solemnity of the septuagintal style and the manifest comparison with Elijah reveal Luke embarking here upon a part of the gospel which he regarded as of the highest importance: in the following chapter Jesus is to be clearly presented as the new Moses, with whom he is connected also by his fulfilment of the Servant of Deutero-Isaiah: for Moses is a type of him who 'made intercession for the transgressors' (Is. liii. 12), many times pleading for Israel (e.g. Ex. xxxii. 31-32; xxxiv. 9; Deut. ix. 26; Num. xiv. 13 ff.). The Lord is indeed more than Elijah, more than one of the ancient prophets (Luke ix. 19)— he is the prophet like Moses (Deut. xviii. 18). Luke claims this in the gospel for him clearly by implication and specifically in Acts iii. 22-23; unmistakable signs in the tradition of which Luke disposed—quite apart from Jesus' final challenge before his accusers—claim for the Lord more even than this: he is greater than Solomon or Jonah (xi. 31-32; cf. Matt. xii. 41-42), he is greater than John the Baptist, himself of the greatest of all mankind (vii. 28). The Child to be born was to be called 'prophet of the Highest' but Luke gave this honour away to John the Baptist, who instead of the Child is to perform the office of 'going before the Lord' (i. 76; vii. 27). Jesus, addressed as 'Lord', sends messengers before his own face (ix. 52).

52   **Samaritans.** Not as a rule in Luke hostile to the Lord. Cf.

x. 33 and **xvii. 16.** Hence Klostermann is perhaps too bold in suggesting that Luke has added the detail that the village was a Samaritan one.

they did not welcome him because he was going to 53
Jerusalem. An entirely normal reaction of Samaritans to Jews on their way to a feast at Jerusalem from Galilee, as Jos. *Ant.* xx. 6. 1 shows, with its account of the serious riot under Cumanus in 52. The incident is likely enough and the point of it for Luke is to show by the Lord's response to the appeal of James and John to the authority of Elijah (see 2 Kings i. 10-12) that he is of another order than Elijah. The text as translated is that of P45 S B sa, etc., and the additions (in verse 54 'as Elijah also did' and in verse 55 'You do not know what sort of spirit you belong to: the Son of Man did not come to destroy lives but to save them') may no doubt be explained as natural attempts to make quite clear what Luke (who does not labour the obvious) was hinting, some part of the addition being due to memory of Luke xix. 10.

Jerusalem. See on xviii. 31.

'I will follow you . . .' In the rest of the chapter Luke has 57 brought together a number of sayings on discipleship to mark the urgency and complete committal required at this time. The saying that the Son of Man, in contrast to the beasts, has nowhere to rest recalls ii. 7, but Luke shares the saying with Matthew (viii. 19-20) as also the following incident.

'Allow me first to go and bury my father.' Whether or 59 not this incident originally recalled to its hearers the call by Elijah of Elisha in 1 Kings xix. 19-21, this was obviously Luke's experience, for he has added the further incident of verses 61-62, recalling that Elisha was ploughing when called by Elijah (1 Kings xix. 19). Whether he invented it himself it is impossible to decide, the vocabulary being Lucan but not exclusively so. Again, the authority and urgency of the Lord's summons cause him to refuse to countenance the delays which Elijah allowed to his disciples. It is not only he, but the **King-** 60
dom of God which gives both him and his situation greater authority than Elijah's.

There are then a number of passages which show the influence of the story of Elijah and Elisha, viz., iv. 25-30; vii. 11-17,

36-50; ix. 51-56, 61-62. While the last might be due to Luke himself, there is reason for regarding the rest as part of a separate tradition according to which Jesus was regarded as the new Elijah. It is not certain that there was such a separate tradition, and in any case Luke has himself enhanced the effect of it. This close association of Jesus with Elijah is paralleled by an equally close association with Moses, in accordance with the way in which the figures accompanying the Resurrection in the Marcan tradition (where indeed there is only one such figure) reappear at the Ascension and with wording which refers the reader back to the Transfiguration where he finds them carefully identified with Moses and Elijah. In the following chapter actions of the Lord are based on those of Moses. Morgenthaler has pointed out the parallel between the rejection at Nazareth as an introduction to iv. 14-ix. 50 and the rejection at Samaria as an introduction to ix. 51-xix. 40. We have emphasized the references to Elijah, Elisha, and Moses: the Lord himself, in Luke iv. 24-25, draws the close parallel between his own rejection at Nazareth and events in the lives of Elijah and Elisha. Stephen, in Acts vii. 35, is to dwell upon Israel's rejection of Moses. Before this, the Lord hints a comparison of himself with Moses, but disclaims Moses' judicial authority (Luke xii. 14). Jerusalem is the slayer of prophets (xiii. 34), but a prophet—he himself—must perish there (xiii. 33). The destiny of Moses, the Servant, and Jesus is—to be rejected. The place where this must happen is also the place of the new Exodus, the place from which the Gospel is to go forth (xxiv. 47). So Moses, when he went up the mountain, was rejected by the people (Ex. xxxii. 1) though it was from this same place that the Law went forth.

CHAPTER X

x. 1-24. THE MISSION AND RETURN OF
THE SEVENTY

After this the Lord chose out seventy others and sent 1
them two by two before his face into every town and place
where he himself intended to come. And he said to them, 2
'The harvest is plentiful but the labourers are few; so
beseech the master of the harvest to send labourers out
into his harvest. Go! See, I send you as sheep in the midst 3
of wolves. Do not carry a purse nor wallet nor sandals; 4
and salute nobody on the road; but in whatever house you 5
enter, first say, "Peace to this house". And if there be 6
there a son of peace, your peace will rest upon him;
but if not, it will return to you. In the same house stay, 7
eating and drinking what they have, for the labourer is
worth his wages. Do not go from one house to another.
And in whatever city you enter and they welcome you, 8
eat whatever is set before you, and heal those in it who 9
are sick, and say to them, "The kingdom of God has
come upon you". And in whatever city you enter and 10
they do not welcome you, go out into its streets and say,
"Even the dust clinging to us from your city on our feet 11
we wipe off at you! But know this—the kingdom of God
has come near!" I tell you, it will be more bearable for 12
Sodom in that day than for that city.

'Woe to you, Chorazin, woe to you, Bethsaida! for if 13
there had happened in Tyre and Sidon the mighty works
which happened among you, long ago they would have
repented sitting in sackcloth and ashes. But it will be 14
more bearable for Tyre and Sidon in the judgment than
for you. And you, Capernaum! "Exalted to Heaven"? 15
"Down to Hades you will go!". Who listens to you listens 16
to me, and who despises you despises me; and he who
despises me despises him that sent me.'

17 The seventy returned with joy saying, 'Lord, even the
18 demons are obedient to us in your name'. And he said to
19 them, 'I saw Satan as lightning fallen from heaven; see,
    I have given you power to tread upon serpents and scor-
    pions, and upon every power of the enemy, and nothing
20 shall harm you. But do not rejoice in this, that the spirits
    are obedient to you, but rejoice that your names have
    been written in the heavens.'
21 At the same time he rejoiced in the Holy Spirit and
    said, 'I give thanks to you, Father, Lord of heaven and
    earth, because you hid these things from the wise and
    understanding and revealed them to babes. Yes, Father,
    for this was good pleasure in your eyes.
22 'Everything has been given to me by my Father, and
    no one knows who the Son is except the Father, and who
    the Father is except the Son and anyone to whom the Son
    wills to reveal him.'
23 And he turned to his disciples and said privately,
24 'Blessed are the eyes which see what you see. For I tell
    you that many prophets and kings have desired to see
    what you see and have not seen them, and to hear what
    you hear and have not heard them.'

1   **seventy.** Farrer (*Apostolic Ministry*, ed. Kirk, pp. 135 ff.)
    has brought out clearly the significance of their appointment:
    in Num. xi. 4-32 Moses is directed by the Lord to appoint
    seventy elders (verse 16) who receive the Spirit of the Lord
    (verse 25) to assist Moses in governing the mixed multitude
    (verse 4). 'The Seventy are apportioned to the seventy nations
    commonly reckoned by rabbinic learning, for whom the Seventy
    Interpreters had already made the Scriptures available' (*ibid.*
    p. 136). The addition of Eldad and Medad in Num. xi may
    mean that the number was seventy-two (cf. the reading of B Θ,
    etc., in Luke x. 1, and of P45 B D it syr. sin. in Luke x. 17).
        two by two. A detail perhaps from Mark vi. 7 or an illus-
    tration of the witness principle of Deut. xix. 15. See Intro-
    duction, p. 8.
2   **harvest is plentiful.** This saying and that of the next verse
    are closely paralleled in Matt. (ix. 38 and x. 16 respectively),

but there the first is in a context of the Lord's own preaching and before the disciples have been chosen for sending. Here it certainly fails to harmonize with the atmosphere created at the end of the previous chapter, and the suggestion that the seventy should have their number increased is nowhere developed. If authentic, the saying would seem to belong more naturally to an earlier period of the Lord's ministry.

Do not carry a purse. ... This injunction is only generally 4 like Matt. x. 9-10a, and is typical of the degree of resemblance in the passage down to verse 11 with passages in Matt. x. Luke has apparently collected together a number of sayings of this character circulating in differing forms, and has added material of his own; for example, **salute nobody on the road**, this time recalling Elisha (2 Kings iv. 29), and the two injunctions to accept the food provided, together with that not to change lodgings. These points also recall the acceptance by Elijah and Elisha of continuous hospitality from the same source (1 Kings xvii. 15; 2 Kings iv. 8).

Peace. So universally the Jewish greeting that Matt. x. 12 5 does not mention the actual word but clearly implies it in the following verse. Luke may be making sure that his Gentile readers know exactly what form of greeting is customary in the Christian church. Moreover, he makes more of the matter than Matthew: apparently even **one** in the house may receive the blessing of the greeting, if he is a **son of peace**, a phrase for 6 which SB do not quote an exact parallel instance in Hebrew or Aramaic, but they argue that it has a future reference; thus a son of peace would be one looking for the peace of God. We may compare Symeon (ii. 25) and Joseph of Arimathaea (xxiii. 51).

The command to announce the **kingdom of God** is a typi- 9 cally Lucan note in his version of the instructions to those whom the Lord sends. See iv. 43 and viii. 1.

more bearable for Sodom in that day. The implication 12 that Sodom has a judgment yet to come beside that already meted out (Gen. xix) illustrates the inexactness of the notion. Judgment takes place in history but also certainly at the end of history. Cf. xiii. 1-3. But the sin of rejecting the Messiah or the kingdom of God is much more disastrous than any other, however notorious.

13   **Woe to you, Chorazin. . . . Bethsaida.** From Q. These woes on the towns of Galilee are not altogether appropriate here, since the seventy report success rather than failure to make their message heard, in verse 17. Chorazin is otherwise unknown, and has been identified with Kerazeh, north of Tell Hum. Bethsaida was rebuilt by Philip as his capital and named Bethsaida Julia after the daughter of Augustus.

14   **Tyre** and **Sidon** seem to be cited as examples of cities of pagan luxury since verse 14 implies that they would be severely judged, and that this was understood by the Lord's hearers. But the Lord had reason to regard them as capable of repentance. Cf. Mark iii. 8 (cf. Luke vi. 17) and Mark vii. 24-31 (cf. Matt. xv. 21-28).

15   **Capernaum! 'Exalted to heaven'?** Both the question and answer are recollections of Is. xiv. 13-15. Chapters xiii-xiv of Is. have long been regarded as no part of the genuine Isaianic oracles, and may be a Hebrew version of an ancient Accadian myth which survived in a number of forms. The passage is not a direct quotation and is necessarily adapted, for in the original the king of Babylon is addressed. It seems likely that the words are proverbial, perhaps often popularly quoted from a poem well known in the Aramaean world. There is thus another reminiscence of Is. xiv. (verse 12) at verse 18 below. (For an account of the Accadian myth see Guillaume, *Prophecy and Divination*, pp. 49 ff.)

16   **despises him that sent me.** Matt. x. 40 gives another version of this no doubt well-remembered saying of the Lord. Rejection of the Lord's messenger was always rejection of God, as Stephen's speech makes very clear (Acts vii. 51, which adds the sting, 'as your fathers, so also you').

17   **even the demons.** The emphasis is surprising: in ix. 49-50 (cf. Matt. ix. 38-41) the Lord expressly welcomes the use of his name in exorcism by one whom he has not commissioned, and in xi. 19 (cf. Matt. xii. 27) appeals to the fact of exorcists working successfully quite apart from himself. The explanation is probably that the authority over demons possessed by the Messiah and bestowed upon the seventy goes beyond the power to exorcise. When it is wielded the demons not only leave the possessed but are permanently obedient to the Messiah and his

agents. They do not return sevenfold increased as in xi. 24-26 (cf. Matt. xii. 43-45).

Satan as lightning fallen from heaven. Verse 15 above 18 appeared to be connected with Is. xiv. The present passage, for which there is no real parallel in the synoptics, may be inspired by Is. xiv. 12; but the notion of the final defeat of Satan might well have been entertained by the Lord himself. It is found in late Judaistic literature, e.g. *The Assumption of Moses* x. 1; *Jubilees* xxiii. 29; and in the *Testaments of the Twelve Patriarchs* at *Test. Sim.* vi. 6 and *Test. Jud.* xxv. 3; but the actual idea of Satan's falling from heaven occurs much later in Jewish literature, for example in the Palestinian Targum (the *Targum Jerushalmi*, which reached its final form about the middle of the seventh century) and in the *Sayings (Pirqé) of Rabbi Eliezer*, a Midrashic work not earlier than the eighth century (*Targ. Jerush.* 1 Gen. vi. 4; *Pirqé R El* xxii. 11c).

power to tread upon serpents and scorpions. SB do not 19 quote any real exact parallel until Rabbi Levi (c. 300) who said Noah had this power. Cf. Ps. xci. 13 and Deut. viii. 15.

written in the heavens. Many passages in the Bible refer 20 to a Book of life or of the living. Cf. Ps. lxix. 28. It is God's book, Ex. xxxii. 32; Ps. lxxxvii. 4-6; cxxxix. 16; in NT cf. Phil. iv. 3; Heb. xii. 23; Rev. iii. 5; xiii. 8; xvii. 8.

he rejoiced in the Holy Spirit. See on i. 14-15 and cf. 21 i. 47. The phrase is unique and well expresses the joy of those who, like Mary and Elizabeth, are permitted to share knowledge of God's plan of salvation. In their case as in that of the Lord here, it is joy at an apocalyptic vision. Luke appears to be responsible for the phrase.

The **babes** are the men of God's **good pleasure** or favour. See the note on ii. 14. Hiding of the revelation from the **wise and understanding** is a firm part of the tradition. (Cf. 1 Cor. i. 18-31.)

The Son. Here best understood by reference to the apo- 22 calyptic literature: thus *Enoch* xlviii. 3 teaches a pre-existent Son of Man who is hidden 'before God' (verse 6), and in Dan. vii. 13-14 the Son of Man represents the saints of the Most High (verses 18, 22, 25, 27). Cf. 2 Esdras xiii. 52. We are not yet moving in the realm of Johannine theology (cf. John x. 15;

xvii. 2) which nevertheless draws ultimately on the same sources.

who the Father is except the Son. Dan. vii. 16 shows Daniel needing an interpreter. In the present saying the Son acts as interpreter for whom he will. Cf. Dan. x. 10, 16, 18, where the mysterious helper might be taken to be an angel but is called 'as a likeness of a son of man' (x. 16—Theodotion's version). The relation between any two of the three, Father, Son, and 'little flock', remains mysterious. Thus the Father does not 'know' or acknowledge as son the outside world. The Lord is therefore alone acknowledged as son at his baptism, and the early church enters into the same relation as her Lord through baptism. Cf. Gal. iv. 5-7 and Rom. viii. 15.

23 **he turned to his disciples and said privately.** Luke makes this addition to a Q passage (cf. Matt. xiii. 16-17) because he wishes it to be understood that the words were not addressed to the seventy but primarily to the twelve, perhaps only to them.

Blessed are the eyes. Cf. Matt. xiii. 16-17. In both Luke and Matthew the saying is separated from the other beatitudes (Luke vi. 20-23; Matt. v. 3-12) although its style would have harmonized with them, perhaps after Luke vi. 22 or even better after Matt. v. 8. This is some slight evidence that the beatitudes of Luke vi. 20-23 and Matt. v. 3-12 were formed early into a collection. For another isolated beatitude cf. Luke xi. 27-28.

24 **prophets and kings.** Cf., e.g., Is. ix. 1-7; xi. 1-9; Jer. xxxiii. 14-16; Zech. ix. 9. Cf. also Luke's quotation of Is. xl. 4-5 ending with the words 'and all flesh shall see the salvation of God' (iii. 4-6) and xi. 31. The thought approaches that of John viii. 56.

x. 25-42. THE LAWYER AND THE PARABLE OF THE GOOD SAMARITAN. MARTHA AND MARY

25 And see—a certain lawyer stood up trying him, saying,
26 'Teacher, what must I do to inherit eternal life?' And he said to him, 'What is written in the Law? How do you
27 read it?' And he said in answer,

'"You shall love the Lord your God with all your heart and with all your soul and with all your strength and with all your mind", and "your neighbour as yourself"'. And he said to him, 'You have answered rightly. Do this 28 and you will live.'

But he, wishing to vindicate himself, said to Jesus: 29 'And who is my neighbour?' In reply Jesus said: 30

'A certain man was going down from Jerusalem to Jericho, and he fell among robbers, who after both stripping him and beating him went away leaving him half dead. By chance a priest was going down by that road, and 31 he saw him and passed by on the other side. In the same 32 way also a Levite who came by that way saw him and went by on the other side. But a Samaritan on his journey 33 came by him and when he saw him took pity on him, and 34 went up to him and bound up his wounds, pouring on oil and wine, and mounting him on his own beast brought him to an inn and looked after him. And on the next day, 35 taking out two denarii, he gave them to the innkeeper and said, "Look after him, and whatever you spend in addition I will repay you on my return". Which of these three 36 seems to you to have been neighbour to him that fell among the robbers?' And he said, 'He that showed pity 37 for him'. And Jesus said to him, 'Go and do the same yourself'.

In their journey he entered a village; and a woman 38 named Martha welcomed him into her house. And she 39 had a sister called Mary, who indeed sat by the feet of the Lord and listened to his word. But Martha was distracted 40 with all the housework and stood by them and said, 'Lord, don't you care that my sister has left me to do the housework alone? Tell her then to give me some help!' In answer the Lord said to her, 'Martha, Martha, 41 you are anxious and make a fuss about a lot of things, but 42 our need is for few things—or one! For Mary has chosen the best dish, and it will not be taken away from her.'

lawyer. The word gives a false impression, but it is impos- 25 sible to find a single term to convey the sense of one expert in the Torah. νομικός is almost exclusively Lucan (at Matt. xxii. 35, the parallel passage, in those MSS. in which it occurs it has almost certainly been inserted from here). Outside the NT it occurs only at 4 Macc. v. 4 and elsewhere than Luke in the NT only at Tit. iii. 9 and iii. 13. The word seems in the gospel to be due to Luke himself, and may well be his way of interpreting γραμματεύς—the more usual term—to the Gentile world. (See *JTS*, April 1950, pp. 56 ff., and October 1951, p. 166.)

trying. 'Trying him out' would be the exact equivalent.

27 **he said in answer.** The answer is a combination of Deut. vi. 5 and Lev. xix. 18, as already found in *Test. Issachar* v. 2; vii. 6; *Test. Dan* v. 3 (c. 109 B.C.), although these passages are not actual quotations. In Mark xii. 29 and Matt. xxii. 37 ff. it is the Lord who associates the two passages, according to common rabbinic practice. Lev. xix. 18 is quoted also at Matt. v. 43; xix. 19; Rom. xiii. 9; Gal. v. 14; Jas. ii. 8.

Luke's form of the quotation from Deut. vi. 5 is interesting: the matter is much complicated by textual questions, but it seems that in the enumeration and order of the human faculties Luke followed a version based on the Hebrew rather than the LXX; the clause, 'and with all your mind', is an addition, and the word for 'mind' is really an alternative translation of the Hebrew for 'heart'; for no version of the OT knows of a form of the commandment in which four human faculties are mentioned. If two versions were current, one with 'mind', the other with 'heart', the text adopted may well be a conflation of the two, and we should perhaps omit 'and with all your mind' with 1241 D a b ff i l Marcion Augustine (⅔).

28 **You have answered rightly.** A rabbinic phrase; cf. vii. 43.
you will live. I.e. gain eternal life. Cf. the use of the verb in Luke xx. 37-38.

29 **neighbour.** According to the Halakah (the Jewish Law) this was every fellow-countryman, but not a non-Israelite. Thus to make a direct answer to the question 'Who is my neighbour?' we might have expected a story in which the Lord taught that a Samaritan should be helped rather than one which showed him as helping. This may well point to the story being here in a context chosen by Luke rather than its original one; but the lack of connexion may easily be exaggerated: a double answer

is given: 'Your neighbour is anyone in need of your help' and
'Strangers are more neighbourly than strict Jews'.

going down. According to Klostermann the fall in height 30
over the 17 miles is just under ¼ mile.

half dead. The Greek word for this and the phrase for **by** 31
chance occur here only in the NT. Such examples of the style
make it possible that Luke is here setting down at least this
version of the story for the first time.

The callous behaviour of the **priest** and **Levite** contrasts 32
with the humane injunctions of the Law which the 'lawyer'
has just quoted and which they should specially cherish (cf.
Deut. xvii. 8 ff.).

oil and wine were mixed and used as an ointment by both 34
Greeks and Jews.

a village. Not Bethany (John xi. 1), if we press the signifi- 38
cance of the place in the narrative which Luke has given to this
incident; but it is at least possible that either the author of the
Fourth Gospel conflated Luke with his other source about
Lazarus, or that both authors were drawing upon a common
source. In such a case, it might seem strange that Luke should
omit so striking a story as that of the raising of Lazarus. J. N.
Sanders has suggested (*NTS*, i. 1. p. 35) that the omission might
be explicable on the ground that Lazarus was only one example
of the Lord's raising of the dead, and one which had caused
controversy; and that there is an allusion to this in the words
at the end of the story of the Rich Man and Lazarus (xvi. 31).

our need is for few things—or one! The reading adopted 42
is that of S and substantially of B. The majority of MSS. read
'but our need is for one thing'; some 'but our need is for a
few things'. Thus the reading adopted might be criticized
as a conflation of variants; but it may be original if we understand that the Lord is making a mild joke: 'we need only a few
dishes—indeed Mary thinks we need only one!' The variant
readings may then be regarded as attempts at simplification.

D, old Latin, and syr. sin. omit the clause about 'our need' and
'for' in verse 42; after 'a lot of things' they read simply: 'Mary
has chosen the best dish . . .' But this does not explain the
presence of the extra words in the vast majority of the MSS.

xi. 1-4. THE LORD'S PRAYER

1 **And it happened that when he was praying in a certain place, when he ceased, one of his disciples said to him, 'Lord, teach us to pray, as John too taught his disciples'.**
2 **And he said to them, 'When you pray, say, "Father,**
3 **may thy name be kept holy; may thy kingdom come; our**
4 **bread for the morrow give us each day; and forgive us our sins, for we ourselves forgive everyone that is in debt to us; and do not bring us into temptation"'.**

1 **when he was praying.** See on v. 16. This first verse is one of the most interesting of the short Lucan introductions to a section from his sources.

One of the disciples. See Introduction, p. 42.

Teach us to pray. See Introduction, p. 59. SB (ii. 186) say that in the days of the Lord's ministry a great part of the Eighteen Benedictions, the official prayer of the old Synagogue, ranked as obligatory, and private prayers were not rare. We have here an example of request for such a special prayer as should express the particular outlook and concerns of a group of disciples. This is supported by the reference to John, who 'taught his disciples' a special prayer and by rabbinic anecdotes of a similar kind (SB i. 466 ff.).

2 **Father.** Occurs in the sixth of the eighteen 'benedictions' of the prayer referred to above; the idea of God as Father to Israel is found frequently in the OT, e.g. Jer. iii. 4; Deut. xxxii. 6; Pss. lxviii. 5; lxxxix. 26; Hos. xi. 1; Is. lxiii. 16; lxiv. 8; individuals may consider God as Father, e.g. Mal. ii. 10; Ps. ciii. 13; in later literature, Tob. xiii. 4; 3 Macc. vi. 4; Wis. ii. 16; xiv. 3. Ecclus. xxiii. 1, 4; li. 10. It was typical of early Christian practice. (Rom. viii. 15; Gal. iv. 6; 1 Pet. i. 17.)

May thy name be kept holy. A petition of inexhaustible significance yet hard to paraphrase; God is above all things holy (cf., e.g., Is. vi. 3) and, as Lagrange well implies, men must preserve this holiness even upon this earth, far below the sphere of the seraphic hymn. Cf. Ex. xx. 7 and Is. xxix. 23b. For a discussion of the variant in D see Introduction, p. 64.

May thy kingdom come. Parallel rabbinic forms pray for the kingdom to be revealed or appear. These are in accordance with the Jewish conception that God's sovereignty is revealed whenever an Israelite does the will of God. Jesus' conception is eschatological and is a desire and prayer for the actual consummation of the Messianic kingdom on earth. For a consideration of the reading found in Gregory of Nyssa see Introduction, p. 59.

for the morrow. The Greek word ἐπιούσιος is not found 3 elsewhere in the NT. It appears as a variant reading in three late MSS. of 2 Macc. i. 8, where it refers to the shewbread. The only other occurrence was in a papyrus document, apparently a domestic account book, discovered by Petrie in 1889 and since lost; this would suggest that the word could describe the daily ration of food issued to domestic slaves (Manson, *JRLB*, vol. 38, no. 1, p. 111). So Bauer (*Wörterbuch*), who refers to the *Sammelbuch Griechischer Urkunde aus Ägypten* of Preisigke (5224: 20).

Origen also knows of an exegesis that the word means 'for the coming age' (*De Or.* xxvii. 13). This is nearer the truth: ἡ ἐπίουσα is found in Prov. xxvii. 1, where it obviously means 'to-morrow', and where it represents the single Hebrew word *yom*—literally 'day' or 'of the day', i.e. 'daily' or 'sufficient for a day'.

Jerome says that 'in the Gospel which is called "according to the Hebrews"' he found the Hebrew word *mahar* ('to-morrow') in the Lord's Prayer here and he interprets the petition as being for the food of the coming kingdom.

If we apply these facts to the use of ἐπιούσιον here, they will justify the usual translation, 'daily bread', and explain the saying of the Syrian father Ephraem (*c.* 306–373): 'The bread of the day shall suffice thee, as thou hast learnt in the prayer'. But they will also justify understanding 'daily bread' as meaning also 'bread for the morrow' or 'for the coming day'. See Black, pp. 149 ff.

each day. Luke has retained ἐπιούσιον from Q and added this phrase, τὸ καθ' ἡμέραν, which brings out one of the meanings of ἐπιούσιον. Black would explain 'each day' as representing the Palestinian Aramaic *yoma den weyomahra*, literally 'to-day and to-morrow', but meaning 'day by day'. Matthew's aorist imperative 'give' (vi. 11) is perhaps nearer the original Q form than Luke's present imperative (lit. 'go on giving').

4   **forgive us** ... The 'Eighteen Benedictions' contain petitions like the first clause; for the second cf. Ecclus. xxviii. 2.

in debt. The Aramaic word behind both **sins** and **debt** is the same, viz. *hobha*.

temptation. Chase ('The Lord's Prayer in the Early Church', *Texts and Studies*, 1891, pp. 60 ff.) suggests on the basis of the Syriac versions that 'do not bring us' had in the original Aramaic the sense of 'do not allow us to come'; Jewish parallels mentioned by SB would suggest that the ordinary temptations of daily life are meant (cf. Luke iv. 13; xxii. 28; Acts xx. 19; 1 Cor. x. 13; Gal. iv. 14; 1 Tim. vi. 9; Jas. i. 2, 12; 1 Pet. i. 6; iv. 12; 2 Pet. ii. 9) and this is the interpretation put on the words by the Embolismos in all the liturgies in which it appears (Brightman, *Liturgies Eastern and Western*, p. 576). Only Matt. xxvi. 41; Mark xiv. 38; Luke viii. 13; xxii. 40, 46; Rev. iii. 10 might refer to the fiery trial, 'the general eschatological time of tribulation', which Schweitzer (*Quest*, p. 362) believes is the correct reference here (cf. *Mysticism*, pp. 239 ff.). A third but less likely explanation in the context is that 'temptation' here is to be understood as man's putting God to the test. (Cf. Luke iv. 12 and the sin of Massah in the OT: Ex. xvii. 7; Deut. vi. 16; Ps. cvi. 13-15; Wis. i. 1-2; Heb. iii. 8-9 (quoting Ps. xcv. 8-9). (See G. F. Allen, *MC*, April 1941, pp. 22 ff.)

xi. 5-28. ON PRAYER. BEELZEBUB CONTROVERSY AND TEACHING ON SPIRITS. TRUE BLESSEDNESS

5 **And he said to them, 'Which of you shall have a friend and shall go to him in the middle of the night and say to**
6 **him "My friend, lend me three loaves, for a friend of**

mine on a journey has arrived at my house, and I have
nothing to offer him!"—and the other, answering from 7
inside, say, "Don't bother me! The door has already
been closed, and my children along with me are in bed.
I cannot get up and give you anything!"—I tell you, even 8
if he will not get up and give him anything because he is
his friend, for his unblushing persistence he will get up
and give to him as many as he needs. And I say to you, 9
ask and it will be given to you; search and you will find;
knock and it will be opened to you. For everyone that 10
asks receives and the seeker finds, and to the knocker it
is opened.

'Which of you that is a father, if his son ask him for a 11
fish, will instead of a fish give him a snake? or again if he 12
ask for an egg, will he give him a scorpion? If then you 13
who are evil know how to give good gifts to your children,
how much more will your father from heaven give the
Holy Spirit to those who ask him?'

And he was casting out a demon, and this demon was 14
dumb; and it happened that when the demon had gone
out that the dumb man spoke; and the crowds marvelled;
but some among them said, 'By Beelzebub the ruler of 15
the demons he casts out the demons'. Others, tempting, 16
required from him a sign from heaven. But he knowing their 17
thoughts said to them, 'Every kingdom divided against
itself is brought to desolation, and house falls on house.
If indeed Satan is divided against himself, how will his 18
kingdom stand—since you say that I cast out demons by
Beelzebub? But if it is by Beelzebub that I cast out demons, 19
by whom do your sons cast them out? On this ground
they will be your judges. But if it is by the finger of God 20
that I cast out demons, then the kingdom of God has
come upon you.

'When a strong man, well armed, guards his own hall, 21
his belongings are undisturbed. But when a stronger than 22
he comes upon him and overcomes him, he takes away
the set of armour in which he had trusted, and distributes
his trophies. He that is not with me is against me, and 23
he that does not gather with me scatters.

24   'When an unclean spirit goes out from a man, he wan-
ders through waterless places looking for somewhere to
rest, and not finding anywhere he says, "I will return to
25   my house, out of which I came". And on going he finds
26   it swept and tidied. Then he goes and takes as well seven
other spirits more evil than himself, and they enter and
dwell there, and the end of that man is worse than the
beginning.'
27   And it happened as he was saying these things that a
woman from the crowd lifted up her voice and said to
him, 'Blessed is the womb that bore you and the breasts
28   which you sucked!' But he said, 'Blessed rather are those
who hear the word of God and keep it!'

5   **Which of you** . . . The interrogative is lost in the pro-
longation of the sentence and the moral drawn from the story
is that a Christian should persevere in prayer (verses 9 and
10). Perhaps this was the original emphasis rather than that
God answers prayer if it is persistent. Verses 11-13 teach rather
that God is willing to answer because of his love. Verses 5-8 are
parallel in their teaching to the parable of the Unjust Judge
(xviii. 1-8), a parable whose position in the gospel has often been
thought difficult to explain but which is probably determined
by Luke's eschatology. Both passages teach perseverance in
prayer at least as persistent as secular seekers after justice or
help, and in each Luke has so used his material that the originally secondary person in the story becomes the more important.
8   **unblushing persistence** translates one word in Greek, lit.
'shamelessness'.
11   **fish.** The words 'bread, will he give him a stone, or again'
before 'fish' are omitted as assimilation to Matt. vii. 9 on the
authority of P45 B Old Latin, syr. sin, sa.
12   The presumption that it is the **Holy Spirit** who is the object
of the disciples' prayer supports the contention that the reading of Gregory of Nyssa at verse 2 is original to the text.
Moreover at Luke xxiv. 49 they are to wait for this gift before
beginning their work of witness. For the Holy Spirit see Introduction, p. 38.
In the Beelzebub controversy Luke has like Matthew con-

flated Mark and Q, the latter apparently introducing the controversy with a miracle.

some among them. Not Pharisees, as in Matt. xii. 24. Luke 15 has reserved verses 37 ff. for controversy with them.

by Beelzebub. The accusation remained a possibility in the minds of many, even apparently including the disciples; cf. xxiv. 38. Beelzebub is the Vulgate's form of the word and its derivation is very uncertain; the name occurs in the NT here and in the parallel passages in Mark and Matt. and at Matt. x. 25; not at all in the OT. If we could read with confidence this form of the name we might connect it with Baal. Cf. βεελζεβούλ and βάαλ μυῖαν at 2 Kings i. 2, 3, 6, and Μυῖαν at Jos. *Ant.* ix. 2, 1. The name would then mean 'Lord of flies', and the god of Ekron in the 2 Kings passage will be a god to turn away the scourge of flies. But Foerster in *TWNT* (i. 605) believes that Josephus shows the meaning of the name was already forgotten in his day. If we may read Zebul at the end of the word the reference may be to a god otherwise forgotten whose name occurs in the Ras Shamra texts as a dying and rising-again god. Certainly in NT times the name is of a leader among the demons, not universally identified with Satan.

Satan is divided against himself if one of his vassals is 18 a rebel.

your sons. I.e. your pupils, who use the exorcisms which 19 you teach. The verse may well be authentic, for it appears from ix. 49-50 that the Lord conceived of others not his followers sharing his powers.

the finger of God. At first sight surprising anthropomor- 20 phism; but Luke is linking the work of the Lord with that of Moses. The OT passages are Ex. viii. 17-19; xxxi. 18; Deut. ix. 10. In the first the point is made that Pharaoh's magicians, able to reproduce the first two plagues by the agency of demons (as the Midrash has it), have to acknowledge that they are unable to reproduce the third and confess that 'This is the finger of God'. Cf. Matt. xii. 28.

a strong man. I.e. Satan.   21

a stronger than he. I.e. Jesus.   22

set of armour. For the custom of taking a panoply or set of armour as a trophy see 2 Sam. ii. 21 (LXX).

distributes his trophies. Cf. Is. liii. 12 (LXX). The reminiscence suggests that it is Jesus as the Suffering Servant who is the conqueror.

24   through waterless places. Cf. Is. xiii. 21, where the inhabitants of the wilderness include demons, in Hebrew, satyrs in a goat-like form. Cf. Is. xxxiv. 14 and Bar. iv. 35.

26   seven other spirits. Cf. viii. 2. The fate of those who do not seek the Holy Spirit (verse 13 above).

27   the womb that bore you. The woman's blessing is of a kind well known both in the Jewish and Gentile world. Cf. i. 42 and 2 Bar. liv. 10. Mary's womb had known the indwelling of the Holy Spirit (i. 35) and this thought provides a link with the previous verses. See also on i. 45, where Mary is blessed because she believed.

28   Blessed rather are those. Mary is temporarily not among them. See on viii. 3 and viii. 19-21. She is not permanently excluded, but her blessedness, like that of others, is dependent on continued obedience, such as she showed at i. 38.

xi. 29-54. SEEKING A SIGN. LIGHT. AGAINST THE PHARISEES

29 The crowds gathering round him, he began to say, 'This generation is an evil generation; it seeks a sign and a sign shall not be given to it except the sign of Jonah.
30 For as Jonah was a sign to the Ninevites, so will the Son
31 of man be to this generation. The Queen of the South will rise up in the judgment with the men of this generation and will condemn them, because she came from the ends of the earth to listen to the wisdom of Solomon, and
32 see—greater than Solomon is here. The men of Nineveh will rise up in the judgment with this generation and will condemn it, because they repented at the preaching of Jonah, and see—greater than Jonah is here.
33   'Nobody after lighting a lamp puts it in a cellar or under a basin, but on a lampstand, so that those who
34 come in may see the light. The body's lamp is your eye.

When your eye is sound, your whole body too is luminous; but when it is bad, your whole body too is dark. Look 35 therefore that the light that is in you is not darkness. If 36 then your whole body is luminous, not having any part dark, it will be as wholly luminous as when the lamp with its bright shining illuminates you.'

While he was speaking a Pharisee invited him to have 37 breakfast with him, and he went in and reclined; and the 38 Pharisee seeing this marvelled that he had not first washed before the breakfast. But the Lord said to him, 39 'Now you, the Pharisees, purify the outside of the cup and the platter, but the inner part of you is full of greed and evil. Senseless men, did not he that made the outer part 40 make the inner part too? But give away as alms the things 41 within and then—all things are pure to you. But woe to 42 you Pharisees, because you tithe mint and rue and every vegetable, and you pass over judgment and the love of God; these latter you ought to have done and not omitted the former. Woe to you Pharisees, because you love the 43 chief seat in the synagogues and salutes in the market-places. Woe to you because you are like concealed 44 tombs, and men walking over them are unaware of them.'

In answer one of the lawyers said to him, 'Teacher, in 45 saying these things you are insulting us too'. And he 46 said, 'Woe to you lawyers also, because you burden men with burdens hard to carry, and you yourselves will not touch the burdens with one of your fingers. Woe to you, 47 because you build the memorials of the prophets, and your fathers killed them. So you are witnesses and show 48 agreement with your fathers' deeds, because they killed them and you build. For this reason the wisdom of God 49 said: "I will send to them prophets and apostles, and some of them they will kill and persecute, that the 50 demand for the blood of all the prophets shed from the foundation of the world may be made from this genera-tion, from the blood of Abel to the blood of Zachariah 51 who perished between the altar and the temple; yes, I tell you, it will be demanded from this generation. Woe 52

to you lawyers, because you have taken the key of knowledge; you yourselves have not entered and those who
53 were trying to enter you have prevented.' When he went
out from that place the lawyers and the Pharisees began
54 to press bitterly upon him and interrogate him on a number of things, lying in wait for him to pounce on something out of his mouth.

29   **The crowds.** In Matt. xii. 38 the passage is introduced by an
express request by the Scribes and Pharisees for a sign. Luke
xi. 16 justifies the mention of crowds here.

    the sign of Jonah. According to verse 32 this is Jonah's
preaching; this is logical since the Ninevites did not witness
Jonah's adventure with the great fish. Matt. xii. 40 has a more
typological interpretation, but cf. verse 41.

31   **The Queen of the South.** See 1 Kings x. 1 ff. The title is
justified by the later tradition (found in Josephus) that she was
the queen of 'Egypt and Ethiopia'.

32   **greater than Solomon . . . than Jonah.** If we pressed
the Greek we should have to say 'something greater', the
saying thus implying that what is greater than the past
great men is Jesus and his kingdom and all that goes with
his work.

33   **a lamp.** The Torah was often thought of as the original light
created by God in the beginning (Gen. i. 3). Cf., e.g., Ps. cxix.
105; Is. li. 4. In the OT God himself is described as light in
Ps. xxvii. 1; Is. lx. 19. In the NT, with the influence of Hellenistic thought, especially of wisdom as the divine light (John i.
7 ff.), the association of God with light as the source of life and
truth is much more marked (John vii-viii; 1 John i. 5; Jas. i. 17).
In the Epistle of James God's constancy as light is compared
to the sun as contrasted with the fickle moon. Luke, who in
verses 35-36 has his peculiar addition to this Q passage, does
not make his thought very clear: the confusion is due to his
placing together two verses probably originally found in different parts of Q: verse 33 (cf. Matt. v. 15) in which the lamp
is the source of illumination, i.e. the Law or the Word of God,
which the scribes have tried to hide in the cellar; and verse 34
(cf. Matt. vi. 22), in which the lamp is that organ by which the

personality grasps this illumination, as a lamp has to be kindled from another source than itself. Cf. John v. 35; Eph. i. 18.

The light that is in you. The light which the eye has ap- 35 propriated from the source into the personality; but it may be darkness if the eye has not clearly grasped that source, but has perverted it, as the scribes had perverted the Word of God.

luminous. Illuminated by the source of light, it will have 36 no part dark, like God himself (Jas. i. 17).

the lamp with its bright shining. Here, as in verse 33, a figure of God, the source of illumination.

The eye is the means (not source) of illumination because with it we read the Word of God, and interpret the world which he made. For this identification of the personality temporarily with the organ most obviously involved, cf. (for the eye) x. 23; 2 Peter ii. 14; 1 John ii. 16; (for the ear) Job xii. 11; xiii. 1; xxix. 11; Jer. vi. 10; ix. 20; Luke ix. 44; Matt. xiii. 16.

a Pharisee. A Lucan introduction to the passage to follow in 37 which the Pharisees are condemned (verses 37-39a). Similarly verse 45 introduces the woes against the 'lawyers'.

the outside of the cup and the platter. Here apparently 39. taken loosely by Luke to stand for the outer man since it is because Jesus has not washed his hands that the host is surprised. Thus he continues with 'the inner part of you'. In Matt. xxiii. 25-26 the metaphor is maintained to the end of the saying. These points illustrate the manner in which Luke has composed his gospel: this saying is not strictly applicable to the question of washing the person, but has been pressed into service and adapted in the process.

Give away as alms the things within. A not altogether 41 successful attempt to translate Luke's τὰ ἐνόντα δότε ἐλεημοσύνην and at the same time to retain the continuity with thought about the inner man which seems to be implied by the Greek and the previous verses. The 'things within' must of course mean 'belongings' but there may be a pun implied. It is more likely that 'give alms' represents the Aramaic *zakko* wrongly read for *dakko* ('cleanse'). Thus Matthew has the correct translation of the Aramaic at xxiii. 26. This was Wellhausen's conjecture, praised by Black (p. 2).

43   Another—Marcan—version of this saying is to be found at
xx. 46. Matt. xxiii. 6 has conflated Q and Mark xii. 39.

44   **concealed tombs.** Matt. xxiii. 27 explains why these are
repugnant: outside they are elegant but inside they are full of
decaying matter.

47   **you build the memorials** (or tombs) **of the prophets.** A
puzzling form of reproach which the scribes could meet with
the retort that they thus dissociate themselves from the deeds
of their ancestors. The explanation probably lies along the lines
suggested by Black (pp. 11-12): Luke's **and you build** goes
back to an Aramaic which might equally well be translated 'and
you are the children' (*sc.* 'of those who killed'). Behind the
saying there seems therefore to have been originally a word-play
in Aramaic, by which the words 'you are their [i.e. the prophets']
builders' sounded the same as 'you are their [i.e. the murderers']
sons'. Thus Matt. in xxiii. 31 has 'you are sons' for Luke's
'you build'. For the reproach cf. also Luke xiii. 34 (Matt. xxiii.
37); Acts vii. 52; Heb. xi. 36-38; 1 Th. ii. 15.

49   **the wisdom of God.** A variant for the normal rabbinic 'the
Holy Spirit' (says) or 'the divine righteousness' (says), meaning 'God says'. Rabbi Eliezer and Rabbi Jehoshua (*c.* 90) both
introduce an exposition of Eccl. iii. 16 by saying of the passage,
'And the Holy Spirit says'; Rabbi Eliezer explains it by Jer.
xxxix. 3, but Rabbi Jehoshua by Ex. xxxii. 27 (SB).

51   **Zachariah.** The R. Eliezer just mentioned, in his exposition
of Eccl. iii. 16, quotes Is. i. 21, and explains the latter by referring to the murder of Zachariah and Urijah in the Temple,
saying that in Eccl. iii. 16 the Holy Spirit justifies the destruction of the Temple by recalling the past profanations there. The
Targum on Lam. ii. 20 refers also to a reproach by the 'divine
justice' for the murder of Zechariah, son of Iddo, a high priest
and prophet, on the Day of Atonement. This identification of
Zechariah with the prophet of the canonical book (see Zech. i.
1) is found also in the parallel Matt. xxiii. 35, but may be dis-
regarded. The Zechariah referred to is probably the son of
Jehoiada the high priest whose witness and murder is described
in 2 Chron. xxiv. 17-22. No other Zechariah (or 'Zachariah'
—which is merely the later form of the same name) need be
sought when we take account of the Talmudic legends that the

blood of this Zechariah boiled at the capture of Jerusalem by
the Babylonians, and of the fact that a supposed trace of this
blood was shown to Jerome, and of the existence of the Tomb
of Zechariah below the Temple walls; this Zechariah and his
murder must have been household words in the time of the
Lord. No doubt the 'traces of blood' shown to Jerome were
invented because of this passage in the gospels, but they would
most probably be ascribed to this notorious murder of Zechariah
of 2 Chron. xxiv.

The alternative is Zechariah son of Bariscaeus, an important
citizen slain by two zealots in the courts of the Temple A.D. 68
(Jos. *B.J.*, iv. 5. 4). In this case the saying is obviously not
authentic.

the key of knowledge. Probably alien to the original. See 52
Black, pp. 193 ff.: the Aramaic original behind this verse and
Matt. xxiii. 13 may well have read, 'You have shut the king-
dom of Heaven before men and taken away the key'.

A similar saying may be quoted from a fragment of a lost
gospel, which is published in *The Oxyrhynchus Papyri* (iv.
23); but in the phrase there, while the word 'key' occurs, there
is no certainty that it was followed by 'of knowledge'. Indeed,
'key of the kingdom' is a very probable restoration (cf. Matt.
xxiii. 13). The phrase in this verse seems then to be due to
Luke, who uses the word 'knowledge' only once elsewhere,
viz. i. 77. This is not direct Hellenization but is due to Luke's
affinity with Wisdom literature, where most of the OT occurrences of the word are to be found.

the lawyers and Pharisees. Luke describes their hostility 53
vividly in these two verses, which are peculiar to his gospel.
This hostility is an important cause, in Luke's account, among
those which led to the condemnation of an innocent man. For
the reading 'lawyers' here see Kilpatrick, *JTS*, April 1950, and
Leaney, *JTS*, October 1951.

xii. 1-34. EXHORTATION TO FEARLESSNESS. THE
RICH FOOL. BE NOT ANXIOUS

1 During this time, a crowd of many thousands having gathered, so that they trod one another down, he began to say
to his disciples first:

'Beware of the leaven, which is the hypocrisy of the
2 Pharisees. But nothing has been hidden which will not be
revealed, and nothing is secret which will not be known.
3 For this reason all that you have said in the darkness will
be heard in the light, and what you have spoken in the ear
4 in your rooms will be proclaimed on the houses. But I say
to you, my friends, do not be afraid of those who kill the
body and after that have nothing further that they can do.
5 But I will show you whom to fear: fear him who after
killing has power to cast into Gehenna. Yes, I tell you,
6 fear him. Are not five sparrows sold for twopence? And
7 not one of these has been forgotten before God. But all the
hairs of your head have been counted. Do not be afraid:
8 you are worth more than many sparrows. But I tell you,
whoever confesses me before men, the Son of Man will
9 confess him also before the angels of God. But he that has
denied me before men will be denied before the angels of
10 God. And everyone who shall speak a word against the
Son of Man, it will be forgiven him; but he who has blasphemed against the Holy Spirit will not be forgiven.
11   'But when they bring you before synagogues and rulers
and authorities, do not be anxious about how to make
12 defence or what to say: for the Holy Spirit will teach you
at that very moment what ought to be said.'
13   Someone from the crowd said to him, 'Teacher, tell
14 my brother to share the inheritance with me'. But he
said to him, 'Man, who has appointed me judge or

distributor over you?' And he said to them, 'See that 15
you keep yourselves from every kind of greed, because it
is not in abundance that anyone's life consists, from his
possessions'.

And he told them a parable, saying, 'A certain rich 16
man's land gave a good crop; and he considered in him- 17
self saying, "What shall I do, for I have nowhere to store
my crops?" And he said, "This is what I will do: I will 18
demolish my barns and build bigger ones, and I will store
there all my corn and my goods, and I will say to my 19
soul, 'My soul, you have many good things laid up for
many years: take a rest! Eat! Drink! Enjoy yourself!'"
But God said to him, "Senseless man! This night your 20
soul is demanded of you: as for the things you have got
ready, for whom will they be?" So it is with the man who 21
stores up for himself but is not rich towards God.'

And he said to his disciples, 'Therefore I say to you: 22
do not be careful for your soul, what to eat, nor for the
body, what to wear. For the soul is more than food and 23
the body than clothing. Consider the ravens, how they do 24
not sow and do not reap, who have not store or barn, and
God feeds them: you are worth much more than birds!
Which of you by care can add to his life's span a cubit? If 25, 26
then you cannot do even the least little thing, why are
you careful about the rest? Consider the lilies, how they 27
do not spin and do not weave; but I tell you, not even
Solomon in all his glory was arrayed like one of them.
But if the grass in the field which is there to-day and 28
to-morrow is thrown into the oven God so clothes,—how
much more you, men of little trust! And do not you search 29
for something to eat and something to drink, and do not
be in suspense. For these things are sought after by all the 30
nations of the world; but you have a father who knows
that you have need of these things. Rather search for his 31
kingdom and these things will be given you in addition.
Do not be afraid, little flock! For your father has been 32
pleased to give you the kingdom.

'Sell your belongings and give alms; make for your- 33
selves purses which do not wear out, an inexhaustible

treasure in the heavens, where no thief approaches nor
34 **moth corrupts. For where your treasure is, there also will**
your heart be.'

1   **leaven.** The symbol of the inner corruption of the Pharisees
(cf. xi. 44) hidden by their hypocrisy. Cf., e.g., Ex. xii. 15, 19;
1 Cor. v. 6 ff. for leaven in this sense.

2   **which will not be revealed.** (Cf. viii. 17, a Marcan context.) This is a prophecy of what will happen at some divinely
ordained time, not a command as at Matt. x. 26. Cf. Luke ii.
35; 1 Cor. iv. 5; Rom. ii. 16.

5   **Gehenna.** Only here in Luke. It derives from the *ge hinnom*,
the valley curving round from south-west to south of Jerusalem, where children were sacrificed to Molech (cf. Jer. vii.
31-32) and which Josiah rendered unusable for religious purposes (2 Kings xxiii. 10), presumably by turning it into a rubbish pit. It thus became both by its horrible associations and
by its present character a symbol for the place of punishment
in the *She'ol* of later Judaism. But it is not necessarily a symbol
for a place of unending punishment, since while the fire is continuous (through the ever smouldering rubbish) what is thrown
there is destroyed.

8   **The Son of Man will confess him.** It should be noted that
the identification of Jesus himself with the Son of Man is by
no means absolute, and the angels appear to have in this picture greater authority than he, as at ix. 26 where (as with the
probably true reading at Mark viii. 38) the Son of Man derives
part of his glory from that of the Father and of the angels. See
on ix. 26.

10   **speak a word against the Son of Man.** Readily understood
as venial for he is not higher than the angels; **but he who has**
blasphemed against the Holy Spirit has blasphemed against
God himself. (Cf. Mark iii. 28-29.)

11   **before synagogues. . . .** If we were certain that the author
was the companion of St. Paul, the list of scenes of persecution
might well be supposed to come from Luke's knowledge of the
Apostle's experience. The clause is added to Q to which must
be assigned the rest of verses 2-12, found in different contexts
in Matthew. See also on xxi. 12 ff.

how to make defence. Omitting 'or what' after **how** with D it syr. cur., pesh., and Clement.

who has appointed me. The Lord explicitly rejects the   14
position of a second Moses, which the man's request seemed to imply. (Cf. Ex. ii. 14.)

greed. Not covetousness, for which the Greek is ἐπιθυμία.   15
my goods. (Cf. Ecclus. xi. 18-19.)   18
soul. A poor if unavoidable translation. See note on i. 47 for   19
the meaning 'self'. No one English word will convey this meaning combined both with that of 'life' in the sense of the ani-
mating principle in a living creature, and with that of 'soul' as
contrasted with body. All these meanings are required here and
in the following verses.

is demanded. Literally 'they demand', a rabbinic peri-   20
phrasis for 'God demands'. For the construction in this sense
see verse 48 and vi. 38.

and he said to his disciples. A Lucan addition to Q; but   22
it is likely that the words which follow here were indeed originally addressed to an inner group of followers. See verses 30 and
31 and cf. Matt. v. 1.

be in suspense. The Greek word occurs only here in the   29
NT. Contemporary usage suggests the meaning, to swing between heaven and earth, thus to have no sure footing, and so
to be anxious.

all the nations of the world. 'ummoth ha-'olam—one of   30
the commonest rabbinic designations of the non-Israelite section of mankind. The words are those of a Jew to Jews whom
he is recalling to their divine mission. Hence the emphatic **you**
at the beginning of verse 29, and the beginning of 30b, in the
genitive, translated 'but you have . . .'

little flock. See on ii. 14 and x. 21.   32

xii. 35-59. BE WATCHFUL. SIGNS OF THE AGE AND A WARNING

'**Let your loins be girded and your lamps alight, and**   35, 36
yourselves like men waiting for their master, when he
comes away from the marriage-feast, that when he has

come and knocked they may immediately open the door
37 for him. Blessed are those servants whom the master on
his coming shall find awake; truly I tell you, he will gird
himself and let them recline, and attend and serve them.
38 And if he come in the second and if he come in the third
watch and find them so, blessed are those servants.

39 'Be sure of this, that if the householder had known at
what time the thief was coming, he would not have
40 allowed his house to be broken into. You too be ready,
because at a time that you do not expect is the Son of Man
coming.'

41 Peter said: 'Lord, is it to us that you address this par-
42 able or to all?' And the Lord said, 'Who then is the faithful
and prudent steward whom the lord will set over his
staff to give out the corn allowance at the proper times?
43 Blessed is that servant whom his master on coming shall
44 find doing so. In truth I tell you, he will set him over all
45 his possessions. But if that servant say in his heart, "My
master is a long time coming", and begin to beat the
46 boys and the maids, to eat and drink and be drunk, that
servant's master will come on a day when he is not
expecting him and at a time that he is unaware, and will
cut him asunder, and will allot him his part with the
faithless.

47 'But that servant who knew his master's wishes and
did not make ready for him and did not act according to
48 his wishes will be flogged with many strokes. But he who
did not know, but did things worthy of lashes, will be
flogged with few strokes; from everyone to whom much
has been given much will be looked for, and from him
before whom much has been set a greater abundance
will be asked.

49 'Fire I have come to cast upon the earth, and how I
50 wish that it were already kindled! I have a baptism to be
baptized with, and how constrained I am until it be
51 finished! Do you suppose that I came to give peace on the
52 earth? No, I tell you, but rather division! For there will be
from now five in one house divided; three against two
53 and two against three will they be divided, father against

son and son against father, mother against daughter and
daughter against mother, mother-in-law against her
daughter-in-law and daughter-in-law against mother-in-
law.'

And he said to the crowds, 'When you see a cloud 54
rising in the west, you say immediately that a shower is
coming, and so it happens; and when a south wind blow- 55
ing, you say that there will be heat, and it is so. Hypo- 56
crites, you know how to interpret the appearance of the
earth and the sky, but this season—how is it that you do
not interpret it?

'But why do you not even of yourselves judge what is 57
right? For as you go with your opponent to an official, 58
on the way devote your energies to getting a discharge
from him, lest he hale you before the judge, and the
judge deliver you to the bailiff, and the bailiff throw you
into prison. I tell you, you will not come out from there 59
until you pay the last farthing.'

your lamps alight. For this and the marriage-feast cf. 35
Matt. xxv. 1-13, but there is not sufficient evidence to assign
for certain these verses 35-38 and the passage in Matt. to Q.

open the door. This and the words 'let them recline' sug- 36
gest a special interpretation of the Messianic Banquet with
which the kingdom is to be inaugurated. The picture is one
of universal application: all should be watchful, awaiting the
coming of the Son of Man; but Luke has not fitted these verses
clearly into his eschatological scheme; it is not clear whether
the time is that between the inauguration of the kingdom and
the final consummation, or whether here he regards these as
simultaneous. Perhaps the source was based on the latter view
while Luke's interpretation certainly envisages more than one
appearance of the Son of Man. (See p. 68.)

serve them. Cf. xxii. 27 and John xiii. 4-5.   37

to us . . . or to all? The insertion of Peter's question by 41
Luke into a Q passage must have some high significance. The
meaning of the parable which prompts it is clear enough on the
surface, and the clue to the meaning of the question must lie
in the answer which the Lord gives in the following verses.

But first we must see what difference there is in Peter's mind (at least as conceived by Luke) between **us** and **all**; see the following note.

42   **over his staff.** The steward is to be in authority temporarily in his Lord's absence. He is therefore a symbol of the Apostles with their authority over the church between the Ascension and the return of the Lord to assume his kingship. The whole passage (verses 41-48) conveys the same warning against misuse of delegated power as xix. 12-27. The answer therefore to Peter's question in verse 41 is that the Apostles have their own special responsibilities. This is sternly emphasized in verses 45-48, especially 47-48. The argument is obscured by the Lord's answer to Peter being in the form of a question: Luke has unskilfully constructed dialogue from traditional material which he has left relatively unchanged.

staff. The Greek word is used in this sense of domestic staff in the LXX of Gen. xlv. 16.

44   **over all his possessions.** Cf. xix. 17, 19, 24-26, the promise of material reward at xviii. 29-30 (cf. Mark x. 29), and the Q passage xxii. 28-30 where a kingdom is assigned to the twelve Apostles.

46   **cut him asunder.** A punishment not unknown for slaves, but the original Aramaic may have had the meaning, 'he will divide him his portion' ('and set it with the faithless'). See Black, p. 190 f.

47-48   These verses, peculiar to Luke, may well have become attached to the dominical sayings, as exegetical commentary, perhaps in a liturgical context. The thought is familiar to the rabbis. For the OT conception of unconscious sin see Num. xv. 22 ff.; Lev. v. 17-19; Ps. xix. 12.

49   **How I wish . . .** τί represents the Hebrew *mah*. Cf. Matt. vii. 14, where it is used with an adjective. Blass is wrong to refer the use to the LXX, where it does not occur. Luke's text may be a mistranslation of an Aramaic original which our text would in fact translate correctly (Black, p. 89). But the Greek is possible: even if the use of τί is bold, that of εἰ can be paralleled at xix. 42. Cf. the LXX of Is. ix. 5 for εἰ after θέλω. The apparent abruptness and the mood are perhaps best paralleled by John xii. 27.

baptism. Cf. Mark x. 38 for baptism as a figure of death.   50

division. See on ii. 14 and 35.   51

from now. Literally, from the period now beginning. Cf.   52
xxii. 69.

son against father. For the phrase and the whole passage   53
cf. Mic. vii. 6, to which Matt. x. 34 f. is even closer.

season. Maintaining the word-play of the Greek, for the   56
word will stand for a season in the natural year and for a period
bearing a special character in the divine plan. This season
demands decision: the Messiah's challenge brings division.

discharge. I.e. from the debt which Luke thinks of as the   58
cause of the dispute. The word for 'bailiff' is constantly used
for an officer charged with collecting debts. The thought loosely
includes the idea that God is the creditor. (Cf. xi. 4.)

on the way. Vital to the argument. The hearers must not
wait for the judgment before making their decision. (Cf. the
sayings in xiv. 25-33.)

CHAPTER XIII

1-35. THE NEED FOR REPENTANCE. HEALING OF
A WOMAN. PARABLES. THE NEED TO ENTER
BY THE NARROW GATE. DEPARTURE FROM
GALILEE. LAMENT OVER JERUSALEM

1 There were some present at that time who were reporting
to him about the Galilaeans whose blood Pilate had mixed
2 with their sacrifices. And in answer he said to them, 'Do
you think that these Galilaeans were sinners above all the
3 Galilaeans because they suffered this? No, I tell you, but
if you do not repent, you will all perish in the same
4 manner. Or those eighteen upon whom the tower fell in
Siloam and killed them—do you think that they were
5 sinners above all the men inhabiting Jerusalem? No, I tell
you, but if you do not repent, you will all perish in the
same way.'
6 And he spoke this parable: 'A man had a fig-tree planted
in his vineyard, and he came looking for fruit on it and
7 did not find any. And he said to the vinedresser, "Look, it
is three years since I have been coming looking for fruit
on this fig-tree and not finding any. Cut it down! Why does
8 it waste the ground?" But the other answered and said to
him, "Master, leave it this year too until I dig round it and
9 manure it; and if it bear any fruit in future—well! But if
not, you shall cut it down." '
10 He was teaching in one of the synagogues on the sab-
11 bath. And there was a woman who had had a spirit of
weakness for eighteen years and was bent double and
12 completely unable to raise herself up. And on seeing her
Jesus addressed her and said to her, 'Woman, you have
13 been released from your weakness'. And he laid on her
his hands; and immediately she was straightened, and
14 glorified God. In response the ruler of the synagogue,
annoyed that Jesus healed on the sabbath, began to say

to the crowd, 'There are six days in which we ought to work: come on those, then, and be healed—and not on the sabbath day'. Jesus answered him and said, 'Hypo- 15 crites, does not each of you on the sabbath untie his ox or his ass from the manger and lead him away and water him? This woman, a daughter of Abraham, whom Satan 16 had tied up—see!—eighteen years, was it not right that she should be untied from her bonds on the sabbath day?' And on his saying this all his opponents were ashamed, and 17 all the crowd rejoiced at the glorious deeds done by him.

He began to say therefore, 'To what is the kingdom of 18 God like, and to what shall I liken it? It is like a seed of 19 mustard which a man took and threw into his garden, and it grew and became a tree, and the birds of the heaven lodged in its branches.' And again he said: 'To 20 what shall I liken the kingdom of God? It is like leaven 21 which a woman took and hid in three measures of meal, until the whole was leavened.'

And he was going on his way through towns and vil- 22 lages teaching, and making his journey to Jerusalem; and a man said to him, 'Lord, are those being saved 23 few?' And he said to them, 'Strive to enter through the 24 narrow doorway, for there are many, I tell you, who will try to enter but be unable. From the time when the 25 householder rises and shuts the door, and you begin to stand outside and to knock on the door and say, "Master, open to us!", he will speak to you, answering, "I do not know where you have come from". Then you will begin 26 to say, "We used to eat and drink in your company, and you have taught in our streets!" And he will speak to 27 you, saying, "I do not know where you have come from. Get away from me, all you workers of wickedness!" There will be wailing and gnashing of teeth when you 28 see Abraham and Isaac and Jacob and all the prophets in the kingdom of God, and yourselves being cast outside. And they will come from the east and the west and the 29 north and the south, and they will recline in the kingdom of God. And see, there are last who will be first and there 30 are first who will be last.'

31   At that time there approached him certain Pharisees saying to him, 'Go away and make your way from here,
32 because Herod wants to kill you'. And he said to them, 'Go and say to that fox, "See, I cast out demons and work cures day by day, and one day soon I shall have com-
33 pleted my task." But to-day and to-morrow and the next day I must be on my way, for it is not right that a prophet should perish outside Jerusalem.
34   'Jerusalem, Jerusalem, killing prophets and stoning those sent to her! How often I have wanted to gather your children in the way a bird gathers her brood under her
35 wings, and you did not want it! See, your house has been abandoned to you! But I tell you, you will not see me until the day comes when you will say, "Blessed is he that comes in the name of the Lord!" '

1   **Galilaeans.** Nothing is known about this incident; but Josephus narrates Pilate's ruse to murder a number of Jews at the time of their opposition to his building of the aqueduct into Jerusalem, a purpose to which he applied funds from the Temple treasury (*Ant.* xviii. 3. 2; *B.J.* ii 9. 4). His soldiers mingled with the crowd, dressed in civilian clothes, and beat them down with clubs which they had concealed. His putting to death some Galilaeans who had come to bring offerings to the Temple is therefore entirely in character: the general impression in the gospels of one who would be just and merciful if he could flatters him immensely. (See Schürer, I. ii. 81-86, Eng. Edn. 1897.)

2   **sinners.** Literally debtors; the noun occurs in Luke only here, but the verb is used in like sense at Luke xi. 4.

4   **eighteen.** Ewald suggested they were the workmen on the aqueduct sacrilegiously paid by Pilate from the sacred treasury (see on verse 1) and who therefore 'owed' their wages to God, but this seems far-fetched.

    tower in Siloam. Not mentioned elsewhere; Luke implies, by not connecting it with Pilate, that it was a pure accident.

5   **you will all perish.** The warning makes the events just mentioned in some sense eschatological. The parable which follows makes the time element clearer.

this year too. Only a short time for the inhabitants to change 8 their ways; the slight difference between this and the immediate execution threatened at iii. 9 (cf. Matt. iii. 10) should not be pressed. The parable is Luke's alternative to Mark xi. 12 ff.

he laid on her his hands. As frequently in healing and 13 blessing, in accordance with OT usage. (Gen. xlviii. 14-20; Lev. ix. 22; in NT, e.g., Mark i. 41; v. 23; vi. 5; vii. 32; Luke iv. 40 for healing, Mark x. 13, 16; Luke xxiv. 50 for blessing.) The Lord does not use the imposition of hands for exorcism; but this and absolution make the chief uses of the action in the liturgy of the early church.

not on the sabbath day. Detailed rules with regard to the 14 kind of work allowed on a Sabbath, according to the urgency of the injury, were published by the rabbis. Cf. the prohibition in the *Damascus Document* (xiii. 22-23): 'No man shall help an animal in its delivery on the Sabbath day. And if it falls into a pit or ditch, he shall not raise it on the Sabbath.' To Jesus these rules were of no more importance than the halter which needed to be untied, and his play on the ties which bind the beasts and those which bind those whom Satan has tied up is maintained to the end of the saying.

a daughter of Abraham. Cf. verse 28 and see the discussion 16 on xix. 9.

glorious deeds. The Greek word is fairly widely used in 17 the LXX, only four times in the NT, of which Luke has one other (vii. 25; cf. Matt. xi. 8) and is the only evangelist to use the word. It is found in Ecclus. (e.g. xliv. 1). The phrase concludes a passage peculiar to Luke (xiii. 1-17).

With verse 18 we enter upon a Q passage (verses 18-21; cf. 18 Matt. xiii. 31-33).

Therefore. Luke's rather artificial suture of his two sources. Luke's townsman hand appears again in the word 'garden', but this is an apt change, for the plant, *sinapis nigra*, which grows wild on the shores of Lake Gennesaret and has a very small seed (proverbial also in the Talmud), attains a great height under cultivation, making its description as a **tree** natural if not strictly accurate. In Dan. iv. 12, 21 the tree in which **the birds lodged** was a figure of Nebuchadnezzar whose glory and kingdom had grown thus great.

21   **leaven.** It transforms from within and its effect is unseen; thus the parable makes a complementary picture to that of the mustard seed.

22   **he was going on his way.** A tardy recollection of the fact that Luke has represented all that has been said and done since ix. 51 as on the journey up to Jerusalem. For a different form of the saying (not necessarily from a different source) see Matt. vii. 13-14. Luke has provided his own introduction.

23   **Are those being saved few?** A not altogether necessary translation, but the present tense may be significant, implying that some thought that the kingdom of God was on the point of appearing (xix. 11). This is not specifically denied in xix. 12-27, where the point as to the time of the kingdom's appearing is that the king has to take his kingdom by entering upon a long journey (which Jesus has already begun with his journey up to Jerusalem), taking the kingdom, and returning. The kingdom therefore is imminent, if not to appear immediately.

24   **Strive to enter.** A command for the present moment, as the urgency of verse 25 shows. In the OT the doctrine of the remnant includes these ideas: Israel is chosen, chosen to be saved, chosen to be a saviour; Israel brings punishment and even destruction on herself, but a remnant will return, or repent, and renew the covenant of God's choosing; this remnant may be the whole nation restored (Ezekiel) or the good part of the nation (as Jeremiah sometimes). The ideas that not all Israel was elect, and not all elect were of Israel, found in Deut.-Is. and Jonah, were preserved in post-exilic times (cf. Zech. ii. 11; viii. 20-23; Ruth i. 16 f.). On the other hand, the period saw the rise of a narrow particularism over-emphasizing the first of these ideas and issuing in sects who confined election to themselves, each sect claiming to be the true Israel. (Thus the Hasidim and Essenes, and—whether to be identified with the latter or not—the sect of Qumran.) Matt. xv. 24 expresses the limitation for his own ministry which the Lord accepted, whether he spoke the words or not; nevertheless verse 29 of our present passage (cf. Matt. viii. 11) teaches that some outsiders will enter the kingdom for which Israel hopes, while many Israelites will not. The question asked here therefore seeks a decision on the question whether all Israel or an elect few (or

remnant) will enter the kingdom of God, and the answer is, a few, and that the time is short for the attempt to make sure of being of this small number.

the narrow doorway. See *4 Esdras* vii. 3 ff., where the broad ways are those of the future world, once the narrow entrance has been negotiated. (Cf. Matt. vii. 13-14.)

the householder shuts the door. The door is shut also in 25 Matt. xxv. 10, as a sign that the fateful hour, when decision is now too late, has struck. Many rabbis held that people seeking admission in the actual days of the Messiah were not to be trusted. (Daube, p. 119.)

Get away from me. . . . The quotation from Ps. vi. 8 occurs 27 also at Matt. vii. 23.

Abraham and Isaac and Jacob, etc. Luke adds **the pro-** 28 **phets** (cf. Matt. viii. 11) and has the saying of these two verses in an order which avoids suggesting that they who **will come** 29 **from the east** and the other corners of the earth are necessarily Gentiles. They might be Jews of the Dispersion; but Matt. viii. 12 contains the definite warning that the 'sons of the kingdom' will be cast out. Luke's warning is only to the Jews of the generation which the Lord is addressing. For the Jewish tone of this part of the gospel see verse 16 above and on xix. 9. Those 'gathered' in Ps. cvii. 3, which is here recalled, are Jews.

there are last. Luke's form of this saying seems to be that 30 of Mark x. 31 expanded slightly (cf. Matt. xx. 16 (Q) and xix. 30 (Marcan)).

Herod. A **fox** because he is a destroyer, not because he is 32 crafty. Ezekiel likens the bad prophets to foxes because they have not gathered the flocks of Israel (xiii. 4). Jesus, on the other hand, is a true prophet (verse 33). Once again the Jewish flavour of the passage is clear.

day by day, and one day soon. Literally 'to-day and to-morrow, and on the third day'. For the translation see Black, p. 152. The Aramaic idiom behind the Greek (for which see on xi. 3) does not refer to two actual days (as Ex. xix. 11) but an indefinite short period followed by a still indefinite but certain event (as Hos. vi. 2).

To-day and to-morrow and the next day. The meaning 33 may therefore be 'on every day', but Black favours the variant of the Peshitta which would give, 'But to-day and to-morrow I must needs work, and on the next go my way' (i.e. pass on, die). Cf. John v. 17 and ix. 4. Verses 31-33 are peculiar to Luke, but the reference to Jerusalem has suggested to him the inclusion here of the two following verses from Q.

34   **How often I have wanted . . .** The expression might make us think that we are listening to the incarnate *logos*; but in Luke it would be more accurate to say that it is to the Wisdom of God that we listen. Cf. ii. 40, 52; vii. 35; xi. 31, 49 (cf. Matt. xxiii. 34), none of which go so far as Paul's 'Christ, the wisdom of God' (1 Cor. i. 24) in identification.

35   **Your house has been abandoned.** It is tempting to see a reference to the Temple, which according to rabbinic tradition was abandoned by the presence of God at the time of the exile when the Temple was sacked and then destroyed; but Jer. xxii. 5, which may be the inspiration of this passage, speaks of the king's house.

Blessed is he that comes in the name of the Lord. This is the cry of those who welcome the Lord on his riding into Jerusalem in Mark xi. 9 and Matt. xxi. 9, but Luke xix. 38 substitutes 'the king' for 'he'. The meaning is not altogether clear, but it seems unlikely that the Lord is either referring or being made to refer merely to the entry into Jerusalem. The clue lies in Ps. cxviii, from whose verse 26 the cry is taken. This psalm may well have been used extensively and early in primitive liturgy (cf. 1 Pet. ii. 6-8; Mark xii. 10-11 and pars.; Acts iv. 11 for occurrences in the NT), as it is known to have been from at least the fifth century; but the words of our passage enter the liturgies relatively late. It seems, therefore, that the words here and at the triumphal entry served to draw attention to the Messianic application of which Ps. cxviii was capable, rather than that liturgical familiarity with the psalm has caused them to be used here.

CHAPTER XIV

1-35. HEALING OF A MAN WITH DROPSY. HUMILITY. THE GREAT SUPPER. THE COST OF DISCIPLESHIP

And it happened upon his entering the house of one 1 of the chief of the Pharisees to eat a meal that they were there watching him. And, see, there was a man with 2 dropsy before him. And Jesus, taking up his speech, said 3 to the lawyers and Pharisees, 'May one heal on the sabbath or not?' And they kept silent; and he took him and 4 healed him and dismissed him. And he said to them, 5 'Which of you, whose son or ox shall fall into a well, will not immediately draw him out on the sabbath day?' And 6 they could give no answer to this.

He spoke a parable to the guests, noticing how they 7 chose out the front seats, saying to them, 'When you are 8 invited by anyone to a wedding, do not recline on the front seat, in case someone of greater honour than you has been invited by the host, and he who has invited both 9 you and him come and say to you, "Make room for this man!" and then you begin shamefacedly to take the last place. But when you are invited, go and recline in the last 10 place, that when your host comes he will say to you, "My friend, go up to a higher place!" Then you will have respect from all those reclining with you. For everyone 11 who exalts himself will be humbled, and he who humbles himself will be exalted.' He said also to the man who had 12 invited him, 'When you arrange a breakfast or supper, invite neither your friends nor your brothers nor your relatives nor your rich neighbours, in case they too invite you back and you get a repayment. But when you arrange 13 a reception, invite the poor, the maimed, the lame, the blind; and you will be blessed, because they cannot repay 14 you; for your repayment will be in the resurrection of the just.'

15 One of those reclining with him, on hearing this, said
to him, 'Blessed is he that eats bread in the kingdom of
16 God!' And he said to him, 'A man was arranging a great
17 supper and he invited many; and he sent his servant at
the time of the supper to say to those invited, "Come
18 along, for we are all ready". And they all began with one
accord to excuse themselves; the first said to him, "I
have bought a field, and it is essential for me to go out
19 and see it; I beg you, allow me to be excused!" And
another said, "I have bought five yoke of oxen, and I am
going to test them. I beg you, allow me to be excused!"
20 And another said, "I have married a wife, and for this
21 reason I cannot come". And the servant came and
reported these things to his master. Then the householder was angry and said to his servant, "Go out at
once into the streets and lanes of the city, and the poor
22 and maimed and blind and lame bring in here!" And
the servant said, "Master, what you ordered has been
23 done, and there is still room". And the master said to the
servant, "Go out into the roads and hedges and force
24 them to come in, that my house may be filled up. For I
tell you that none of those men who were invited shall
taste of my supper!"'

25 There were travelling with him great crowds, and he
26 turned and said to them, 'If anyone comes to me and
does not hate his father and his mother and wife and
children and brothers and sisters, yes, and his own life,
27 he cannot be my disciple. Whoever does not carry his
own cross and come after me cannot be my disciple.
28 For which of you, wishing to build a tower, does not first
sit down and reckon the expense, to see if he has enough
29 for its completion? So that it does not happen that when
he has laid the foundation and is not able to finish it, all
30 the onlookers begin to make fun of him saying, "This is
the man who began to build and was not able to finish it!"'
31 Or what king, going to join battle with another king does
not first sit down and consider whether he can with ten
thousand meet the king coming against him with twenty
32 thousand? And if not, while he is still at a distance, he

sends an embassy and asks for terms of peace. So then 33
everyone among you who does not say farewell to all that
belong to him cannot be my disciple. Salt then is good, 34
but if even the salt has become insipid, with what can it
be seasoned? It is usable neither for soil nor for manure. 35
They throw it away! He who has ears, hear well!'

May one heal on the sabbath or not? See SB, i. 623. From 3
rabbinic evidence of a slightly later time the answer would be,
'If there is danger to life, yes; otherwise, certainly not'. But
much casuistry was possible on the ground that certain things
had a medicinal value but could be enjoyed by a healthy man
as food or be used for the care of his health. Such foods did not
count as medicine, and might therefore be given to a sick man
on the Sabbath.

they kept silent. Perhaps because there was a difference of 4
opinion among them on this matter.

son or ox. An incongruous pair, as Black remarks (p. 126). 5
He offers as the original: 'Which of you shall have an ox
(*be'ira*) or an ass (*bar hamra*) fallen into a well (*bēra*). . . .' This
would give a play on words in the original Aramaic and the
phrase for ass, literally 'son of the yoke' (cf. Matt. xxi. 5), would
account for the word 'son' here. The variants in the MSS. are
apparently corrections of the text translated, but the reading
'ass' gives the right sense.

front seats. Literally first reclining-places.   8

then you will have respect. This may seem an unworthy 10
reason for humble behaviour and indeed to take away its
humility, if the parable is taken to be a piece of instruction for
this world. It is rather the utterance of a truth about the eternal
world in the form of something going on before the speaker's
and listener's eyes; it is God alone who can allot places in the
heavenly kingdom. (Cf. Mark x. 40 and Matt. xx. 23.)

This verse occurs again at xviii. 14 and is found in a slightly 11
different form at Matt. xxiii. 12. The teaching is found often
in the NT, notably also at Jas. iv. 6, 10; 1 Pet. v. 5; Phil. ii. 5 ff.

the resurrection of the just. Not necessarily implying that 14
only the just would rise. Acts xxiv. 15 represents Paul as believing in the resurrection of both just and unjust, as taught by

15   213

Dan. xii. 2 and some parts of *Enoch*. The *Testaments of the Twelve Patriarchs* envisages the ultimate resurrection of all, though perhaps not all at the same time. But Luke's own view has more in common with the *Psalms of Solomon*, which contemplate only a resurrection of the just, and with 2 Macc. (cf., e.g., vii. 9) where the resurrection is the reward of martyrs. This is strikingly brought out in Luke's treatment of Mark xii. 18-27, by his significant addition at xx. 35.

15   **in the kingdom of God.** The pious exclamation of the fellow-guest continues the Lord's thought: the Messianic kingdom was to be inaugurated by a banquet. The just would be raised in order to partake of it.

17   **sent his servant.** The oriental custom: exact time for arriving was not given at the time of invitation.

18   **began to excuse themselves.** Their reasons are all more or less valid, as excuses for not following Christ usually are. Nothing is gained by seeking to find parallels in actual history to these men.

20   **married a wife.** A better excuse than the rest, obeying punctiliously Deut. xxiv. 5.

21   **The householder.** Again a type of God, as at xiii. 25. The kingdom is even at the time the Lord is speaking being filled with all whom the strict thought of as outcast.

24   **None of those who were invited shall taste of my supper.** Since they had themselves refused to come this apparent punishment is not apt at the end of the parable, and comparison with Matt. xxii. 1-10 suggests that the ending is due to Luke, who has thus made it an answer to the pious guest's remark in verse 15. Matt. xxii. 1-14 conflates the parable with another one. See Kilpatrick, *op. cit.* p. 30.

26   **If anyone comes to me.** This series of sayings is most appropriate to the time when Jesus had set his face to go to Jerusalem and he therefore must warn would-be followers of the cost of sharing his destiny. Verse 25 appears to be a Lucan introduction, while verses 26-27 are Q, Luke having preserved in verse 26 what seems to be the more original form of a saying which Matthew has adapted to a later time at x. 37.

hate his father and his mother. The words are startling, but Luke's arrangement of these sayings allows them to take

the meaning which alone makes sense: if a man is to follow
Jesus to the end he must hate and despise his own greater desire
and love for all natural objects of affection.

carry his own cross. This saying also is in place and belongs 27
to the immediate situation. Luke has 'universalized' it at ix. 23.
The parables which follow are all intended to point one moral
only: a disciple must be sure that he can see his discipleship
through to the end. In the words of verse 29, he must be 'able
to finish it'.

salt. The introduction of the saying is equally abrupt in 34
Mark ix. 50; but the form here appears to be that of Q. Cf. Matt.
v. 13, which alone gives a good connexion with a context.
Matthew's identification of the Lord's disciples with the salt
of the earth would make excellent sense here.

CHAPTER XV

1-32. THE LOST SHEEP AND LOST COIN.
THE PRODIGAL SON

1 There were drawing near to him all the tax-gatherers and
2 sinners to listen to him. And both Pharisees and scribes
murmured saying, 'This fellow welcomes sinners and
3 eats with them!' And he spoke this parable to them say-
4 ing, 'What man of you who has an hundred sheep and has
lost one of them does not leave the ninety-nine in the
5 wilderness and go after the lost one until he finds it? And
when he has found it he sets it on his shoulders rejoicing,
6 and when he has come home he calls together his friends
and neighbours and says to them, "Rejoice with me, for
7 I have found my sheep, the lost one". I tell you that there
will thus be joy in heaven over one repentant sinner
rather than over ninety-nine just men who have no need
8 of repentance. Or what woman who has ten drachmas,
if she lose one drachma, does not light a lamp and sweep
9 the house and search carefully till she find it? And when
she has found it she calls together her friends and neighbours and says, "Rejoice with me, for I have found the
10 drachma I had lost!" Thus, I tell you, there is joy in the
presence of the angels of God over one repentant sinner.'
11 And he said: 'A man had two sons; and the younger of
12 them said to his father, "Father, give me the portion of
property which falls to me". And he divided their liveli-
13 hood among them. And after not many days the younger
son gathered everything together and left for a distant
country, and there he frittered away his capital by living
14 in extravagance. And after he had spent everything, there
was a severe famine in that country, and he began to be
15 in need. And he went and joined one of the citizens of
that country, and he sent him into his fields to feed pigs.
16 And he longed to fill his stomach with the carob pods

which the pigs ate, and no one gave anything to him. And 17
when he came to himself he said, "How many of my
father's hired men have food to spare, and I am dying
here of hunger! I will get up and go to my father and say to 18
him, 'Father, I have sinned against heaven and before you;
I am no longer worthy to be called your son: treat me as 19
one of your hired men'." And he got up and came to his 20
father; but while he was still a long way off his father saw
him and was moved, and ran and fell on his neck and
kissed him. And his son said to him, "Father, I have sin- 21
ned against heaven and before you. I am no longer worthy
to be called your son—" But the father said to the ser- 22
vants, "Quick, bring the best robe and put it on him, and
put a ring on his finger and sandals on his feet, and bring 23
the fattened calf, kill it, and let us eat and enjoy ourselves,
because this my son was dead, and has come to life 24
again, he was lost and has been found". And they began to
enjoy themselves. But his elder son was in the field, and 25
as he came and drew near to the house, he heard music
and dancing, and he called to him one of the boys and 26
inquired what this might be. And he said to him, "Your 27
brother has come and your father has killed the fattened
calf, because he has got him back safe and sound". And 28
he was angry and would not go in; and his father came
out and tried to persuade him. But he said in answer to 29
his father, "Look, all these years I have been your slave
and have never disobeyed your orders, and to me you
never gave a kid for me to enjoy myself with my friends!
But when this son of yours, who has consumed your 30
capital with harlots, has come, for him you have killed
the fattened calf!" But he said to him, "My boy, you are 31
always with me, and everything I have is yours. We had 32
to enjoy ourselves and rejoice, because this brother of
yours was dead, and has come to life again, and was lost
and has been found."'

welcomes sinners. For Jesus as host see on v. 29.   2
murmured. The reproach is founded on an ancient rule not
to associate with the godless. Cf. the Midrash on 2 Chron. xx. 37

and the quotation of Is. lii. 11 at 2 Cor. vi. 17. The whole chapter is designed to oppose this rule by collecting those sayings of the Lord which appeal to the naturalness of rejoicing over a repentant sinner, equal to that of joy over finding something precious which had been lost. The argument is then always to the hearers, inviting them to admit the inevitability of Jesus' own joy at having been able to make friends with the sinners; they would in parallel cases do the same. Hence the appeal, 'What man of you . . .'

5   **when he has found it.** The Lord 'finds' tax-gatherers and sinners to bring them back.

11   **two sons.** Each is equally important to the argument and it is a mistake to take the elder son and his anger as a mere appendix to the story. This, with the father's reply to him, is the climax.

15   **to feed pigs.** The Lord is aware of the degradation to which those he is befriending have sunk.

16   **he longed to fill his stomach.** But the picture is not necessarily that he did so (though we might translate, 'he was glad to . . .'); to eat the fruit of this tree (*ceratonia siliqua*), still common in Palestine and round the Mediterranean, was, according to the rabbis, the equivalent of being in the direst need.

17   **when he came to himself.** He saw that he was his own enemy. It is a mistake to suppose that the Lord, who made the great sacrifice of life and death for his fellow-men, either neglected or despised the self-regarding instinct. Cf., e.g., the teaching on prayer, xi. 5-13; and the young man called to give up all, yet promised 'treasure in heaven' (Mark x. 21; Luke xviii. 22; Matt. xix. 21).

18   **against heaven.** The Greek may rather be 'up to heaven', as though his sin were piled up that high. (Cf. Ezra ix. 6 and 1 Esd. viii. 72 (LXX).)

Father. An appeal which would seem natural to the hearers, for the idea of a forgiving father is common in Jewish literature. Cf. Is. lxiii. 16-19 for this idea applied to Yahweh.

22   **But the father said.** The prepared speech is cut short.

24   **my son was dead.** The notion of one spiritually 'lost' being regarded as 'dead' and yet capable of being brought 'to life again' is Jewish, as Ezek. xxxvii. 1-14 powerfully shows.

boys. For this translation see on vii. 7 above.   26

Look, all these years. The elder son's indignation is 29
natural: it is false to the whole spirit of the story to represent
him as a monster of hidden selfishness. His father does not rebuke him but reminds him that he is 'always with' him: the
relation between them never needed mending.

this brother of yours. With exquisite economy the point is 32
made that the tax-gatherers and sinners are brethren of those
who murmur at Jesus' associating with them; this responsibility
cannot be shelved by calling the sinner 'this son of yours'.

has been found. In as true a sense as those other less precious
things mentioned in verses 4-9, rejoicing over whose restoration
seemed so natural. So the elder brother, who needs no repentance, is challenged to rise above his natural ethic to that in
which forgiveness leads to joy, with the constant suggestion
that this higher ethic is no less natural than the other.

CHAPTER XVI

1-31. THE UNJUST STEWARD. HYPOCRISY OF
PHARISEES. ABOUT THE LAW AND DIVORCE.
THE RICH MAN AND LAZARUS

1 He began to say also to his disciples. 'There was a certain
rich man who had a steward, and this steward was
2 accused to him as a waster of his property. And he called
him and said to him, "What is this that I hear about you?
Render an account of your stewardship: for you can be
3 steward no longer." And the steward said within himself, "What shall I do, for my master is taking away
the stewardship from me? Dig I cannot, begging I am
4 ashamed to do. I know what to do, so that when I am
removed from my stewardship they will accept me into
5 their houses." And he called to him each one of his
master's debtors and began by saying to the first, "How
6 much do you owe my master?" And he said, "An hundred baths of oil". And he said to him, "Take your
7 account and sit down quickly and write fifty". Then he
said to another, "And how much do you owe?" And he
said, "An hundred kors of corn". And he said to him,
"Take your account and write eighty".
8 'And his master praised the dishonest steward because
he had acted wisely. For the sons of this age are wiser in
9 their society than the sons of light. And I say to you, make
for yourselves friends out of the dishonest mammon, that
when it fails they may accept you into eternal lodgings.
10 'He that is faithful in very little is faithful also in much,
and he that is dishonest in very little is dishonest also in
11 much. If then in the dishonest mammon you were not
12 faithful, who will entrust to you the genuine? And if with
what belonged to another you were not faithful, who will
13 give to you our own? No servant can serve two masters:
for either he will hate the one and love the other, or be

loyal to one and despise the other. You cannot serve God and mammon.'

All this was heard by the Pharisees, who were money- 14 lovers, and they derided him. And he said to them, 'You 15 are the men who justify yourselves before men, but God knows your hearts; for what is exalted among men is an abomination in God's presence.

'The law and the prophets were until John; from then 16 the kingdom of God is preached and everyone oppresses it. But it is easier for heaven and earth to pass away than 17 for one letter-hook of the law to be dropped.

'Everyone who dismisses his wife and marries another 18 commits adultery, and he who marries her who has been dismissed commits adultery.

'There was a rich man, and he was dressed in purple 19 and linen, enjoying himself luxuriously every day. A poor 20 man named Lazarus was cast at his doorway in an ulcerous condition and wanting to be fed with what fell from 21 the rich man's table; indeed the very dogs came and licked his ulcers. It happened that the poor man died and 22 was carried by the angels into the bosom of Abraham; the rich man also died and was buried. And in Hades he 23 lifted his eyes, being in tortures, and saw Abraham from a distance and Lazarus in his bosom. And he called out 24 and said, "Father Abraham, pity me and send Lazarus to dip the tip of his finger in water and cool my tongue, for I am in agony in this flame". But Abraham said, "My 25 son, remember that you have had your good things in your lifetime, and Lazarus in the same way miseries; but now he is here being comforted, but you are in agony. And with all this, between us and you a great gulf has 26 been fixed, so that those wishing to cross hence to you are not able, nor pass over thence to us." And he said, 27 "I beg you then, father, to send him to my father's house: for I have five brothers; so that he can testify to them, so 28 that they too do not come into this place of torture". But Abraham said, "They have Moses and the prophets: 29 let them listen to them". But he said, "No, father 30 Abraham, but if someone goes to them from the dead,

31 they will repent". But he said to him, "If they do not listen to Moses and the prophets, not even if someone rises from the dead will they be convinced".'

6   **baths.** The Greek is a transliteration of the Hebrew *bath*, a liquid measure, the same as the *ephah*, about 40 litres.

   Take your account. The steward could have seen, then, since he holds the debtor's receipts, how much each owed: his questions are more useful to convey information to the listener than as part of the story. The change had of course to be written in the debtor's hand.

7   **kors.** Another transliteration; the Hebrew *kor* is a dry measure, equivalent to the *homer*, about 10 bushels.

8   **the sons of this age.** An expression which does not occur in rabbinic writing, although 'a son of the age to come' is common.

   the sons of light. Cf. John xii. 36 and 1 Th. v. 5; and 'children of light' at Eph. v. 8. The only Judaistic source known for an exact equivalent of the former phrase is the Qumran *Manual of Discipline*, i. 9; ii. 16; iii. 13. The same work has also 'sons of darkness' (i. 10).

   in their society. Taking γενεά as representing the Hebrew *dor* rather than the meaning of *toledoth*. See Brownlee's note on *Man. Disc.* iii. 14 where the phrase *betholedoth* has just been used: 'The distinction between the *doroth* is one of character rather than chronology. There are basically two so-called generations (really societies), the righteous and the wicked.' He cites for this meaning of *dor* Pss. xiv. 5, xxiv. 6, cxii. 2; Deut. xxxii. 5, 20; Prov. xxx. 11-14; Matt. xii. 39; xvii. 17. (Cf. also *Man. Disc.* iv. 15, and Luke ix. 41.)

9   **friends out of the dishonest mammon.** The advice is startling and the interpretation of the whole passage difficult. The following is perhaps the most reasonable solution: the parable ended originally at verse 8, and was intended only to emphasize the necessity to come to terms with the times, which so urgently demanded a decision (cf. xiv. 26-33). The unjust steward is commended for recognizing this fact; he showed intelligent self-interest (see on xv. 15-17 above). He is not commended for the method he used, which is only incidental to the

story. While Luke no doubt understood this, he thought that lessons should be drawn even from the dishonest course taken by the steward. Verses 9-13 are therefore an assorted collection of sayings brought here to explain points in the parable, a task for which they are not well fitted.

The saying in verse 9 is probably ironic, perhaps originally addressed to Pharisees (cf. verse 14): 'Yes, make friends by your dishonest wealth (in your absurd belief) that they may welcome you into eternal lodgings!' Unexpressed is the conviction that eternal lodgings cannot be thus secured.

mammon. See Black, p. 102: the word is found in the Targums and Talmud in the sense of 'profit', or 'money'.

He that is faithful in very little. This does not seem a 10 natural lesson to draw from the story, for the steward was *unfaithful* in much: but Luke seeks in this and the following three verses to modify the impression that a dishonest action has been commended. The verse may well be inspired by Q: cf. Luke xix. 17; Matt. xxv. 21, 23.

our own. The reading of B and Origen, and perhaps to be 12 preferred for its very unexpectedness, although 'your own' would have sounded strange. **'Our own'** balances **'the genuine'** in the previous verse, and must mean the true riches of membership in the Christian fellowship and the knowledge imparted with it.

No servant. Again Q. (Cf. Matt. vi. 24.)   13

everyone oppresses it. Black provides the warrant for this 16 translation (p. 84), taking βιάζεται as transitive and εἰς as representing an Aramaic preposition not required in Greek but just intelligible ('everyone oppresses against it'). Cf. the reading of D at xix. 44. This brings the meaning into harmony with that of Matt. xi. 12 and it is possible that the original, as Black suggests, read 'violent men oppress it'. Those who oppress the kingdom are the Pharisees and scribes (or 'lawyers'), as is clear from the woes pronounced against them in xi. 37-52 (especially 52). On the other hand, if the correct translation is 'everyone forces his way into it', the reference must be in part at least to the crowds of xiv. 25; or to those who are preparing violent action to obtain the kingdom. In this case the preaching will not be that of Jesus himself, but would refer to others who are not recorded in the gospel but who were advocating revolt, such as apparently happened at some time contemporary with the events of the gospel story, perhaps with the Passover which was the background of Jesus' arrest. (Cf., e.g., Mark xv. 7 and see note on Luke xxiii. 19.) A third possibility is to take the whole of the passage from verse 15 or even from verse 13, as a veiled reference to the support given by the Pharisees and their scribes to Herod Antipas, whose offence against Jewish morality had brought him the enmity of John the Baptist (iii. 19; cf. especially Mark vi. 14-29).

Daube (p. 300) suggests an interpretation of the whole passage (verses 16-18) on the basis of two points found in later Judaism: one is the warning by the *Mekhilta* (the Midrashic commentary on Exodus of the early second century A.D.) that even a single person might by over-eager anticipation of God's good time 'impair the entire community', as the people at Mount Sinai would have done if they had 'broken through' (Exod. xix. 21, 24). The second is the story of Simeon ben Johai (about the middle of the second century) according to which the Book of Deuteronomy accuses Solomon in heaven of having altered the phrase in Deut. xvii. 17, 'he shall not multiply wives to himself', to 'to a multitude of wives for himself'. The interpretation of Luke here will then proceed: 'John is Elijah and the prophet promised in Deuteronomy. Miracles are performed . . . the age foretold in the scriptures is dawning', but 'at this transitional stage much violence is still done to the kingdom' by those who anticipate God's appointed time. 'Nothing has occurred' to 'cancel the duty of observing the Law. . . . The faithful will not disregard even the *yodh* in the precept' in Deut. xvii. 17 and thus imitate Solomon (verses 17 and 18). 'Man and woman by sexual union return to, or re-approach, the ideal androgynous state. A husband remarrying after divorce, or a man marrying a divorced wife, commits adultery.'

As already argued (pp. 41 f.) Luke avoids identification of the Baptist with Elijah except at i. 17 and 76, and the evidence from rabbinic tradition is comparatively late; but the interpretation is attractive and if true need not conflict with that which would see here an attack on Antipas. See next note.

18   **everyone who dismisses his wife.** Antipas had dismissed the daughter of Aretas and married Herodias, who herself had

already been married to his half-brother. 'Dismisses' describes
the action of a husband desiring a divorce for personal reasons
when his wife has committed no actual offence, as permitted by
Deut. xxiv. 1. The following verse in Deuteronomy allows a
woman thus dismissed to marry another man. Both courses of
action are expressly forbidden here, and Antipas is thus condemned on two counts. Luke's gospel does not raise the question whether divorce on any ground was recognized by the
Lord, but condemns the heartless form of it allowed by Deuteronomy. For a fuller account of the Lord's teaching on divorce
see Mark x. 2-12 (cf. Matt. xix. 3-12) where also reference is
made to the procedure of Deut. xxiv. 1. With the present verse
cf. Matt. v. 32.

a rich man ... dressed in purple. Such as would be found 19
in a palace (cf. vii. 25). Perhaps another reference to Antipas.

Lazarus. The only occasion on which a character in a 20
parable receives a proper name; since Luke knew of Martha and
Mary (x. 38 ff.) it is at least possible that he both knew their
brother Lazarus and that he was reported to have been raised
by the Lord from the dead. This would give considerable point
to verses 30-31, but there remains the great difficulty of Luke's
silence about this miracle and indeed about Lazarus the brother
of Martha and Mary altogether. These points suggest that the
connexion between the two traditions (Luke x. 38 ff. and John
xi) is one of a common source which by the time it had reached
either of the evangelists had become much changed; for it would
be hard to argue the dependence of Luke upon John on any
likely view of the dates of the two gospels, and there seems no
hint in Luke to suggest to the author of the Fourth Gospel that
the two sisters had a brother named Lazarus. (For a discussion
of the question see J. N. Sanders, *NTS*, i, 1. pp. 29 ff.)

carried by the angels. In the older angelology it was the 22
angel of death, i.e. Satan or Sammael, who took away the soul.
That angels in God's service took the souls of the righteous
and the Despoiler those of the godless is a tradition which
appears first *c.* A.D. 150. It may not be too fanciful to compare
Wis. iii. 1 with the conception here: Lazarus is without torment
and reclines not indeed in the hand of God but in 'the bosom
of Abraham', used here perhaps as a more concrete expression

of being 'gathered to his fathers' (Gen. xv. 15; xlvii. 30; Deut. xxxi. 16; Judg. ii. 10). But it may imply reclining at a meal, a concrete picture of blessedness for poor Lazarus. Cf. Matt. viii. 11 for reclining with Abraham at a meal (not retained by the Lucan parallel, xiii. 28).

23   **Hades.** Usually the equivalent of *She'ol*, the place of departed shades in the OT; but here used as the equivalent of Gehenna (see note on xii. 5).

from a distance. Cf. the gulf of verse 26. The rabbinic Eden (reserved for the righteous) and Gehenna (the place of torment) were to lie close to one another, so that after the final judgment each party could view the other. The distance and gulf are therefore distinctive features of this story. For fuller comment on the idea of Paradise see on xxiii. 43.

24   **water.** Enoch xxii. 9 mentions a well of water in the righteous' division of *She'ol*, and also testifies to the separation between the two parts.

26   **gulf.** See on 23 above.

27   **five brothers.** Not necessarily a reference to historical persons; but the number may be correct for the brothers of Antipas surviving at the time of the composition of the story.

29   **They have Moses and the prophets.** The very authorities set aside by both Pharisees and Antipas. See on verse 16 above and cf. John v. 46.

31   **not even if someone rises from the dead.** If the saying is authentic but not a reference to the historical Lazarus (see on verse 20 above), it must be added to the Lord's predictions about his own Passion and Resurrection. If not authentic it may be a tilt by Luke at the Pharisees, who gave lip-service to belief in the Resurrection (Acts xxiii. 8), a doctrine which was indeed taught by 'Moses and the prophets' (Acts xxvi. 22-23).

xvii. 1-19. STUMBLING-BLOCKS. FORGIVENESS.
FAITH. THE POSITION OF SERVANTS. HEALING
OF TEN LEPERS

He said to his disciples, 'It is impossible for stumbling- 1
blocks not to come, but woe to him through whom they
come! It would be better for him for a millstone to be 2
hung round his neck and for him to be thrown into the
sea than that he should make one of these little ones
stumble. Look to yourselves. If your brother sin, rebuke 3
him, and if he repent, forgive him. And if seven times in 4
a day he sin against you and seven times turn to you
saying, "I repent", you shall forgive him.'

And the apostles said to the Lord, 'Make our faith 5
stronger'. The Lord said, 'If you had faith like a mustard 6
seed, you would say to this mulberry-tree, "Be uprooted
and planted in the sea!" and it would have obeyed you.

'Which of you who has a servant ploughing or shep- 7
herding, will say to him when he has come in from the
field, "Come straight in and recline!" and will not rather 8
say to him, "Get my supper ready, and gird yourself and
serve me while I eat and drink, and after that you shall
eat and drink"? Does he thank the servant because he 9
has carried out his orders? So you, too, when you carry 10
out all your orders, say, "We are unprofitable servants:
what we were bound to do we have done".'

And it happened in the journey to Jerusalem that he 11
was passing through the border country of Samaria and
Galilee. And on his entering a village there met him ten 12
lepers who stood at a distance; and they lifted up their 13
voices saying, 'Jesus, master, have pity on us!' And when 14
he saw them he said to them, 'Go and show yourselves
to the priests'. And it happened that while they went they

15 **were cleansed. And one of them, seeing that he was**
16 **healed, turned back, with a loud voice glorifying God,**
and he fell on his face at his feet, thanking him; and he
17 **was a Samaritan. In answer Jesus said, 'Were not all ten**
18 **cleansed? Where are the nine? Were there not found any**
to turn back and give glory to God except this alien?'
19 **And he said to him, 'Rise and go. Your faith has saved**
you.'

1 **He said to his disciples.** The verse begins with a typical
Lucan introduction and proceeds with Q material (cf. Matt.
xviii. 7), but verse 2 is derived from the Marcan form of the
saying (Mark ix. 42).

2 **The little ones.** Not to be interpreted literally, as Matt.
xviii. 6. They are the people who from the worldly point of view
are unimportant. Cf. LXX use, e.g. Gen. xix. 11; 1 Sam. v. 9.
See also Introduction, pp. 21 f.

3 **If your brother sin.** The Lucan version of the teaching on
forgiveness is free from the ecclesiastical legislation with which
it is obscured in Matt. xviii. 15-18 and 21-22.

7 **Which of you who has a servant.** This passage could have
been originally addressed only to men of some wealth. Mark i.
20 shows that Zebedee could afford to hire men, but none of the
disciples were landowners with slaves, as far as we know. The
original address seems to have been then to wealthy Jews, perhaps to Pharisees, whose religion was confined to mere carrying out of orders.

10 **unprofitable servants.** SB show that Rabban Jochanan b.
Zakkai (d. *c.* A.D. 80) had a similar saying with regard to the
fulfilling of the Law.

11 **the border country.** Making the best possible sense of μέσον
('the middle'). The verse illustrates Luke's ignorance of the
geography of Palestine: the Lord has already left Galilee and
entered Samaria (ix. 52) and if on his way to Jerusalem cannot
now be near Galilee. See separate note after the text of ix. 62.

12 **stood at a distance.** Obeying the Law (Lev. xiii. 46). On
the regulations for showing oneself to the priests see on v. 14.

16 **thanking him.** This passage and xviii. 11 furnish the only
two examples in the synoptics of εὐχαριστεῖν in a context

228

neither eucharistic nor quasi-eucharistic; but the verb occurs in a non-eucharistic sense at John xi. 41 and frequently in Paul. Luke uses εὐλόγησεν at ix. 16 (cf. Mark vi. 41) and it appears that εὐχαριστεῖν had not yet acquired an exclusively liturgical connotation. See further on xxii. 17 ff.

this alien. Cf. Naaman the Syrian, the only leper healed by 18 Elisha (iv. 27 and see the note on ix. 51). Samaria and its people are important as representative of the alien world. (Cf. ix. 51-56; x. 33.)

xvii. 20-37. THE KINGDOM OF GOD AND THE DAYS OF THE SON OF MAN

Asked by the Pharisees when the kingdom of God was 20 **coming he answered them and said, 'The kingdom of God does not come with observation, nor will they say,** 21 **"Look, here it is!" or "There it is!"—for, look—the kingdom of God is among you!'**

He said to the disciples, 'The days will come when you 22 **will long to see one of the days of the Son of Man and you will not see one; and they will say to you, "Look, there** 23 **he is, look, here he is!"—do not go after them, do not follow them. For as the lightning when it lightens shines** 24 **from one part under the sky to another part under the sky, so will the Son of Man be. But first he must suffer** 25 **much and be rejected by this generation. And as it was in** 26 **the days of Noah, so will it be in the days of the Son of Man: they were eating, drinking, marrying, and being** 27 **given in marriage, until the day when Noah entered the ark and the flood came and destroyed them all. It was the** 28 **same in the days of Lot: they were eating, drinking, buying, selling, planting, and building: but on the day when** 29 **Lot left Sodom, fire and brimstone rained from the sky and destroyed them all. It will be the same on the day** 30 **when the Son of Man is revealed. On that day whoever is** 31 **on the top of his house and his belongings in the house, let him not come down to fetch them; and the man in the field in the same way let him not turn to look behind him.**

16

32,33 Think of Lot's wife! Whoever seeks to possess his life
  34 shall lose it, and whoever loses it will keep it alive. I tell
      you, on that night there will be two on one bed, one will
  35 be taken away and the other will be left. Two women will
      be grinding at the same mill, one will be taken away and
  37 the other will be left.' And in answer they said to him,
      'Where, Lord?' And he said to them, 'Where the body is,
      there also will the eagles be gathered together'.

  20 **observation.** The verb is not common even in the LXX
      and the noun is known in biblical Greek only here and in
      Aquila's translation of Ex. xii. 42; but the use of the verb in the
      LXX is enough to show that here there is word-play between
      two senses of it: 'watch for' (i.e. try to catch), and 'observe'
      (i.e. keep, *sc.* regulations). Cf. xi. 53-54 for the Pharisees'
      watching in the first sense: the kingdom of God comes
      neither through meticulous keeping of the tradition, nor
      by hostile watching of Jesus. There is irony in this, for their
      watching of him would show them the kingdom if they
      looked aright, if they were able to discern the signs of the
      times (xii. 56).
  21 **the kingdom of God is among you.** C. H. Roberts has
      argued on the evidence of a papyrus that the Greek should be
      understood as almost 'within your grasp' or 'within your
      power' (*HTR*, xli. 1, Jan. 1948). That for which the Pharisees
      imply they are looking lies before their very eyes. There is also
      a message for Luke's own contemporaries: the Church possesses
      in its account of Jesus its inalienable example or picture of the
      kingdom. Therefore it can hold out in the world (xviii. 1-8): its
      kingdom does not come with observation: it has it potentially
      already (Conzelmann). The first part of the verse bears signs of
      Lucan composition: he appears to have extracted it from Mark
      xiii. 21, which he omits in its context.
  22 **one of the days of the Son of Man.** An expression which
      cannot be explained on the basis of Aramaic. Black does not
      discuss it. If there is any connexion with the Day of the Lord,
      it is with that conception of it as a day of salvation and life for
      God's holy ones, found in *Pss. Sol.* (xii. 7; xiii. 9-11; xiv. 2-7)
      rather than with that of doom as found, for example, in Jer. iv.

23-25 and Zeph. ii. 3; for these days will be welcome to the disciples. See Introduction, pp. 68 ff., where it is argued that the Days of the Son of Man are days of revealing the glory of the Son of Man, beginning with the Transfiguration, and to be ended in the final consummation.

lightning. The comparison is with its brightness rather than 23 its suddenness. Cf. verses 23-24 with Matt. xxiv. 26-27: the Son of Man will shine with unmistakable brightness as at the Transfiguration.

But first he must suffer. An important part of the Lucan 25 eschatology, inserted here as an echo of ix. 22. Cf. ix. 44 and xviii. 32-34. All these three passages are in Marcan contexts, and their main thought Luke inserts here into a Q context: it is laid down by scripture that the Messiah must suffer in order to enter into his glory (cf. Is. liii. 3, 8). The teaching is emphasized by the risen Christ at xxiv. 26, 46.

Noah entered the ark. See Gen. vii. 7, where Noah's wife, 27 sons, and sons' wives are mentioned. This may account for the reference to marrying, etc., here.

Lot. Mentioned by Luke alone; the catastrophe in Lot's days 28 was by fire, and Luke may have thus arranged the sayings to follow the hellenistic tradition of alternate catastrophes by flood and fire, a tradition going back to Plato's *Timaeus*, where it is ascribed to Egyptian lore (21 E—22 D). (Knox, *Hellenistic Elements*, p. 10.)

fire and brimstone. The sentence is composed from words 29 occurring in Gen. xix. 24, where θεῖον, as elsewhere in the LXX, represents *gophrith*, a foreign word of uncertain derivation but apparently denoting some combustible material, possibly oil.

when the Son of Man is revealed. For the significance of 30 these words see Introduction, pp. 70 f.

On that day. Luke anticipates his treatment of Mark xiii. 31 14-20 (Luke xxi. 20-24) by adapting here verses 15-16 of the Marcan passage, which his own interpretation does not require in ch. xxi.

let him not turn to look behind him. As Lot's wife did (Gen. xix. 26). The words may have suggested to Luke verse 32, found only in his gospel.

33   **whoever seeks to possess his life.** Luke has used here
the Marcan form of the saying, which he has also at ix. 24
(rather than the form found at Matt. x. 39); but he has made
some interesting changes: 'possess' for 'save', and 'keep it
alive' for 'save it'. Indeed, the warning against trying to turn
one's life into a possession, a belonging which could be jealously
guarded, would accord with translating ἀπολέσει by 'destroy'.
There is no word in English which has the double meaning of
the Greek, 'lose' and 'destroy'.

34   **on that night.** A Lucan touch, comparable to placing the
Transfiguration at night (ix. 32), but perhaps due here to the
reference to 'two on a bed'; Matt. xxiv. 40 has 'two in a field'.
The verse is added in some texts of Luke as verse 36, perhaps
by assimilation to Matthew, although it is possible that the verse
is genuine and has been omitted by homoioteleuton.

37   **eagles.** However originally intended, the 'eagles' apparently
taken by Luke to be the Roman standards (see on i. 74). This
is further evidence that the day to which Luke looks forward in
this passage (xvii. 22-37) is that of the destruction of Jerusalem,
the consummation of the 'seasons' of the Gentiles, after which
the Son of Man will appear (xxi. 24-27).

CHAPTER XVIII

1-43. THE UNJUST JUDGE. THE PHARISEE AND THE
TAX-GATHERER. THE CHILDREN. THE RICH
YOUNG MAN. THIRD PREDICTION OF THE
PASSION. THE BLIND MAN AT JERICHO

He spoke a parable to them on the necessity of their 1
always praying and not giving up, saying, 'There was a 2
judge in a city who did not fear God and took no notice of
man; and there was a widow in that city, and she used to 3
come to him saying, "Give me justice from the person
who has wronged me!" And for a time he was unwilling, 4
but after that he said to himself, "Even if I do not fear
God and take no notice of man, yet because of this widow 5
bothering me I will see justice done for her, so that she
does not by her coming finally wear me out".' And the 6
Lord said, 'Listen to what the unjust judge says! Will not 7
God do justice for his chosen ones who cry to him day
and night, while he is slow to help them? I tell you that 8
he will do justice for them soon; but when the Son of
Man comes, will he find faith on the earth?'

And he spoke this parable to some who trusted in them- 9
selves that they were righteous and despised the rest:
'Two men went up to the Temple to pray, one a Pharisee 10
and the other a tax-gatherer. The Pharisee took his stand 11
and prayed like this to himself: "God, I thank you that I
am not like the rest of men, greedy, wicked, adulterers,
or even like this tax-gatherer; I fast twice every week, I 12
tithe all my income." But the tax-gatherer, standing at a 13
distance, would not lift up even his eyes to heaven, but
struck his breast, saying, "God, have pity on me, a
sinner". I tell you, this one went down to his home 14
accounted righteous rather than the other. For everyone
who exalts himself will be humbled, and he that humbles
himself will be exalted.'

15 They began to bring to him even the babies, for him to touch them. On seeing it, his disciples were angry with
16 them. But Jesus called the babies to him saying, 'Allow the children to come to me and do not stop them. For of
17 such as these the kingdom of God consists. Truly I tell you, whoever does not accept the kingdom of God as a child does, will not enter it.'

18 And a ruler asked him, 'Good teacher, what shall I do
19 to inherit eternal life?' Jesus said to him, 'Why do you
20 call me good? No one is good, except one,—God. You know the commandments: "Do not commit adultery, do not murder, do not steal, do not witness falsely, honour
21 your father and your mother".' But he said, 'All these
22 things I have kept from my youth'. Hearing this, Jesus said to him, 'You still lack one thing: all that you have sell, and distribute to the poor, and you will have treasure
23 in the heavens; and come and follow me'. When he heard this he became very sad, for he was extremely
24 rich. Jesus observed him and said, 'With what difficulty
25 do those who have riches enter the kingdom of God! It is easier for a camel to enter the eye of a needle than for a
26 rich man to enter the kingdom of God.' Those who had
27 been listening said, 'Then who can be saved?' But he said, 'Things impossible with men are possible with
28 God'. Peter said, 'See, we have left our own and have
29 followed you', and he said to them, 'Truly I tell you that there is no one who has left home or wife or brothers or parents or children for the sake of the kingdom of God,
30 who will not receive them many times over at this time, and in the coming age eternal life'.

31 Taking aside the twelve he said to them, 'See, we are going up to Jerusalem, and there will be completed every-thing that has been written through the prophets for the
32 Son of Man; for he will be delivered to the Gentiles and
33 mocked and insulted and spat upon, and after flogging him they will kill him, and on the third day he will rise
34 again'. And they understood nothing of this, and this matter was concealed from them, and they did not know what was being said.

It happened that as he was approaching Jericho a blind 35
man was sitting by the wayside begging. Having heard 36
the crowd passing through he inquired what this was. It 37
was reported to him that Jesus the Nazarene was passing
by; and he shouted, 'Jesus, son of David, have pity on 38
me!' And the people in front angrily told him to keep 39
quiet; but he all the more cried, 'Son of David, have pity
on me!' Jesus stopped and bade them bring him to him; 40
and as he approached he asked him, 'What do you want
me to do for you?' And he said, 'Sir, for me to see again!' 41
And Jesus said to him, 'See again: your faith has saved 42
you'. And immediately he did see again, and he began 43
to follow him glorifying God; and all the people, having
seen this, gave praise to God.

not giving up. Persistence was taught also by the rabbis: 1
Simeon ben Halaphta (latter half of second century) cites the
saying, 'The impudent conquers the wicked one, how much
more the Good One of the World'.

There was a judge. The whole story of verses 2-5 shows 2
links of style and subject with xi. 5-8 (see note on xi. 5). Luke
has deliberately placed the parable here in an eschatological
context (cf. verses 6-8). The Lord exhorts his hearers (the disciples—cf. xvii. 22) to prayer of the kind suitable to times of
distress. Verse 1 is not a general injunction only: the disciples
are to pray increasingly when they look longingly and in vain
for one of the Days of the Son of Man.

And the Lord said. A patent Lucan addition begins here: 6
verses 6-8 are either homiletic tradition or composed by Luke
himself as words of comfort in his own day. He represents the
Lord as anticipating these times in such passages as the present
section (xvii. 22-xviii. 8) and xxi. 20-28.

his chosen ones who cry. I.e. those whom Rev. vi. 9 calls 7
'those who have been slain for the word of God and the
witness which they have given' but who in this passage are still
suffering on earth. Parallels with Rev. vi. are noticed also in
the other great eschatological section of Luke, at xxi. 24 and
xxiii. 30.

while he is slow to help them. The καί is Semitic and the clause continues the description of the condition of the 'chosen ones', which is begun by a participle. LS seem right therefore in the translation offered for the verb here.

8   **will he find faith on the earth?** Or the same sort of situation as is described in xvii. 27, 28? Faith here is the kind of life which is lived by faith in the future, especially a future vindication. (Cf. xxii. 32.)

9   **some who trusted in themselves that they were righteous.** These are in the greatest danger, since they do not heed the double warning of xvii. 21 (given to inquiring and probably sneering Pharisees) and xvii. 26 ff. It is an alien's faith which saves him in xvii. 19, faith in Jesus; those warned in this parable have faith in themselves, and this is not the sort of faith acceptable to the Son of Man (verse 8).

11   **I thank you.** A type of prayer not unknown to the rabbis, though SB's examples (*ad. loc*) do not date earlier than 70.

12   **I fast twice.** Sabbath and feast days must be free from fasting; otherwise the pious could choose any days, but the custom grew up of observing those days in the week—the second and fifth—which were the days of public fasts. Cf. *Didache* viii. 1, where the 'hypocrites' are said to fast on the second and fifth days (Mondays and Thursdays) and Christians are bidden to fast on the fourth and 'preparation' days (Wednesdays and Fridays).

   I tithe all my income. More than was required. Assuming the Pharisee did not deal in beasts, he was required to tithe, according to Deut. xiv. 22 ff., corn, wine, and oil, and rabbinic exegesis extended this to include pulse and greens. (Cf. Matt. xxiii. 23 and Luke xi. 42.)

13   **would not lift up even his eyes.** In *Enoch* xiii. 5 the fallen angels are similarly downcast and Enoch pleads for them.

14   **accounted righteous.** The Pauline phrase is necessary for the verb; it means one whose sins had been forgiven, though rabbinic thought would insist on the sinner making good the wrongs he had done. (Cf. Zacchaeus' promise, xix. 8.)

   everyone who exalts himself. See on xiv. 11.

15   **the babies.** Luke here follows Mark x. 13 ff. closely, and it is perhaps only at ix. 46-48 that he conveys a further meaning. (See Introduction, p. 57.) But see next note.

for of such as these the kingdom of God consists. 16
Apparently the original conclusion, verse 17 being a separate
saying. The babies are a symbol of those who form the kingdom of God, i.e. of 'the little ones' (see on xvii. 2). Luke does
not bring out the value of the babies for their own sake, but
omits Mark x. 16.

as a child does. The verb is added to make clear that the 17
meaning is not 'in childhood'. (Cf. John iii. 3, 5.)

Why do you call me good? Luke does not alter the ques- 19
tion in Mark x. 18 (contrast Matt. xix. 17) but his whole gospel
—like that of Mark, indeed—is proof that the author believes
the word 'good' is applicable to Jesus. Yet it is not enough to
say that Jesus is merely testing the 'ruler's' sincerity. See
following notes.

No one is good, except one,—God. Jesus is as unconscious
of his sinlessness as he is free from a sense of sin. Cf. the saying
attributed to Jesus in the *Gospel according to the Hebrews*, as
cited by Jerome, *Contra Pelagium* iii. 2: Jesus, invited by his
family to be baptized with them by John the Baptist, answers,
'What have I committed that I should be baptized by him,
unless it be that in saying this I am in ignorance'.

the commandments. They are given in an order instruct- 20
ive for the study of Lucan use of sources: a synopsis will show
at first sight a possible agreement of Matt. and Luke against
Mark x. 19 (cf. Matt. xix. 18); but in the order of the first two
commandments quoted Luke is unique and is following the
order of B in the LXX (Ex. xx. 13 f.; Deut. v. 17 f.) and of the
Nash papyrus. (Cf. Rom. xiii. 9; Jas. ii. 11.)

You still lack one thing. This verse is perhaps the best 22
testimony by the synoptics to the faithfulness of Paulinism to
the essential gospel: cf., e.g., Phil. iii. 7; Rom. iii. 21 ff.

or wife. A Lucan addition to Mark x. 29 in a verse where 29
Luke otherwise abbreviates Mark; was Luke thinking of Paul?
Cf. 1 Cor. ix. 5 which shows that in fact the wives of the
Apostles were not left but shared their wanderings and work,
except in the case of Paul, who appears to have been unmarried
(1 Cor. vii. 8).

for the sake of the kingdom. A typically Lucan alteration:
for him the establishment of the kingdom is a process begun

by Jesus and continued by the Apostles with his authority and power. (See Introduction, p. 34.)

30   **many times over.** Luke slurs over the promise in Mark x. 30 of a reward consisting in just those normal human relations which had been renounced, together with material possessions also.

at this time. The promise is to the Apostles, who will receive (according to Luke) many times over the *equivalent* of what they had given up, being endowed with great powers during the present age, here in this world (cf. Luke xxiv. 49; Acts i. 8; ii. 1 ff.; v. 1-16). Luke had no doubt seen evidence of these powers, but none of temporal and material wealth such as Mark seems to promise.

eternal life. Here Mark and Luke agree; the form of the promise in both envisages reward for the Apostles both in this age and in that to come, while Matthew understands no promise of a kingdom of this earth during the present age. According to him the Apostles will have a high position in the age to come, which will dawn at the same time as the establishment of the kingdom (xix. 28 ff. in which Matthew employs the Q saying found in a Lucan form at Luke xxii. 29-30).

31   **we are going up to Jerusalem.** Mark x. 33: Luke omits here Mark x. 32 (but cf. xix. 28), having begun the journey to Jerusalem at ix. 51. Jesus twice visits the Temple as a child, exciting the wonder of those who meet him there (ii. 22, 27 ff.; ii. 41 ff.) and Luke makes the climax of the temptations that associated with the temple at Jerusalem. Jesus is to fulfil his 'exodus' at Jerusalem on the authority of Moses, Elijah, and himself (ix. 31; xiii. 33; cf. ix. 51, 53). The journey is further noticed at xiii. 22; xvii. 11; xix. 11, 28, and after the accomplishment of the 'exodus', Jerusalem is the centre from which the work of establishing the kingdom is to begin (xxiv. 47). The same religious importance is attached to the city in the story of St. Paul, who also sets himself to go up to Jerusalem (Acts xix. 21; xx. 22; xxi. 4, 11 ff.).

through the prophets. It cannot be said that they had prophesied the suffering of the Son of Man, but ill-treatment of the servant at the hands of the Gentiles may be said to be foreshadowed in Is. l. 6 and liii. 8 and the rising the third day in

Hos. vi. 2. This theme of the necessary fulfilment of the scriptures through the Messiah's suffering recurs at xxiv. 25 f. and xxiv. 47; the application of it to the Son of Man originates with the gospels or their sources (perhaps Jesus himself), and is most striking at xxii. 69 (q.v.).

they understood nothing of this. See on ix. 45. Luke's 34 representation of the Apostles' dullness enhances the moments of the enlightenment in chapter xxiv (especially verses 16, 25, 26, 27) and helps to explain the contrast in their conduct before and after the resurrection.

a blind man. He symbolizes the Apostles. Like him, they 35 do not yet see, but their eyes will be opened by the Messiah himself (xxiv. 31).

son of David. The Messianic title is dangerous and the 39 crowd naturally try to stop him using it; but it is appropriate: his faith is in Jesus as the Messiah. See iv. 18; vii. 22, and notes.

On the Lord's descent from David see on xx. 44.

glorifying God. These words and the rest of the verse are 43 added by Luke. They emphasize that the miracle is from God, and make the passage suitable for liturgical use.

CHAPTER XIX

xix. 1-27. ZACCHAEUS. PARABLE OF THE POUNDS

1, 2 And he entered and passed through Jericho; and see, there was a man called by name Zacchaeus; and he was
3 a chief tax-collector, and he was rich. And he sought to see who Jesus was and was unable because of the crowd,
4 being short. And he ran on ahead and climbed a syca-
5 more to see him, for he was about to pass that way. And when he came to the place, Jesus looked up and said to him, 'Zacchaeus, hurry and come down! For to-day it
6 is in your house that I must stay.' And he hastened and
7 came down, and welcomed him with pleasure. And on seeing it all grumbled saying that he had gone into the
8 house of a sinner to lodge. But Zacchaeus stood up and said to the Lord, 'See, Lord, half of my possessions I give to the poor, and if there is anyone from whom I have obtained anything by false accusation, I restore it four-
9 fold'. Jesus said to him, 'To-day this house has received
10 salvation, just as he too is a son of Abraham. For the Son of Man came to seek and save the lost.'
11 As they were listening to this he added a parable, on account of his being near to Jerusalem and their think-ing that the kingdom of God was immediately going to
12 appear. So he said: 'A nobleman went into a distant country to receive for himself a kingdom and to return.
13 He called his ten servants and gave them ten pounds, and said to them, "Be occupied with business till I come".
14 But his fellow-citizens hated him and sent ambassadors after him to say, "We do not want this man to be king
15 over us". And it happened that on his return after receiv-ing the kingdom that he gave orders for those servants to be called to him, to ascertain what each had gained by
16 business. The first came in and said, "Your pound, sir,

has earned ten pounds in addition". And he said to him, 17
"Well done, good servant! As you have proved trustworthy in a very small matter, you shall be one with
authority over ten cities." And the second came saying, 18
"Your pound, sir, has made five pounds". And he said 19
to him too, "And you shall be over five cities". And the 20
other came saying, "Sir, here is your pound, which I kept
wrapped up in an handkerchief; for I was afraid of you, for 21
you are a hard man—you take what you have not deposited and reap what you have not sown". He said to 22
him, "Out of your own mouth I will condemn you, wicked
servant! So you knew that I was a hard man, taking what
I had not deposited and reaping what I had not sown?
Why did you not give my money into the bank and when 23
I came I would have drawn it with interest?" And to the 24
attendants he said, "Take his pound from him and give
it to him who has the ten pounds". And they said to him, 25
"Sir, he has ten pounds!" "I tell you that to everyone 26
who has shall be given, but from him who has not there
shall be taken from him even what he has. But as for 27
those enemies of mine who did not want me to be king
over them, bring them here and kill them before me!"'

Zacchaeus. For the name cf. Ezra ii. 9; Neh. vii. 14; 2 Macc. 1
x. 19. The incident is related with a wealth of Semitisms, which
continue into the parable of the pounds. Verse 2 is an excellent
example of Semitic construction.

all grumbled. It was not only the Pharisees who were 7
offended by Jesus' friendship with the tax-collectors, whom all
regarded as traitors.

Zacchaeus stood up. If this was in the house, this is no 8
answer to the grumbling. Possibly verse 8 is a homiletic addition, by Luke or by his source. In that case Jesus' reply in
verse 9 was originally addressed to the grumblers.

he too is a son of Abraham. This notion of salvation as 9
promised only to Jews is found also at xiii. 16 and perhaps also
at xiii. 28; it left its mark upon the Apostles' conception of the
kingdom, according to Acts (cf. i. 6, ii. 39). The consistent idea
that the Apostles, as Jewish vicegerents, would reign over this

kingdom, is found in Q (Luke xxii. 29-30; Matt. xix. 28). This
judaizing notion cannot have been invented by Luke, who saw
clearly that salvation was for Gentiles also, and records in Acts
(e.g. x. 45) the surprise of Jewish Christians at this fact; nor is
it Luke alone who sometimes represents the Lord's gifts of
healing and forgiveness as normally to be restricted to his
fellow-countrymen. This is clear from the story of the Syro-
Phoenician woman, which Luke omits (Mark vii. 24-30; Matt.
xv. 21-28). These gifts were on occasion available to Gentiles,
as to the centurion (vii. 1-10); yet even he acts through Jewish
representatives. This is then a notion which Luke found in his
sources. For a discussion as to the extent of these, see pp. 17 ff.
and 31 ff.

10   **seek . . . the lost.** Cf. Ezek. xxxiv. 16, where the picture is
of the shepherd restoring the flock. Such a picture enhances the
conception discussed in connexion with verse 9, and also recalls
the theme in the gospel represented by ii. 14; x. 21; xii. 32.

11   **near to Jerusalem.** This verse is of great interest since it
makes clear two related points: (1) The Lord's followers expected Jerusalem shortly to be the scene of the establishment
of the kingdom, i.e. of the *parousia*. Note especially the word
'appear' (not 'come'). They expected a kingdom of this world,
a restoration of Israel (Acts i. 6). (2) Luke corrects this notion:
Jerusalem is to be the scene rather of the Passion and Resurrection. The disciples had already failed to understand this (ix.
45 and xviii. 34).

Luke therefore adds a second theme to the parable: the kingdom which is the reason for the nobleman's journey, and the
rebels against him. This is clearly an addition to the story, which
may be found without it in Matt. xxv. 14-30.

12   **went into a distant country to receive a kingdom.** This
may appear strange until we reflect that the Jews of this time
were familiar with pretenders travelling to Rome to obtain
Roman support and authority for their thrones. Thus Herod
the Great in 40 B.C. was successful in such a mission (Jos. *Ant.*
xiv. 14. 1-4). On his return he executed several opponents
(*Ant.* xv. 1. 2). Archelaus, succeeding with the title of king but
without the permission of Augustus, went to Rome to obtain it
in 4 B.C. He was joined there by Antipas who sought the same

prize for himself and by Jews who came to plead against his claims (*Ant.* xvii. 9. 3-4. *B.J.* ii. 2. 1-3). Finally Philip, Herod's third son, made the journey to assist Archelaus against a new Jewish delegation (*Ant.* xvii. 11. 1). Cf. verses 14 and 27. But the country to which Jesus is to travel is that of death, at the hands of Romans.

He called his ten servants. It is not unlikely that the 13 original parable, shorn of the additions (verses 12b, 14, 27), also had an eschatological significance: for they are to 'be occupied' till he returns. Like those addressed in xii. 35 ff. they are in positions of authority in a period immediately preceding their Lord's return, and like them are to be severely punished if they abuse that authority. Chapter xii warns against waste and tyranny, the present passage against timidity and sloth.

The number ten has probably no positive significance; being the number of fingers, it is a common round number among many peoples; it is so frequently in the OT (e.g. ten patriarchs before the Flood, Gen. v.; ten commandments, Ex. xx.; Deut. v.; ten plagues, Ex. vii.-xi.) and is used in this way at Luke xv. 8 and Matt. xxv. 1. Negatively Luke's use of it is significant; he has avoided the three servants found in Matt. xxv. 14-15, with their graded gifts, too reminiscent of gnostic systems; three was clearly the original number in Luke's source, for only three servants are called to account (verses 16, 18, 20). See also on viii. 8.

And they said to him, 'Sir, he has ten pounds!' Is this 25 an echo of the opponents of Archelaus? It is possible that the parable originally ended at verse 24, more probably with verse 26, without verse 25 intervening. If the first is correct, then both Matthew and Luke have added a floating saying found also at Mark iv. 25, in which context Luke (viii. 18) changes its form. Cf. Matt. xiii. 12 and for his parallel to this passage, xxv. 29.

enemies. The harsh treatment assigned to them should not 27 be so pressed that we have to find a parallel for it in the scene of the coming inauguration of the kingdom. In Matt. xxv. 30 it is not the enemies (who of course do not appear in that version) but the timid servant who is cast into the outer darkness: in that gospel there is no period between the beginning of the kingdom and the final consummation.

28 And after saying this he went forward, going up to Jeru-
29 salem. And it happened that when he came near to
Bethphage and Bethany towards the hill called the Hill
30 of Olives, he sent two of his disciples, saying, 'Go into
the village opposite, on entering which you will find a
colt tethered, upon which no man has ever yet sat; and
31 when you have unfastened him, bring him. And if anyone
asks you, "Why are you unfastening him?"—this is what
32 to say: "The Lord has need of him."' Those who were
33 sent went away and found it as he had told them: as they
were unfastening the colt his owners said to them, 'Why
34 are you unfastening the colt?' And they said, 'The Lord
35 has need of him'. And they brought him to Jesus and after
throwing their cloaks on the colt they mounted Jesus on
36 him; and as he went along they spread their clothes
37 underneath, in the road. As he was approaching the
actual descent of the Hill of Olives the whole crowd of
disciples began to rejoice and praise God with a loud
voice for all the acts of power which they had seen,
38 saying, 'Blessed is the king who comes in the name of the
Lord! In heaven peace and glory in the highest!'
39   And some of the Pharisees from the crowd said to him,
40 'Teacher, rebuke your disciples!' And he answered, 'I
41 tell you, if they are silent, the stones will cry out!' And
as he drew near, seeing the city, he wept over it, saying,
42 'If you had known at this day, if only you had known
what was for your peace! But now it is hidden from your
43 eyes. For the days will come when your enemies will
build an entrenchment against you, and will encircle
44 you and keep you in from every side, and they will raze
you to the ground, and your children within you, and
they will not leave one stone on another in you, because
you did not recognize the time of your visitation.'
45   He entered the temple and began to cast out the sellers,
46 saying to them, 'It is written: "And my house shall be a

house of prayer"; but you have made it "a den of robbers"'.

He taught daily in the temple; now the chief priests 47
**and the scribes, along with the prominent members of
the people, sought to destroy him, and could not find** 48
anything to do, for all the people hung upon him listening.

forward, going up to Jerusalem. Cf. Mark x. 32. The 28
journey to Jerusalem which Luke so strongly emphasizes has
its root in the Marcan tradition. Luke is now following Mark
but makes, as we shall see, many changes of order and emphasis.

on which no man has ever yet sat. Cf. Mark xi. 2. The 30
fulfilment of the prophecy of Zech. ix. 9, somewhat laboured by
Matt. xxi. 1-5, is told with extreme reverence. The words would
in actual fact be very strange and irrelevant in the real situation.

if anyone asks you. The instructions seem to be founded on 31
plans previously made, but we are left tantalizingly without a
clue as to how or when.

the actual descent. This added verse seems by its vocabu- 37
lary to be Luke's own; but the topographical detail, especially
in view of Luke's usual indifference to it, is extremely interesting. Plummer remarks that it is at the top of this descent that
the south-east corner of the 'City of David' (but not the
temple) comes into sight, and quotes Stanley's guess that this
may have prompted the hymn. If so, we may suppose that it
proceeded from hearts trusting implicitly in the imminent kingship of their hero (cf. verse 38 below) and ignorant still of the
warning which Luke would have us believe was conveyed in
xix. 11 ff.

for all the acts of power. The Lord comes to his city and
his temple, having been long on the journey. This is the crown
and climax of his ministry, and the praise sums up all that he
has done which leads to, and deserves, this day. See also on
verse 42.

the king. It is clear that the original contained this word, 38
although there are variant readings here. It is lacking altogether
only in some Caesarean MSS. The fact is significant: it illustrates
once more Luke's insistence on the Christian claim to the kingship of Jesus, even though none is more alive than he to the

17   245

necessity of testifying to the political innocence of Christianity.
The first line of the cry of welcome is from the LXX of Ps.
cxvii. 26. Luke omits 'Hosanna' (Mark xi. 9) as unintelligible
to Gentile readers.

in heaven peace. A phrase unique in the NT. See on ii. 14.
Peace is a favourite word with Luke, occurring in several
passages peculiar to his gospel. In two of these, xiv. 32 and xix.
42, it is peace as opposed to war. In the others, i. 79; ii. 14; x.
5, 6, it is a gift of God, a state of total well-being. The unusual
variant here of the Tuscan Gospel quoted by Black, 'pace sia
in terra', is no doubt caused by reminiscence of ii. 14, strongly
recalled by 'glory in the highest'.

40   **stones will cry out.** Cf. Hab. ii. 11.

42   **what was for your peace.** The king comes to his city. Some
echo the cry of welcome uttered by the angels at his birth, but
his city rejects him. A rabbinic tradition derived the name
Jerusalem by mingling Gen. xiv. 18 and xxii. 14, claiming it
contained the word *shalom*, peace.

But now. Referring back to 'this day'; but the English conceals another meaning of the Greek, viz. 'but in fact'. (Cf. 1 Cor.
vii. 14; xii. 20; xv. 20.)

43   **an entrenchment.** The language of this verse is derived
from the LXX of such passages as Is. xxix. 3; xxxvii. 33; Ezek.
iv. 1-3; Jer. lii. 4-5. See also following note.

44   **raze.** Cf. Hos. xiii. 16, and for other elements in the verse,
Hag. ii. 15 and Ps. cxxxvii. 9; but the prophecy is not a mere
citation. No doubt by itself it fails to justify the conclusion that
the gospel was written after A.D. 70, but it is support for the
strong evidence afforded by Luke's treatment of Mark xiii. 14
at xxi. 20.

46   **it is written.** Strangers are to be made joyful in 'my house
of prayer', according to Is. lvi. 7. Jer. vii. 11 calls the temple
'a den of robbers' in the midst of a prophecy of its destruction.

47   **He taught daily.** A justifiable inference from a careful reading of Mark xi. 15-19, especially verses 16-17, which imply that
for some days the Lord not only taught in the temple but also
actively prevented its desecration in order to establish the new
reverence on which he insisted. Cf. Luke xx. 1, and xxi. 37 for
further details of the Lord's practice at this time.

the people. Distinguished from their 'prominent members'. 48
The people were an indispensable support for the Lord in the
days during which his authority prevailed in the temple. He
lacked rabbinic authority and was attacked on this ground. Cf.
xx. 1 f., and for the people's support, xx. 6, 19, 26, 45 ff.; xxi. 38.
The people are the λαός, contrasting in all the passages with
Mark's 'crowd' (ὄχλος), except in xx. 26a and xxi. 38 (which
are peculiar to Luke).

CHAPTER XX

1-47. CONTEST BETWEEN THE LORD AND HIS
OPPONENTS FOR AUTHORITY. PARABLE OF
WICKED FARMERS. TRIBUTE. RESURRECTION.
DAVID'S SON. WARNING OF PEOPLE AGAINST
PHARISEES

1 And it happened on one of the days when he was teaching
the people in the temple and preaching the gospel, the
chief priests and scribes with the elders came upon him,
2 and spoke to him in these words: 'Tell us with what
authority you do this, or who it is who gave you this
3 authority'. In answer he said to them: 'I too will ask you
4 a question and do you tell me: the baptism of John—was
5 it from heaven or from men?' Now they reasoned among
themselves in these words: 'If we say "From heaven",
6 he will say, "Why did you not believe him?" But if we
say "From men" the whole people will stone us, for they
7 are convinced John was a prophet.' And they answered
8 that they did not know from whence it was. And Jesus
said to them, 'Nor do I tell you with what authority I do
this'.

9 And he began to speak this parable to the people: 'A
man planted a vineyard, and hired it out to farmers, and
10 went away for a considerable time; and at the season he
sent to the farmers a servant, for them to give him some
of the fruit of the vineyard; but the farmers beat him and
11 sent him away with nothing. And he again sent another
servant, and they beat him too, and insulted him and
12 sent him away with nothing. And he again sent a third;
13 but him too they wounded and threw him out. Now the
owner of the vineyard said, "What shall I do? I will send
my son, my beloved one; perhaps they will respect him."
14 When they saw him the farmers reasoned with one
another saying, "This is the heir: let us kill him so that

the inheritance may be ours'. And they threw him out 15
of the vineyard and killed him. What then will the owner
of the vineyard do to them? He will come and destroy 16
those farmers and give the vineyard to others.' When
they heard this they said, 'God forbid!' But he looked at 17
them and said, 'What then does this scripture mean?—
"the stone which the builders rejected is the one which
has become the head corner-stone". Everyone who falls 18
on that stone will be crushed and it will grind to powder
any upon whom it falls.' And the scribes and chief priests 19
tried to lay hands on him at that very moment, and they
were afraid of the people; for they knew that he had
spoken the parable against them. And after keeping 20
watch on him they sent as spies some men pretending to
be sincere, to seize on his word, so as to hand him over to
authority and the power of the governor. And they ques- 21
tioned him, saying, 'Teacher, we know that you speak
and teach rightly, and show no favour, but in sincerity
teach the way of God: is it right for us to give tribute to 22
Caesar or not?' But he perceived their craftiness and said 23
to them, 'Show me a denarius. Whose image and inscrip- 24
tion has it?' And they said, 'Caesar's'. And he said to 25
them, 'Well, then, render Caesar's to Caesar and God's
to God'. And they were not able to seize on his word 26
before the people and marvelling at his answer were
silent.

Some of the Sadducees approached, they who deny 27
that there is a resurrection, and questioned him saying, 28
'Teacher, Moses wrote for us, "If anyone's brother dies,
having a wife, and he be childless, his brother is to take
his wife and raise offspring for his brother. There were 29
seven brothers, then! and the first took a wife and died 30
childless,—and the second, and the third took her, and 31
in the same way the seven left no children and died.
Lastly the woman too died. The woman then in the 32,33
resurrection—of whom among them will she be the
wife? For the seven had her as a wife.' And Jesus said to 34
them, 'The sons of this age marry and are given in marriage, but those counted worthy to attain that age and the 35

resurrection from the dead neither marry nor are given
36 in marriage. For indeed they can no longer die, for they
are like angels, and are sons of God, being sons of the
37 resurrection. But that the dead are raised, Moses too
showed at the bush passage, when he says, "the Lord the
God of Abraham and the God of Isaac and the God o
38 Jacob". But he is God not of the dead but of the living; for
39 all live, for him.' In answer some of the scribes said,
40 'Teacher, well spoken!' For they no longer dared to ask
him anything.
41   And he said to them, 'How is it that they say that the
42 Christ is son of David? For David himself says in the book
of Psalms, "The Lord said to my lord, 'Sit at my right
43 hand until I set your enemies as a footstool beneath your
44 feet!'"' David then calls him "lord", so how is he his
45 son?' In the hearing of all the people he said to the
46 disciples, 'Beware of the scribes who like to walk in robes
and who love greetings in the squares and front seats in
47 the synagogues and chief seats at dinners, who devour
the houses of widows and for a pretence pray at length.
They will receive a greater sentence.'

2   **authority.** See on xix. 48.
4   **the baptism of John.** The submission of the Lord to his
baptism shows that he regarded it as 'from heaven', i.e. bearing
God's authority. Indeed, he saw the Baptist as the originator
of the movement which he now led. See on vii. 18.
6   **John was a prophet.** The Lord endorsed this belief (vii. 26).
9   **planted a vineyard.** Cf. Mark xii. 1. Luke shows little
awareness of the reference to Is. v. 2.
11   **he again sent.** The Gk. here and in verse 12 has a septuagintal style contrasting with Mark xii. 4.
    servants. In view of the emphasis on the son in verse 13 it
seems that there might be a reference here to the prophets, the
parable approaching more nearly to an allegory in this respect
than most parables; but there is no need to find any historical
parallel in the fates of the three servants.
13   **my son, my beloved.** Cf. Mark xii. 6. The particular phrase
must recall the baptism in all three synoptics (Mark i. 11; Matt.

iii. 17; Luke iii. 22). This strengthens the impression that there is a reference to the Lord himself here.

they said. Who are 'they'? The parable is addressed to the 16 people (verse 9), but cf. verse 19 for the presence of those against whom it was directed. Luke appears to mean that the scribes and others made no further remark after verse 7 and the 'they' here must be the audience of people. Their exclamation is Luke's addition to Mark; like Matthew he has noticed the obscurity of the connexion between Mark xii. 9 (which would end the parable quite naturally) and the OT quotation in Mark xii. 10-11, and seeks to remove it.

looked at them. A natural sequel to what Luke has already 17 added in verse 16. He uses the verb only here and at xxii. 61, and in both passages effectively. In Mark it is slightly more usual: in both it reflects severity or reproval. Luke significantly omits it where the object of the look is the twelve, at xviii. 27. (Cf. Mark x. 27.)

the stone. Even in the versions of Matthew and Luke the connexion between the parable and the quotation is difficult: in the parable the emphasis is finally on the coming rejection of the farmers by the owner of the vineyard, that is of the official representatives of Judaism by God; but the quotation, which is certainly from Ps. cxvii. 22-23 (LXX), places the emphasis on the object of their rejection. Matt. xxi. 43 suggests that the rejected stone will be a nation which does the will of God and therefore receives the vineyard (i.e. the kingdom); Luke adds a reference which underlines the other OT conception of the stone, ultimately from Dan. ii. 34, 35, 44, or Is. viii. 14-15, or both, though perhaps immediately from a late Judaistic work unknown to us.

at that very moment. For the translation see Black, p. 79. 19
the people. See on xix. 48 above.

authority. Presumably the Sanhedrin, while the **governor** 20 is of course the procurator. See on xxiii. 1.

show no favour. A Hebrew expression crudely translated 21 into Greek, meaning literally 'do not lift up the face', i.e. make the countenance rise by flattery. Cf. Rom. ii. 11, and Ecclus. iv. 27 where the phrase is used in an injunction not to 'raise the face of an official'. Jesus is here being tempted to flatter the emperor or his representatives by a reply favourable to Caesar, while his tempters subtly make that way out of their supposed dilemma impossible.

25   **Caesar's to Caesar.** The use of the coinage is a small example of the machinery of a civilization which the Jews had to accept; but this acceptance was an uneasy compromise with a principle rather than based upon one. According to the prophets foreign rule might be the will of God (e.g. Jer. xxvii. 6) though the foreign ruler might well be unaware of this (Is. x. 5-7); but such a doctrine was naturally resisted, and was remote from that of such popular leaders as Judas of Galilee, who led a rebellion in opposition to the census of A.D. 6 (Acts v. 36. See Introduction, p. 45 f.). Indirect taxation could be collected without a census, which was a necessary preliminary to direct taxation, carried out for Judaea since A.D. 15 by the Roman procurator. The silver *denarius*, which was the form in which the tax was paid, was therefore a mark of political subjugation; further, the inscriptions on it were reminders of the cult of the emperor and therefore also religiously abhorrent.

The Lord's answer suggests that it was just to demand payment from subject states as a general principle; the *denarius* is to be rendered—given back, not merely given—in return for the services of government. This is the theme of Rom. xiii. 1-7; 1 Pet. ii. 13 ff.; Tit. iii. 1. But the doctrine that rulers are owed obedience because God has given them their authority clearly lies behind this teaching in Rom. xiii. and 1 Pet. ii., and a telling example of this direct dependence of earthly authority upon God is given in John xix. 11. The Lord was as acutely aware of the religious objection to the *denarius* as his questioners: thus the words, 'and God's to God', besides reminding them positively of their highest duty, also imply that the worship which the emperor demanded can be rendered to God alone. Cf., e.g., Ex. xx. 3 ff.; Ps. lxxvi. 11 f. Jewish scruples in this matter were officially respected, but individuals, such as Pilate, often caused trouble by offending them. See on xiii. 1; and for a critical attitude towards Rome, on xvii. 37 and xxiii. 28.

The changed attitude to Rome and its government in the book of Revelation is due not only to the persecution which the author believes is destined ultimately to subject all Christians to martyrdom, but also to the sense of horror aroused by the observation that this cruelty derived from a perverted worship, which included the imperial cult and, setting the emperor in the place of God, afforded a ghastly parody of the divinely constituted order of God, angels, and men. Nevertheless, almost all Christians in the centuries following NT times held fast to the duty of obedience, including the payment of taxes, to the emperor, while ready to suffer martyrdom rather than render to Caesar what God alone may rightly command.

his brother is to take his wife. Deut. xxv. 5-10 teaches that 28 where brothers live together and one dies childless, his brother is to beget a child for him by the widow, and that he will be disgraced if he refuses to do this. It is not commanded that he must marry the widow; but Gen. xxxviii. 8 ff. implies that the widow had a right to the brother as a husband if he were free, and the book of Ruth (iii-iv) implies that at that date convention demanded that the act of begetting a child for the dead husband would imply marriage; this was part of the duty of the next of kin, one of whose other duties was to redeem an inheritance in danger of being lost to the family. Lev. xxv. 25 ff. defines this last duty but says nothing of the other custom. The conception of a next of kin's duty as embracing these and other duties is very ancient, evidence of it having appeared in the Nuzu documents and in Egypt.

those counted worthy. As at xiv. 14 (q.v.) Luke appears to 35 hold the doctrine that only the righteous dead rise, and thus makes a significant addition to the Marcan version here (cf. Mark xii. 25).

they can no longer die. Another Lucan addition but one 36 which does no more than bring out the meaning implicit in the latter half of Mark xii. 25.

they are like angels. Cf. *2 Bar.* li. 10; the source of both passages is thought by Charles (*Apoc.* and *Pseudep.* ii. 480) to be *Enoch* civ. 4, 6, but literary dependence is insufficient comment on the important development of thought; Luke, like Mark (xii. 25), makes the risen righteous equivalent to the heavenly beings who wait upon God. Cf. Acts vi. 15; Matt. xviii. 10. This confusion, not to say identification, of the righteous dead with angels, i.e. with the innocent beings of the other world, might be caused in popular thought by an early passage of Paul, I Th. iv. 14, where God 'brings with him' not angels but Christians who have died.

37   **Moses too.** Jesus sympathized with the reverence for the original Mosaic law which characterized the Sadducees, and thought that the tradition of the Pharisees and their learned men often obscured its true message. (For the first point cf., e.g., Mark x. 3 ff.; for the second Mark vii. 3 ff.) But his own acceptance of the prophets and of apocalyptic placed him in this matter nearer the view of the Pharisees. Here he appeals to a scripture which the Sadducees would certainly respect, viz. Ex. iii. 6. Those who are in relation to God must be living; God has no relation to the dead.

38   **for all live, for him.** Added by Luke to his Marcan material, possibly derived from 4 *Macc.* xvi. 25 ('Those who have died for God live for God like Abraham and Isaac and Jacob'). If Townshend is right in arguing (in *Apoc. and Pseudep.* ii. 654) that the date of 4 *Macc.* must be between 63 B.C. and A.D. 38, Luke may have known it, though Plummer entertains the possibility of 4 *Macc.* having imitated Christian phraseology.

41   **and he said to them.** Luke omits here the question about the great commandment which he has in his own form (though derived from Mark xii. 28-31) at x. 25-28. The Lord passes straight to a counter-attack after surprising his opponents with his complete answers to their hard questions. Luke follows Mark closely but makes some interesting slight changes.

42   **in the book of Psalms.** For Mark's 'in the Holy Spirit'. Luke is not objecting to Mark's theory of inspiration (as Acts i. 16 will show) but merely helping his readers. The psalm is cx. 1, its original meaning being, 'The Lord said to my lord, "Sit at my right hand, etc. . . ."' where the psalmist's lord may have been Simon, high priest from 141 until his murder in 135, or his son John Hyrcanus, who actually took the royal title. It was in the autumn of 141 that the people ratified the nomination to the high priesthood made by Gentile kings. Cf. the language of I Macc. xiv. 41 with the psalm. If Melchizedek is the right original reading in verse 4 (which Cheyne doubted), the plea is that there is precedent for a valid high priesthood without

election. But the psalm may well have a longer history which would take back its origin to a pre-exilic enthronement psalm, making it easier to understand how it had come to be taken as 'Messianic' in the interpretation of our Lord and his contemporaries; it is of course the promise of the Lord to make the person addressed victorious over his enemies which led to the interpretation that this person was the Messiah: the exile and many years since had completely obliterated knowledge of the origin of the psalms, and Jesus and his contemporaries shared common ground in ascribing them to David. SB show (iv. 1. 452-65) that in rabbinic literature this Messianic interpretation is not found until the second half of the third century, when it appears as something new in interpretation. This later rabbinic reluctance is no doubt due to the fact that the passage was so often used in the Christian church, e.g. Acts ii. 34-35; vii. 56; 1 Cor. xv. 25; Heb. i. 3, 13; 1 Pet. iii. 22.

how is he his son? The question is challenging and hard 44 to interpret; but it clearly implies that the Lord did not share the popular belief that the Messiah must be descended from David. This in turn may imply either that although himself descended from David, he made no claim to be the Messiah; or that he claimed to be the Messiah, but not by virtue of descent from David.

If the Lord was repudiating any claim to be descended from David, we have to explain the tradition that he was so descended, represented by Rom. i. 3; Luke i. 32; iii. 23 ff. (especially 31); Acts ii. 30-31; Matt. i. 1; Rev. xxii. 16. The tradition is not found in Mark but Rom. i. 3 is early. Its explanation may be that the claim that Jesus was the Messiah led quickly to the claim that he was of Davidic descent.

If the Lord was indeed descended from David, the explanation of the saying here may be that the Lord repudiated any claim to be the Messiah which was founded on this descent. Elsewhere he does not repudiate the Messiahship outright, but rather that conception of it held by his followers (Mark viii. 29-33; Luke ix. 20-22), accepting it only when this means suffering (Mark xiv. 62; Luke xxii. 69; Matt. xxvi. 64) and even then qualifying the claim by reference to the different concept of the Son of Man.

46 **front seats in synagogues.** This second half of the verse
is paralleled by Luke xi. 43 (q.v.).

in robes. The *tallith* was 'the resplendent coat of men distinguished by piety or scholarship' (Daube).

47 **devour the houses of widows.** By taking them as pledges
for debts which cannot be repaid. Note the connexion with the
following short passage.

xxi. 1-4. THE WIDOW'S FARTHINGS

He looked up and saw rich people throwing their gifts 1
into the treasury-box; and he saw a poor widow throwing 2
there two farthings, and he said, 'Truly I tell you that 3
this poor widow has thrown in more than all; for all these 4
threw for gifts from their surplus, but she from her want
has thrown in all the living that she had'.

treasury-box. Cf. 2 Kings xii. 9. 1

xxi. 5-38. COMING DESTRUCTION OF THE
TEMPLE AND APOCALYPTIC TEACHING

And when some were saying about the temple that it had 5
been adorned with fine stone and monuments, he said,
'These things at which you are looking,—the days will 6
come when a stone will not be left upon another which
will not be broken apart'. They asked him, 'Teacher, 7
when therefore will this be, and what is the sign when it
is about to take place?' And he said, 'See that you are 8
not led astray; for many will come in my name saying,
"I am he" and "The time has come". Do not go after
them. But when you hear of wars and revolutions, do not 9
be frightened, for these must happen first, but the end
will not come immediately.'

Then he began to say to them: 'Nation shall rise against 10
nation and kingdom against kingdom, and there will be 11
great earthquakes and in places plagues and famines, and
there will be both terrifying portents and great signs from
heaven.

'But before all these things they will lay hands on you 12

and persecute you, handing you over to synagogues and
jailors, to be led away before kings and governors for my
13 name's sake. The result for you will be a testimony:
14 settle therefore in your hearts not to concern yourselves
15 beforehand with your defence, for I will give you utterance and wisdom, which none of your adversaries will
16 be able to withstand or gainsay. But you will be delivered
up even by parents and brothers and kinsmen and friends,
17 and they will put some of you to death, and you will be
18 hated by all because of my name. And not a hair of your
19 head will be destroyed: by your endurance you will
purchase your lives.

20   'But when you see Jerusalem encircled by armies,
21 then be sure that her desolation has come. Then let those
in Judaea flee to the hills, and those in the centre of her
make their way out, and those in the country districts not
22 go into her, because these are the days of vengeance for
23 the fulfilling of all the scriptures. Woe to women with
child and giving suck in those days! For there will be great
24 distress in the land and wrath for this people, and they
will fall by the edge of the sword and be taken prisoner
into all the nations, and Jerusalem will be trodden down
by the nations until the times of the nations be fulfilled.

25   'And there will be signs in the sun and moon and stars,
and on earth peoples' confusion with despair at the roar-
26 ing waves of the sea, men fainting from fear and apprehension at what is coming on the world; for the powers
27 of the heavens will be shaken; and then they will see the
Son of Man coming in a cloud with power and great glory.
28 When all these things begin to happen, look up, and lift up
your heads, because your redemption is drawing near.'

29   And he spoke a parable to them: 'See the figtree and all
30 the trees: when they put forth, you look at them and know
31 of yourselves that already summer is near; so too, when
you see these things happening, be sure that the kingdom
32 of God is near. Truly I tell you that this generation will
33 not pass away until all happen. Heaven and earth will
pass away but my words will not pass away.

34   'Beware for yourselves that your hearts are not weighed

down with debauchery and drunkenness and worldly
cares, and that day come upon you suddenly, like a snare; 35
for it will come upon all who dwell on the face of the
whole earth. Be watchful at all times praying that you 36
may be strong to escape all that is going to happen, and
to stand before the Son of Man.'
During the days he taught in the temple, and for the 37
nights he went out and lodged on the hill called the Hill of
Olives. And all the people came early to him in the temple 38
to listen to him.

some were saying. Luke places the scene of this chapter's 5
discourse in the temple itself: there has been no note of leaving
it since xx. 1; Luke omits the reference to going out to the Hill
of Olives found in Mark xiii. 3, but uses it in verses 37-38.

They are still the **some** of verse 5, the names carefully given 7
in Mark xiii. 3 being omitted. The discourse is therefore according to Luke addressed to the people.

what is the sign? It is hard to say whether this question is
really answered in the discourse as it follows in Mark; but in
Luke's account the sign for the coming destruction of the temple
is given at verse 20, and the language there is definite. Other
signs are given at verses 25 ff. (again more definitely than in
Mark): these are to presage the deliverance of the persecuted.

See that you are not led astray. By representing the Lord 8
as addressing the people Luke has subtly conveyed a sense of
the words being addressed to the readers of his gospel. Here,
too, he has shortened the opening of Mark xiii. 5 to a mere 'and
he said', making the discourse continuous.

I am he. I.e. 'The Messiah is present'. Daube (p. 325)
claims that the origin of the saying with this sense is the Passover *Haggadah*. Cf. Mark xiii. 6, and the references in the Fourth
Gospel where there is often a reminiscence of the treatment of
the formula in the OT as equivalent to the divine name (e.g. Is.
xliii. 10; xlviii. 12). See John iv. 25 f.; viii. 24, 28, 58; xiii. 19; xviii. 5,
6, 8, and Dodd, *The Interpretation of the Fourth Gospel*, pp. 93 ff.

the time. Or 'season', the eschatological period in God's
plan: a Lucan addition. The season meant is that of the desolation of Jerusalem (verse 20), which is the inauguration of the

times of the nations (verse 24). The next 'time' is that of the redemption (verse 28). All these are Lucan insertions or transformations.

9   **revolutions.** Such as the rebellion of the Jews which led to the desolation of their city: another Lucan addition. The prediction has already been made at xix. 41 ff. just before the Lord entered the city, and is now made as he sits in the temple.

the end will not come immediately. Not even the destruction of Jerusalem is the final event. Cf. Mark xiii. 7: 'the end is not yet'. Luke's emphasis is that these events do lead to the end, though not at once.

10   **Then he began to say to them.** A Lucan insertion, introducing a detailed description of what has been so far only sketched.

12   **But before all these things.** Another precise indication by Luke, for which Mark gives no hint at Mark xiii. 9. Luke is calling attention, in the apocalyptic manner, to events in his own day. The work of spreading the gospel (Mark xiii. 10) is even now being carried out, and inevitably means the persecution of those who proclaim it.

synagogues and jailors. Cf., e.g., 2 Cor. vi. 5; xi. 24; Acts xvi. 22 f. ; xxii. 19.

Kings and governors. Cf. Acts xxiv; xxv. 7-12, 23 ff.

13   **the result for you will be a testimony.** Cf. Acts iv. 5-22, 25-26.

15   **I will give you utterance and wisdom.** In Acts iii. 12-26 Peter makes an eloquent speech before the people; in Acts iv. 8-13 he is filled with the Holy Spirit and surprises the Sanhedrin with his eloquence. They are unable to 'gainsay' him. (The Greek verb occurs in the NT only here and at Acts iv. 14.)

What is probably the Q version of this teaching is found at xii. 11-12 (cf. Matt. x. 19).

16   **you will be delivered.** Contrasting with the impersonal form of the saying in Mark xiii. 12; Luke had perhaps known of just such unnatural treachery, perhaps in 64, in the persecution under Nero.

some of you. Including Peter (see on verse 15). Luke also no doubt thinks of Paul.

17   **hated by all because of my name.** This might refer to the

calumny fastened by Nero upon Christians, which gave great impetus to hatred of them throughout the empire. Cf. Acts xxviii. 22.

not a hair of your head will be destroyed. So soon after 18 verse 16, this cannot mean that those addressed will all escape death. It must be interpreted in the light of verse 19.

you will purchase your lives. Luke has subtly altered 19 Mark xiii. 13b. The clue to his meaning lies in Luke ix. 24 and xvii. 33: the lives which may be purchased by endurance are their lives in the age to come.

Jerusalem encircled by armies. There is no need to see 20 evidence here for a separate source, as, for example, Dodd, *JRS*, 1947. Luke is reinterpreting Mark throughout the Little Apocalypse, and at every point we can see both his reason for so doing and his retention of a link with his Marcan original. Here the word 'desolation' recalls Mark xiii. 14. The reason for reinterpretation is more than Luke's knowledge of the fate of Jerusalem at the hands of Vespasian and Titus: he is deliberately urging his readers to see that the eschatological events which they had been led to expect had been in part exactly fulfilled; and where others warn of similar events to come, Luke warns of further 'times' to come. (See on verses 8 and 9 above.)

those in the centre of her. I.e. of Jerusalem. For the phrase 21 cf. Ezek. ix. 4: the desolation of Jerusalem is so much the main theme that Luke once again departs slightly from Mark (xiii. 15-16) though he has borrowed from Mark xiii. 16 at xvii. 31.

the days of vengeance. Cf. Deut. xxxii. 35, and especially 22 Ezek. ix. 1.

for the fulfilling of all the scriptures. Here is Luke's warrant for his imaginative interpretation of his Marcan original: the doom of Jerusalem was a theme of the prophets, and the cause of it might be summed up in the words of the last of the prophets to prophesy her doom: she did not know the things which were for her peace (xix. 42).

wrath for this people. For the words cf. 2 Kings iii. 27. 23 Verses 23b-24 are Luke's own.

taken prisoner into all the nations. Testified by Jos. *B.J.* 24 vi. 9. 3.

18 261

Jerusalem will be trodden down by the nations. The vocabulary is again supplied by the OT, viz. Zech. xii. 3 f. (LXX), the former reappearing at Rev. xi. 2.

until the times of the nations be fulfilled. That each nation has its appointed time is part of the theme of apocalyptic in many writings, e.g. Dan. *passim*; cf. the Qumran *Manual of Discipline*, iv. 18: 'Now God through the mysteries of his understanding and through his glorious wisdom has appointed a period for the existence of wrongdoing; but at the season of visitation he will destroy it for ever; and then the truth of the world will appear for ever'.

25   **there will be signs in the sun and moon and stars.** Cf. Is. 13. 10. But the stars will not fall from heaven, as in Mark xiii. 25. Here Luke's motive for substituting a passage of his own (verses 25-26) is his desire to invest the fall of Jerusalem, not the end of the world (as Mark), with catastrophic solemnity. That he is not identifying the end of the world with the fall of the city is shown by his omission of Mark xiii. 27 and the substitution of his own verse 28.

the roaring waves of the sea. Cf. Ps. lxiv. 8 (LXX); and for the fainting from fear see Deut. xxviii. 28 and *2 Bar.* lxx. 2.

26   **the powers of the heavens.** Cf. Is. xiii. 26; xxxiv. 4, 13; Joel ii. 10.

27   **the Son of Man coming in a cloud.** Not 'in' or 'with clouds', as Mark xiii. 26. For Luke the cloud is that which enshrined the glory of the Lord at the Transfiguration; he is the only evangelist to make this identification, giving the word always in the singular. See xvii. 22 and Introduction, pp 68 ff., especially p. 70, where it is argued that this event is not the final judgment, but the same event as is referred to in xvii. 30, the appearance of the Son of Man ('one of the days of the Son of Man') which presages the deliverance of the nation, and the coming of the kingdom (see verse 31). For **cloud** see pp. 36 f.

28   **lift up your heads.** For the vocabulary in a different context cf. Is. viii. 21.

redemption. Here not personal salvation only, but an event wrought by God in history. Cf. Eph. iv. 30. The same idea is expressed in the phrase, 'consolation of Israel' at ii. 25, and at ii. 38 in almost the same words as here; there the phrase is, significantly, 'the redemption of Jerusalem'.

parable. Luke takes it over from Mark xiii. 28 f. with some 29
alterations, of which the most important is the provision of a
subject for the verb 'is near', in verse 31.

the kingdom of God is near. A manifest correction of 31
Mark's implication that not only the Son of Man but the end
of the age is to be expected after the signs described (Mark xiii.
27). For Luke, the coming of the kingdom of God on earth is
but one step towards the final consummation.

this generation will not pass away. Luke's retention of 32
almost all Mark xiii. 30-31, in spite of much rewriting of the
Marcan Little Apocalypse, is a powerful witness against the
theory of a separate source. The words take on a different meaning from that which they bear in Mark by the omission of 'these
things' after 'all'. (See next note.) In view of Luke's reinterpretation and deliberate extension of the times of the end,' generation'
cannot for him mean one generation of history, as it does for
Mark: Luke has forced it to bear the meaning 'mankind'.

until all happen. That is, the whole of God's plan, not only
the events described here (Conzelmann).

Beware for yourselves. The warnings which follow strike 34
an odd note: would there be any opportunity for debauchery in
a city so hardly beset? One is tempted to think that these warnings are meant for the time after the establishment of the kingdom, when the Apostles will have power (xxii. 29-30). The same
doubt exists for the interpretation of xii. 37 (q.v.). If the suggested view is right, 'that day' does not refer back to verse 31
but is used absolutely as an alternative title for the Day of the
Lord; the OT warrant for this is in Is. ii. 11, 17, quoted 2 Th.
i. 10; Matt. vii. 22; 2 Tim. i. 12, 18; iv. 8 are further certain
uses of the title, but Luke x. 12 is uncertain.

like a snare. Is. xxiv. 17.   35

in the temple. The last two verses of the chapter once more 37
make clear that the discourse just ended is represented by Luke
as taking place in the temple. See the reference to Mark xiii. 3
in the note on verse 5. See on xix. 48 for the necessity to lodge
at night on the Hill of Olives.

xxii. 1-13. THE BETRAYAL. PREPARATION FOR THE PASSOVER

1 The Feast of Unleavened Bread called the Passover
2 was drawing near, and the chief priests and scribes were
looking for a way to destroy him; for they feared the
3 people; but Satan entered into Judas called Iscariot, being
4 of the number of the twelve, and he went away and
conferred with the chief priests and commanders on
5 how to deliver him to them. And they were delighted and
6 agreed with him to give him money. And he swore an
oath and looked for an opportunity to deliver him to them
away from the crowd.

7 The day of Unleavened Bread came on which the
8 Passover must be sacrificed; and he sent Peter and John
saying, 'Go and prepare the Passover for us, so that we
9 may eat it'. And they said to him, 'Where do you wish us
10 to prepare for it?' And he said to them, 'Look, when you
have entered the city there will meet you a man carrying
a water-pot: follow him into the house where he is going
11 and say to the owner of the house, "The teacher says to
you, 'Where is the lodging where I am to eat the Passover
12 with my disciples?'"' And he will show you a large upper
13 room ready strown. Make ready there.' They went away
and found it as he had told them and they prepared the
Passover.

1   **Unleavened Bread called the Passover.** Josephus in *Ant.*
iii. 10. 5 distinguishes the feasts, saying that the one succeeds
the other, but in xiv. 2. 1 he writes of the feast of Unleavened
Bread 'which we call the Pascha'. Ex. xii. 3 ff. enjoins the
eating of the Passover lamb on 14th of Nisan and the eating of unleavened bread to start that evening and to con-

tinue until the 21st (verse 18). Lev. xxiii. 5-6 does not really
contradict this with its 'fifteenth day of the same month' for the
beginning of Unleavened Bread, for the fifteenth day began on
the previous evening. (Cf. verse 5.)

Satan. See the notes on iv. 2 and iv. 13. For Satan entering 3
Judas cf. John xiii. 27.

of the number. One of several Lucan additions in this passage (verses 3-6), perhaps emphasizing that he was only of the
number, not of them in spirit. Luke is later to give the narrative
of his replacement (Acts i. 15-26).

commanders. I.e. of the temple guards, allowed to the 4
Sanhedrin (cf. Matt. xxvii. 65).

away from the crowd. An interpretation of Mark xiv. 2, 6
'not among the feast', i.e. not among the festival crowds, rather
than 'not on the feast day'; the actual time of the betrayal was
the feast day.

Peter and John. Substituted for 'his disciples' in Mark xiv. 8
12, thus making them already representatives in chief of the
twelve, as they are in Acts iii. 1, 3, 11; iv. 19; viii. 14. (Cf. Luke
viii. 45.)

a man carrying a water-pot. Slightly less usual than a 10
woman doing so and therefore easily distinguished. It is difficult
to guess when the elaborate preparations for this secrecy were
made, but they point to knowledge or at least suspicion on
Jesus' part of the untrustworthiness of Judas. While the temple
stood, inhabitants of Jerusalem were under obligation to give
free hospitality to pilgrims.

xxii. 14-38. THE LAST SUPPER

And when the time came, he reclined, and the Apostles 14
with him; and he said to them, 'I have longingly desired 15
to eat this Passover with you before I suffer, for I say to 16
you that I will not again eat of it until it be fulfilled in the
kingdom of God.'

And he took a cup and after giving thanks said, 17
'Take this and divide it among yourselves, for I say to 18

you, I will not drink from now of the fruit of the vine until the kingdom of God come'.

19 And he took bread and after giving thanks he broke it and gave it to them saying, 'This is my body which is given for you; do this for my memorial'.

20 And the cup in the same way after supper, saying, 'This cup is the new covenant by my blood, which is shed for you.

21 'But see, the hand of him who is delivering me up is
22 with me on the table. For the Son of Man goes according to what is destined, but woe to that man through whom
23 he is delivered up!' And they began to debate among themselves as to which of them therefore it could be who was going to do this.

24 There also arose strife among them as to which of them
25 had claim to be the greatest; but he said to them, 'The kings of the nations lord it over them, and those who
26 exercise power over them are called benefactors. Not so you, but the greater among you, let him become as a
27 younger, and the leader as one serving. For which is the greater, he that reclines or he that serves? Is it not he that reclines? But I am among you as one serving.

28 'You are they who have continued with me in my
29 temptations, and I assign to you as my father assigned to
30 me a kingdom, for you to eat and drink at my table in my kingdom, and you shall sit on thrones judging the twelve tribes of Israel.

31 'Simon, Simon, see, Satan has demanded you all, to
32 sift you like wheat; but I have prayed for you, for your faith not to fail, and do you, once you have turned back,
33 strengthen your brothers.' But he said to him, 'Lord, I am
34 ready to go with you both into prison and to death'. But he said, 'I tell you, Peter, the cock will not crow to-day until you have thrice denied that you know me'.

35 And he said to them, 'When I sent you out without purse or wallet or sandals, did you lack anything?' And
36 they said, 'Nothing'. And he said to them, 'But now, he that has a purse, let him take it, and in the same way his wallet, and he that has no sword let him sell his cloak

and buy one. For I say to you that this scripture must be 37
fulfilled in me: "And he was reckoned with the lawless
men". For indeed all that concerns me finds fulfilment.'
And they said, 'Lord, see, here are two swords'. And he 38
said to them, 'It is enough'.

Apostles. With S* B D and the Old Latin: the word occurs 14
already in the gospel six times (and frequently in Acts) as against
once only in each of the others. Its use here is another sign of
Luke's thinking of the twelve as they appear in Acts (cf. on
verse 8 above). For Luke's treatment of Marcan material see
also verse 16.

longingly desired. The Greek is probably a Semitism; even 15
though the form of expression is found in papyri, its entrance
into Greek is probably from Judaism.

until it be fulfilled. I.e. the Passover, as is demanded by the 16
grammar. The feast is the anticipation of the Messianic Banquet
which the Apostles are promised in verse 30. The variant in D
for 'fulfilled', viz. 'be eaten new', suggests that this interpretation was shared by this early codex.

in the kingdom of God. Luke brings the kingdom into
prominence at many places in his gospel; both this feature and
the connexion made between the Passover, the Lord's suffering,
and the kingdom are so typical of Luke that it is unnecessary
to see here any evidence for a separate source from Mark.

And he took a cup. The verse is remarkable by its position 17
rather than its substance (cf. Mark xiv. 23). It is discussed in
the Introduction, pp. 72 ff.

from now. See R. H. Lightfoot, *History and Interpretation* 18
in the Gospels, p. 180: discussing Mark xiv. 60-62 and parallels,
he draws attention to Luke's use of ἀπὸ τοῦ νῦν here and at
verse 69, and the similar use of ἀπ' ἄρτι by Matt. xxvi. 29 and
64. He concludes that there is in both Matthew and Luke 'a
vital connexion between the divine office and authority of Jesus
referred to' at Mark xiv. 62; Luke xxii. 69; Matt. xxvi. 64, and
his death, which is the subject of the saying here. Luke presents
the 'vital connexion' in this way: Jesus is Messiah but does not
rule as such over the kingdom of God until he has entered into
his glory through his suffering. This is implicit in verse 69, and

the force of 'from now' here, and of the vow which contains the words, is that the Lord now consecrates himself for that suffering. He has earnestly desired to eat the Passover before he suffers, but he abjures wine before it. He will drink when the kingdom of God has come and has released him from this vow. Such a vow is in accordance with Jewish practice (cf. Lev. x. 9; Num. vi. 3; Ezek. xliv. 21).

until the kingdom of God·come. Cf. Mark xiv. 25: 'new in the kingdom of God'. According to Luke there will be no such transformation of the vine; for him the coming of the kingdom is not yet the consummation of creation.

19 **And he took bread.** See Introduction, pp. 72 ff., for the whole passage and especially for discussion on the authenticity of the longer or shorter text; comments here are designed to interpret the Textus Receptus.

This is my body. See Introduction, p. 72 ff.

given for you. Non-Marcan. Cf. 1 Cor. xi. 24. Since the Lord **broke** the bread, one meaning of the words 'This is my body which is given for you' must be 'My body is sacrificed for you'.

do this for my memorial. (Cf. again 1 Cor. xi. 24.) 'Do this to recall me to yourselves until the Passover be fulfilled in the kingdom of God.' For the OT injunction connected with the original Passover cf. Ex. xii. 14; xiii. 9; Deut. xvi. 3 (especially the phrase 'for a memorial' in the first two references). The Passover will now always have this new character of celebrating the sacrifice of Jesus.

20 **and the cup in the same way after supper.** For the critical significance of the lack of a main verb see Introduction, p. 73. The whole verse as far as the word **'blood'** has obvious affinities with 1 Cor. xi. 25.

the new covenant by my blood. The broken bread links the Lord's death with the Exodus through the Unleavened Bread element of the feast, and the blood symbolism links it with the sacrificed lamb which saved the Israelites at the time of the Exodus by blood (Ex. xii. 7, 13, 22-23); but the immediate reference is clearly to Ex. xxiv. 8, 'the blood of the covenant'. No better commentary on the words can be found than Heb. ix. 11-28, especially verses 16-22.

which is shed for you. The significance of the grammatical difficulty is observed, Introduction, p. 73. The words again bring out the meaning implicit in those which precede them.

is with me on the table. A Lucan variant for Mark xiv. 18, 21 possibly a recollection of Ps. xli. 9. John xiii. 18 quotes the psalm but at xiii. 26 appears to follow the Marcan tradition, thus giving some slight negative evidence on the question of a separate source for Luke here. Mark xiv. 18 is also aware of the psalm.

as he is destined. The words imply that Luke knew of no 22 scripture which, as Mark implies, prophesies his betrayal. This explanation of Luke's rejection of Mark xiv. 21 ('as it has been written about him') is of course inconsistent with that given for Luke's departure from Mark in verse 21. For the verb cf. Acts ii. 23; x. 42; xvii. 26, 31; this is the only use of it in the gospel, though the kindred 'counsel of God' is found not only in Acts (xiii. 36; xx. 27) but also in Luke vii. 30.

And they began to debate. The verse is a natural addition 23 to Mark (cf. Matt. xxvi. 25) especially as a link with the following passage.

strife. The material for verses 24 26 and possibly for verse 27 24 is Mark x. 41 ff. Luke's reason for bringing the passage here is probably the thought that only in the imminent kingdom will the Apostles be accorded any position in which they will be tempted to exercise too much power over others (verse 29).

kings. The introduction of the word is typical. See Intro- 25 duction, p. 7, for the argument that Luke deliberately meets the challenge that Christians acknowledged another king than Caesar (cf. xxiii. 2).

are called benefactors. Giving the Marcan phrase a sting of irony which any reader of Greek in the Hellenistic world would appreciate, the honorific phrase *Euergetes* being used of kings in Syria and Egypt.

not so you. The language is strange but the general meaning 26 is that of Mark x. 43-44. Several causes may account for the form of the saying here: the terms 'younger' and 'leader' may well 'reflect the concern of the Hellenistic Churches with the differentiation of the members in the local congregations'

(Fuller, *The Mission and Achievement of Jesus*, p. 57). For 'younger' cf. 1 Tim. v. 1, 2, 11, 14; 1 Pet. v. 5; and for 'leader' cf. Heb. xiii. 7, 17, 24. Again, Luke may be assimilating the saying to ix. 48, where the child is a symbol of Jesus. If the Lord was the youngest of the company the fact would lend extra point to vii. 28, ix. 48, and this passage.

27   **one serving.** Keeping the force of the participle; Luke never uses the noun deacon, perhaps because by his time it had already acquired its technical meaning.

28   **temptations.** Or trials, ordeals. See on xi. 4 and verse 3 above. The verse may have a common origin with Matt. xix. 28 (who has 'you who have followed me'), verse 30 being parallel to some extent with the last part of Matt.'s verse.

29   **I assign to you . . . a kingdom.** See Introduction, p. 75.

30   **eat and drink at my table in my kingdom.** The words for 'at my table' are the same in Greek as those in verse 21: for Luke the present table has a great significance as the forerunner or type of the table at the Messianic Banquet which is to inaugurate the kingdom.

   thrones. In Matt. xix. 28 they will be occupied at the time of the 'regeneration' when the Son of Man sits on his throne, evidently to judge, for the Apostles in that passage are 'also' to sit judging. The association of the work here with the kingdom makes clear that for Luke the Apostles will judge in the sense of the Judges in the OT, i.e. they will rule. The twelve are the new Israel, perhaps the new twelve patriarchs.

31   **Satan has demanded.** The verb is found nowhere else in the NT or LXX, but at *Test. Benj.* iii. 3.

   you all. The Greek is plural. Satan has demanded all, but the responsibility for strengthening them will be Simon's.

32   **I have prayed for you.** Because Simon is the leader. Cullmann conjectures this to be the original context of the saying in Matt. xvi. 18 (which he regards as authentic; see *Peter, Disciple, Apostle and Martyr*, pp. 176 ff.). Elements in this passage recall the book of Job in which Satan is permitted to subject Job to trial; but the sifting here has eschatological significance: it is the testing time preceding the kingdom, whose final victory depends on the endurance of the Apostles, especially Peter, their leader. For this position of Peter in Luke see viii. 45; ix. 32; xii. 41;

xxii. 8, 61; xxiv. 34, and on v. 1-11 in the Introduction, p. 54, where it is argued that Luke is there giving prominence to the call of Peter in a way which secured his authority.

strengthen your brothers. Cf. Mic. v. 3-4; John xxi. 15 ff. These words, preceding Peter's declaration and the Lord's warning of his coming denial, render the latter less emphatic than in Mark (xiv. 29-31) or Matthew (xxvi. 34 f.).

into prison and to death. For Luke, no empty boast: Peter 33 had suffered imprisonment (Acts iv. 3; v. 18; xii. 3 ff.) and probably by now a martyr's death.

the cock. Cf. Mark xiv. 30. Cockcrow is the third watch of 34 the night, before the fourth and last ('early morning').

But now. Perhaps because the devil is once again active. See 36 on verse 3 above.

Sword. The simplest explanation for this unexpected insist- 37 ence seems to be as follows: the tradition was firm that at the time of the arrest at least one sword was used by the Lord's disciples (Mark xiv. 47; Matt. xxvi. 51; Luke xxii. 49-51). This caused Luke embarrassment since he was eager to assure his readers of the political harmlessness of Christians; but if the Messiah's followers looked and acted like 'lawless men', an explanation could be found in the fact that this was only in order to complete the fulfilment of scripture.

this scripture must be fulfilled. Is liii. 12, certainly regarded as Messianic by Luke and others before him. Mark xv. 28, of doubtful authenticity but found in a number of ancient authorities, makes a very similar use of Is. liii. 12.

It is enough. Two swords are enough to fulfil the scripture. 38 The Lord does not require them to be used, as verses 49-51 show clearly.

xxii. 39-53. THE ARREST

And he went out and went according to his custom to 39 **the Hill of Olives, and his disciples also followed him. When he came to the place he said to them, 'Pray not to** 40 **enter into temptation'. And he was withdrawn from them** 41 **about a stone's throw, and he knelt and prayed, saying,** 42

'Father, if you will, take this cup away from me; but let not my will but yours be done'.

43 There appeared to him an angel from heaven strength-
44 ening him; and he was in agony and prayed more earnestly, and his sweat was like drops of blood falling
45 on the earth. And he rose up from prayer, and came to
46 his disciples and found them sleeping from grief, and said to them, 'Why are you asleep? Rise and pray, so that
47 you do not enter into temptation!' While he was still speaking, see, a crowd! And the one called Judas, one of the twelve, approached them and came near to Jesus to
48 kiss him. But Jesus said to him, 'Judas, is it with a kiss
49 that you deliver up the Son of Man?' When those around him saw what was about to happen, they said, 'Lord, shall
50 we strike w. ·h the sword?' And one from among them did strike the high priest's servant and cut off his right ear.
51 Jesus answered, 'Stop! No more!' And he touched the ear
52 and healed him. And Jesus said to those who had come upon him, the chief priests and commanders of the temple and elders, 'Have you come out with swords and clubs as
53 against a robber? I was with you daily in the temple but you did not stretch out your hands towards me. But this is your hour and it is the power of darkness.'

39 **according to his custom** as described xxi. 37-38. Cf. verse 53 below. Luke does not mention Gethsemane but makes the arrest take place on **the Hill of Olives.** See further on verse 40.

the disciples. Perhaps more than the twelve; cf. xix. 37.

40 **the place.** As Luke has described the events, this must be their encampment. It is hard to decide whether this is a deliberate alteration of Mark xiv. 32 or merely a stylistic avoidance of local names. If the former, it is certainly evidence for at least Luke's knowledge of another, non-Marcan, tradition.

Temptation. I.e. the fiery trial which should precede the kingdom, as, e.g., Dan. xii. 10; Zech. xiii. 9; xiv. 1-3, and often in the OT and later Judaistic works. See on xi. 4 for passages in the NT where the word bears this meaning.

41 **And he was withdrawn from them.** The differences in vocabulary and the addition of verses 43-44 to the Marcan out-

line are all explicable on the basis of Luke's own conceptions
and interpretations.

he knelt. More reverent than Mark xiv. 35, 'fell on the
ground'.

cup. A symbol of death; cf. Mark x. 38.   42

There appeared to him an angel. Verses 43-44 omitted by 43
some important authorities, including B A W fam 13 Clem Or,
may well be genuine: their omission may be due to some copyists thinking them incompatible with the Lord's divinity (cf.
Streeter, pp. 123, 137). But the passage makes real both the
suffering and its divine control and acceptance; the vocabulary
is also Lucan. For the angel see pp. 43 ff.

sleeping from grief. An unskilful attempt to adapt the 45
Marcan story so as to spare the reputation of the Apostles.
Grief keeps awake. Luke similarly spares them the shame of
being found asleep three times.

shall we strike with the sword? Luke's addition of this 49
verse is amply explained by reference to verses 35-38. See note
on verse 37.

Stop! No more! See verse 38 and note. This command and 51
the healing of the ear confirm the impression that the Lord did
not wish the swords to be actually used.

commanders. See on verse 4.   52

in the temple. Cf. xxi. 37-38.   53

the power of darkness. Cf. iv. 6 and the notes on iv. 2 and
13. Cf. also Col. i. 13; John xii. 31; xiv. 30; xvi. 11; 2 Cor.
iv. 4; Eph. vi. 12; 1 Pet. ii. 9; *Ep. Barn.* xx. 1 (cf. ix. 4). These
references are given by Brownlee in his translation and notes
on the *Manual of Discipline* (B.A.S.O.R. Suppl. Studies, Nos.
10-12) on iii. 20 ff. where the doctrine lying behind this saying
is clearly stated: 'In the hand of the prince of lights is the rule
over all the sons of righteousness: in the ways of light they
walk; and in the hand of the angel (*malakh*) of darkness is all
the rule over the sons of folly and in ways of darkness they
walk; and by the angel of darkness are led astray all the sons
of righteousness; and all their sins and wickednesses and their
guiltinesses and transgressions of their deeds are in his rule
according to the mysteries of God until his end (time)'. (Independent transl.)

xxii. 54-71. BEFORE THE SANHEDRIN.
PETER'S DENIAL

54 They seized him and took him away and took him into
the house of the high priest, and Peter followed at a dis-
55 tance. As they had lit a fire in the middle of the court and
56 were sitting together round it, Peter sat among them; a
maid saw him sitting by the light and gazing at him said,
57 'This one too was with him'. But he denied it with the
58 words, 'I do not know him, woman!' And after a short
time another saw him and said, 'You too are one of
59 them'. But Peter said, 'Man, I am not!' And after an
interval of about one hour another insisted, saying, 'Certainly this one was also with him. Why, he is a Galilaean!'
60 But Peter said, 'Man, I do not know what you are talking
about!' And immediately while he was still speaking the
61 cock crowed. And the Lord turned and looked at Peter,
and Peter remembered the Lord's word, when he said to
him, 'Before the cock crows to-day, you will deny me
62 thrice'. And he went out and wept bitterly.
63 And the men who were holding him were mocking
him and slapping him, and covering him up and asking
64 him, 'Prophesy, which is the one who struck you?'
65 And many other things they said as they blasphemed
against him.
66 And when day came, the elders of the people were
assembled, high priests and scribes, and they led him
67 away into their Sanhedrin and said, 'If you are the
Christ, tell us'. He said to them, 'If I tell you, you will not
68, 69 believe: if I question you, you will not answer. But from
now the Son of Man will be seated at the right hand of
70 the power of God.' They all said, 'Are you then the Son of
71 God?' And he said to them, 'You say that I am'. And they
said, 'Why do we still need witnesses? For we ourselves
have heard it from his own mouth.'

54   the house of the high priest. In Mark xiv. 55 ff. the house
is immediately the scene of some sort of trial or inquiry, of

which the details are given; another council is held in the early
morning (Mark xv. 1) of which the only detail given is the
result, that they bound Jesus and took him to Pilate. Luke re-
serves the proceedings (which he shortens by omitting Mark
xiv. 55-61) to the early morning council, whose result is the
same as in Mark xv. 1 (Luke xxiii. 1). This account is based on
Mark so closely as to the incidents themselves that there is no
need to postulate another source: it seems like a correction of
the unlikely procedure in Mark of holding an inquiry in the
middle of the night and another meeting in the early morning.
But if this seemed to Luke unlikely, it may be nearer the truth,
since the proceedings in the night would be with a few who
could be gathered, the formal morning council being held to
make their proceedings legal. By his rearrangement Luke has
brought Peter's denial to the front of the narrative, during the
time that Jesus is being held a prisoner and mocked by his
guards until the morning, without any officials being present.

another. In Luke altogether three different people accuse 58
Peter of being of the company; in Mark xiv. 66, 69, 70, the maid
speaks twice and the bystanders once.

The Lord turned and looked. Apparently from the inside 61
of the house: Luke indeed, who has added this incident with
telling force to the Marcan outline (cf. verses 43-44), is not
concerned with topographical details.

wept bitterly. The whole of this verse is omitted by 0171 62
and the Old Latin and may be due to assimilation to the text
of Matthew (xxvi. 75). If it is genuine, the repentant tears mark
the beginning of Peter's 'turning back' (verse 32).

elders. The Greek word is a collective singular. As at Acts 66
xxii. 5, it means the Sanhedrin.

Sanhedrin. This council cannot be traced earlier than
198 B.C. when it is mentioned in a letter written by Antiochus
III after the battle of Panion (Jos. *Ant.* xii. 3. 3); its purpose
was to assist the high priest and it could not be assembled as
a judicial court without the consent of the procurator (Jos. *Ant.*
xx. 9. 1. Cf. John xviii. 31).

If I tell you. The Lord's answer here is the Lucan substitute 67
for his silence in Mark xiv. 61. Silence might be thought by
Gentile readers to imply lack of effective defence.

68 **If I question you.** A recognized way of self-defence. Cf. xx. 41-44.

69 **But from now.** See the note on verse 18.

The Son of Man will be seated. Contrast 'You will see the Son of Man' (Mark xiv. 62; Matt. xxvi. 64). For Luke the event is cosmic and hidden from unbelieving eyes. As in the other synoptics, the Lord is challenged as to his Messiahship and answers about the Son of Man, whose destiny he has associated with suffering (ix. 22; ix. 44; xviii. 31); but after the Resurrection the suffering, now triumphantly past, is attached to the Messiahship (xxiv. 26, 46). See also the following note.

at the right hand. Cf. Ps. cx. 1, which at xx. 42 is taken to be Messianic. The conception of the Son of Man is therefore here joined with that of the Messiah, and suffering is joined with exaltation.

Power of God. 'Power' in Mark xiv. 62 means 'God', and Luke has expanded the phrase for his Gentile readers rather than translated it. He uses the recollection of Dan. vii. 13 in such a way as to exclude the picture of the Son of Man being conveyed by clouds. This is consistent with his substitution of 'the Son of Man will be seated' for Mark's 'you will see the Son of Man'. See on xxi. 27 and Introduction, p. 68 ff.

70 **Son of God.** A Messianic title; cf. Ps. ii. 7 (and Luke iii. 22).

You say that I am. 'You' is emphatic. Luke has drawn out what he takes to be the force of Mark xiv. 62: the Son of Man is the corporate personality of which the Lord and his disciples are the representatives; at this moment the Lord is the sole representative: in him the true Israel, the 'little flock', 'the saints of the Most High' are 'from now' exalted to God's right hand. The Sanhedrin misunderstood this to mean that Jesus identified himself exclusively with the Son of Man, and that the claim to the exaltation of the Son of Man must be a claim to be the Son of God.

71 **from his own mouth.** Substituted for the word 'blasphemy' in Mark xiv. 64. Luke has made the words of the Lord a disclaimer: there is thus no question of blasphemy and no need for the rending of clothes (Mark xiv. 63). Again any attentive reader may see that the words are not from the Lord's own mouth, and therefore that the charge of xxiii. 2 is false.

CHAPTER XXIII

xxiii. 1-25. TRIALS BEFORE PILATE AND BEFORE
HEROD

And the whole crowd of them rose and brought him to 1
Pilate. And they began to accuse him saying, 'This man 2
we have found perverting our nation and preventing the
payment of taxes to Caesar, and saying that he is Christ,
a king'. And Pilate questioned him, saying, 'Are you the 3
king of the Jews?' And he in answer said to him, 'Do you
say that?' And Pilate said to the high priests and the 4
crowds, 'I find no case against this man'. But they per- 5
sisted, saying, 'He stirs up the people, teaching throughout the whole of Judaea, and beginning from Galilee as
far as this place'.

Pilate on hearing this asked, 'Is the man a Galilaean?' 6
And on ascertaining that he was under Herod's authority, 7
he sent him back to Herod who was also himself in
Jerusalem during those days; Herod on seeing Jesus was 8
greatly pleased, for he had for a considerable time wished
to see him through having heard about him, and he hoped
to see some sign occurring through him. He questioned 9
him on a number of things, but he gave him no answer.
The high priests and scribes stood there continuously 10
accusing him. After treating him with contempt and 11
mockery, Herod, along with his soldiers, cast a fine robe
round him and sent him back to Pilate. Herod and Pilate 12
became friends with one another on that day (for before
they had been in enmity against one another).

Pilate after summoning the high priests and rulers of 13
the people, said to them, 'You brought this man to me as 14
a misleader of the people and, you see, I after examining
him before you have found no case against this man from
the things of which you accuse him; neither has Herod. 15

19

For he has sent him back to us; and see, nothing deserv-
16 ing death has been done by him. I will flog him therefore
and release him.'

18   But the whole crowd cried out saying, 'Away with this
19 man and release to us Barabbas!'—a man who through
some rising which had occurred in the city and through
20 murder had been thrown into prison. Pilate again ad-
21 dressed them, wishing to release Jesus, but they shouted
22 again, saying, 'Crucify, crucify him!' A third time he said
to them, 'Why? What wrong has he done? I have found
no case for death in him. I will flog him therefore and
23 release him.' But they urged on with great shouts demanding that he should be crucified, and their shouts
24 prevailed. And Pilate decreed that their demand should
25 be carried out, and released the man thrown into prison
for insurrection and murder, whom they were demanding, while Jesus he delivered up to their will.

1   **brought him to Pilate.** Luke avoids the Marcan 'delivered
him up' (xv. 1; cf. Matt. xxvii. 2): his purpose is to make clear
that the Roman power had nothing against Christianity or its
founder; he will not therefore represent this action as the
supreme betrayal which it was for the Jewish (i.e. early) Christian tradition. Luke cannot of course make the Jews responsible
for the actual crucifixion and has to admit that it was done 'by
the hands of men without the law,' but in Acts ii. 23, iv. 10, he
does apply the main verb in his accusation to the Jews themselves, while Pilate is consistently and persistently shown as
trying to secure the release of Jesus, which the crowd themselves
refused (verses 16, 20, 22; Acts iii. 13). For the synoptic tradition about the 'delivering up' see Mark ix. 31; Luke ix. 44;
Matt. xvii. 22 (where it is to be 'into the hands of men') and
Mark x. 33; Luke xviii. 32; Matt. xx. 19, where it is to be 'to
the Gentiles', Luke there taking over the Marcan phraseology.
His careful rewriting is indeed never so apparent as in the
Passion Narrative, but he returns to an identification of sinners
with Gentiles at xxiv. 7.

2   **accuse.** The charge which follows is obviously false, in
direct opposition to the evidence (xx. 20 ff.). The Jews' false

witness hides their own political rebelliousness. Their choice is
for a murderous rebel (verses 18 ff.).

Do you say that? To take this as a question obtains the best 3
sense; there is no evidence that the words imply assent: there is,
as at xxii. 70, a refusal to speak in the same language. In Mark
xv. 2 the words are immediately followed by the many accusa-
tions of the high priests, implying that the answer of the Lord
had not incriminated him, as it would have done if it had been
a mere assent. The question is full of meaning: it is a challenge
to Pilate to see for himself whether by his actions in the past
or present Jesus is or claims to be the king of the Jews: and it
is for Luke and his readers a challenge of a different kind, to
decide, as Pilate had to, what the answer to the question is. An
alternative and kindred explanation is that of John xviii. 33-38,
which also takes the words as a question, expanding them in
order to interpret them.

Luke omits once more the reference to the silence of the Lord
in Mark xv. 4-5. See on xxii. 67. Verses 4-5 are his own, and he
begins some free writing, moved here by his desire to emphasize
the virtual acquittal by Pilate.

the crowds. The fickleness of crowds perhaps requires no 4
explanation, but it is interesting to speculate when they changed
their allegiance. The 'crowd' (πλῆθος) of verse 1 is only a contemptuous way of referring to all those who in the house of the
high priest had condemned the Lord, so that the 'crowds' of
the ordinary people are mentioned here in the Passion Narrative
of this gospel for the first time; the reason for their change of
loyalty is slurred over by the absence of the noun as a subject
of the cry in verse 18, so that one might imagine that it was
merely the original accusers who cried out in a body for the
release of Barabbas and then for the crucifixion of Jesus (verse
21). But this is only literary: Luke is well aware that the whole
people were responsible and makes this point with emphasis at
Acts iii. 13 ff. The last point in the narrative when the people
were an effective defence for the Lord was xxii. 2.

I find no case. Pilate's words are abrupt in their acquittal,
and this is made a further three times (cf. verses 16, 20-22).
Luke emphasizes to his Roman readers that their governor did
not believe Jewish lies, as they do now.

7 **Herod.** The 'trial' before Herod is Lucan vocabulary, and does not suggest any other hand than Luke's: either it is free writing, in which case we must suggest a motive for its intrusion into the tradition, or it is oral tradition which Luke has set down in his own words, and which had not before been committed to writing. For the view that it was a tradition which Luke had been given we have the fact that ix. 9 suggests that Luke knew of either a fact or a tradition that Herod was curious about Jesus, and thought it more likely and less sensational than that he identified him with John the Baptist risen from the dead (Mark vi. 16; Matt. xiv. 2). But the common-sense attitude of Herod on that occasion is in very marked contrast to the picture of a credulous and garrulous princeling which Luke draws here. The clue to the passage may therefore lie in the desire of Luke to show that the Lord was acquitted by both the king (whom some Jews at least would acknowledge) and the Roman governor. The same motive underlies Acts xxv. 13 ff. (cf. especially verses 15, 16, 22, and for an echo of Luke xxiii. 4-5 see Acts xxv. 25; cf. also the words of Agrippa, playing a part in the 'trial' of Paul like that of Herod's in the Passion of the Lord, at Acts xxvi. 31). Luke has his dual audience in mind: both Jew and Gentile are invited to share in the official acquittal of the Lord, which was overridden by the action of the high priests and their supporters. Indeed, this may well be an example of the principle of witness which Luke claims to observe (i. 2) and which Morgenthaler believes to determine the arrangement of the Lucan writings: the rule of twofold witness (Deut. xix. 15), quoted Matt. xviii. 16 ff.; John viii. 17; 2 Cor. xiii. 1; 1 Tim. v. 19; Heb. x. 28; 1 John v. 6 ff., is observed also in the written gospel. For the association of Herod with Pilate in creed-like writing cf. Acts iv. 27 and Ignatius, *Ep. Smyr.* i. 1-2 (Kelly, *Early Christian Creeds*, p. 69).

18 **crowd.** See on 4 above.

Barabbas. This is a patronymic and implies he had another name. The Caesarean tradition, supported by syr. sin., at Matt. xxvii. 16, is that his own name was also Jesus. This would easily be dropped by copyists out of reverence.

19 **some rising.** Dismissing in a different manner from that of Matt. xxvii. 16 the problem raised by Mark's ' in the rising ' (xv. 7. It is at least possible that there had been a rising con-

nected with the Lord's presence at the Passover, on the part of
the more nationalistic of his followers. That the twelve had expected a literal restoration of the kingdom seems certain from
Acts i. 6; iii. 21, and is justified in a way by Luke xxii. 29-30
(cf. Matt. xix. 28). To this we may add the presence of the
sword among the Lord's followers, a tradition which Luke
found embarrassing. (See on xxii. 36-38.) If this was the case,
the popular desire for the release of Barabbas may be due to the
fact that he had struck a blow for national independence, while
the crowd were disappointed in Jesus for failing to do so.

their demand. Luke omits entirely the explanation that this 24
was customary (Mark xv. 6. Verse 17 in Luke is not authentic).
Not even he can acquit Pilate of weakness and allows himself
an emphasis on his injustice in the words in verse 25, 'the man
thrown into prison for insurrection and murder'.

delivered up to their will. The verb Luke can here take 25
over from Mark xv. 15 where the theme of deliverance into the
hands of Gentiles is intensified, because it is to the will of Jews
that the deliverance is made; but this again is merely literary,
for the actual crucifixion is of course carried out by Romans.

xviii. 26-56. CRUCIFIXION, DEATH, AND BURIAL

And as they led him away, they seized a man called 26
Simon, a Cyrenian, who was coming from the country,
and laid the cross on him, to carry it behind Jesus. There 27
followed him a great crowd of the people and women
who mourned and lamented him. Jesus turned to them 28
and said, 'Daughters of Jerusalem, do not weep for me,
but weep for yourselves and your children, for, see, the 29
days are coming in which they will say, "Blessed are
the barren and the wombs which have not borne, and
the breasts which have not given suck".

'Then they will begin to say to the mountains, "Fall on 30
us!" and to the hills, "Hide us!" For if they do these 31
things when the tree is tender, in its dryness what shall

32 happen?' There were also others, two criminals, led with
him to be executed.

33   And when they came to the place called Skull, there
they crucified him and the two criminals, one on his
34 right and the other on his left. Jesus kept saying, 'Father,
forgive them; they do not know what they are doing'.
35 Parting his clothes they cast lots for them. And the people
stood looking on. The rulers also mocked him, saying,
'Others he saved, let him save himself, if this is the
36 Christ of God, the chosen'. The soldiers also made sport
37 of him, approaching and conveying to him poor wine and
saying, 'If you are the king of the Jews, save yourself!'
38 There was also a placard upon him:'This is the king of the
Jews'.

39   One of the hanged criminals began to blaspheme him:
40 'Aren't you the Christ? Save yourself and us!' The other
answered him with a rebuke and said to him, 'Don't you
even fear God, since you are in the same condemnation?
41 And we indeed justly enough, for we are getting the
penalty for what we have done; but this fellow has done
42 no crime.' And he said, 'Jesus, remember me when you
43 come into your kingdom'. And he said to him, 'Truly I
tell you, to-day you will be with me in paradise'.

44   And it was already about the sixth hour and there was
45 darkness over the whole land until the ninth hour, the
sun having failed; and the veil of the temple was split in
46 the middle. And after crying with a loud voice Jesus said,
'Father, into your hands I commend my spirit'. And after
47 saying this he breathed his last. On seeing what happened
the centurion gave glory to God, saying, 'This man really
48 was innocent!' And all the crowds who had gathered for
this spectacle, after seeing what happened, turned away
49 beating their breasts. All his acquaintances stood at a
distance, as also the women who had together followed
him from Galilee, observing these things.

50   And see, a man named Joseph, being a member of the
51 council, a good and just man—he was one who had not
concurred with their decision and action—from Arimathaea, a Jewish city, a man who was expecting the king-

dom of God,—he approached Pilate and requested the 52
body of Jesus, and he took it down and wrapped it in a 53
sheet, and laid him in a tomb hewn out of the rock, where
no one was as yet lying. And it was the day of preparation 54
and the sabbath was drawing on. Those women who had 55
come with him out of Galilee followed and they saw the
tomb and how his body was laid, and went back and 56
prepared spices and perfumes. And on the sabbath they
rested according to the commandment.

Simon. From Mark xv. 21 which tells us that he was the 26
father of Alexander and Rufus. Rufus may be the person mentioned in Rom. xvi. 13.

Verses 27-31 are certainly independent of Mark; although
appropriate here, they are not essentially part of the Passion
Narrative, since verses 29-31, to which the rest are introduction, are akin to xiii. 34-35 and xix. 41-44.

Weep for yourselves. The Lord's words are a strikingly 28
clear example of his fears for the victims of Roman harshness.
See on xvii. 37 and for the destruction of Jerusalem xxi. 24-27.

say to the mountains. The verse quotes Hos. x. 8 in which 30
Cod. B, etc., of the LXX follow the Hebrew closely; Luke's
version follows Cod. A in the order of the verbs. The quotation
may therefore be due to Luke's own hand. Luke has not lost
sight of the fact that the woes brought by Roman harshness
bring deliverance in their train by the coming of the Son of Man
(cf., e.g., xxi. 28). This is suggested by the obvious affinity of
this passage with xxi. 23. The quotation from Hos. x. 8 is used
at Rev. vi. 16 as an example of what will be said by the rulers
of this world when faced with judgment.

when the tree is tender. Lagrange is right to protest that 31
Jer. xi. 16 and Ezek. xx. 47 are irrelevant here, but himself
strains the sense in regarding the passage as bearing the same
meaning as Prov. xi. 31 and 1 Pet. iv. 17 f.: the emphasis is upon
the times, for now the *kairoi* of the Gentiles are but beginning;
they will bring great distress on the land and wrath on the
people (xxi. 23) and Jerusalem will be trodden down (xxi. 24)
until the times of the Gentiles are fulfilled, that is, in the tree's
'dryness'. The times of the Gentiles are compared to the life

of a tree in their duration: in the spring they do but begin their oppression, in the autumn they will finish it with total destruction. Cf. xxi. 29-31. The words therefore connect the Lord's prophecy of the coming catastrophe with the present event, his own crucifixion. See on xxii. 69-70, where the point is made that the exaltation of the Son of Man begins now, with his suffering; and verse 45 of this chapter.

32 **two criminals.** Luke brings them to the forefront, perhaps because they are important as fulfilment of prophecy (Is. liii. 12; cf. Mark xv. 27 and see on xxii. 36-37).

34 **Father, forgive them.** The words have the support of S* A C Old Latin vg syr. cur and pesh, Mcion Iren Or Aug, and their omission in other MSS. may be due to the conviction, common in Gentile Christian circles, that God did not forgive the Jews for the crucifixion, but punished them for it by the destruction of Jerusalem. Cf. Origen, *Contra Celsum*, viii. 42. Luke is in the main following Mark closely here, and the words ascribed by him to the Lord may well be due to his own pen, the motive being to show that the prisoner himself did not condemn the Romans for their part in his execution. (Cf. Acts iii. 17; xiii. 27; 1 Cor. ii. 8.)

Parting his clothes. Cf. Ps. xxii. 18. The Psalm influenced Mark's Passion Narrative strongly; Luke makes further use of it in verse 35.

35 **looking on ... mocked.** Pss. xxii. 7; lxxx. 6; on 'mocked' see also below.

let him save himself. Cf. Wis. ii. 13, 17-20.

the chosen. See on ix. 35. The title associates Jesus with Moses against whom the people murmured (e.g. Ex. xv. 24; xvi. 2); the stronger word 'mocked' is used at 1 Esd. i. 51.

36 **The soldiers.** Made the subject of the verb of mocking rather than the passers-by (Mark xv. 29); Luke apparently wished to soften or obliterate if possible any impression that the people were hostile (cf. verse 48). The soldiers' mockery is natural to the scene of a crucifixion and does not do much to destroy the general impression that nearly all the witnesses of this crucifixion were sympathetic to the victim.

conveying to him poor wine. A hint that in spite of his omission of Mark xv. 34-36 Luke was using Mark here. The

wine in question was rough and sour but probably not offered
in mockery, since it was a drink commonly used. But Luke
follows the mood of Ps. lxix. 21 (Mark xv. 36) rather than that
of John xix. 29.

King of the Jews. Reference to the claim, typical of Luke, 37
replaces the taunt in Mark xv. 29, which is about the claim to
destroy the temple and rebuild it in three days.

One of the hanged criminals. The last words of Mark xv. 39
32 suggest the possibility of the passage which follows, the
material of the criminal's mocking being suggested by Mark xv.
32b, otherwise not represented in Luke.

hanged. Cf. Gal. iii. 13, quoting Deut. xxi. 23.

Jesus, remember me when you come into your king- 42
dom. Most authorities read 'with (ἐν) your kingdom', but Luke
elsewhere avoids the notion that the kingdom can be conveyed
from one place to another; we therefore follow B L 372, a number of Old Latin, and Augustine. The reading of D ('in the
day of your coming') falls under the suspicion of doctrinal
alteration equally with that of the majority reading.

The words need not imply a complete faith in the criminal;
they are gently ironic, a courageous jest which the Lord takes
up seriously.

Truly I tell you. Luke introduces the phrase at the most 43
three times himself (iv. 24; xii. 37; and here), always omitting
'truly' in nine Q passages, and leaving the phrase in Marcan
material only three times out of nine. It must therefore mean
considerable emphasis on his part, or a conviction that the words
are authentic.

in paradise. See Jeremias in *TWNT*, on which the following
is based. Paradise is a loan word from old Iranian for an en-
closing wall and then for a park, which by the third century
B.C. was used in Greek for park. In the LXX (incl. Gen. ii.
and iii.) it is used for the garden of (planted by) God (Gen.
xiii. 10; Exek. xxviii. 13; xxxi. 8; cf. Is. li. 3): in this and in the
phrase 'a dainty luxurious garden' (Gen. ii. 15 (according to a
variant reading); iii. 23 f.; Is. li. 3 (according to a variant reading); Ezek. xxxi. 9; Joel ii. 3) it bears in the LXX a strongly
religious meaning, which is older than the biblical Garden of
Eden, going back to the cultic garden containing the Tree of

Life whose waterer and libation-priest is the king, in Mesopo-
tamia, Syria, and Canaan. (The idea of the king as waterer finds
striking reference in the NT in John vii. 38.)

The use of paradise alone, with the technical meaning of the
part of She'ol reserved for the righteous, occurs first in *Test.
Levi* xviii. 10, where the priestly Messiah 'shall open the gates
of paradise'. The word thus enters the NT from the LXX and
late Judaistic literature; the phrase in Hebrew and Aramaic for
the paradise of the time before history and after its end, as for
the paradise of the time between the beginning of the end and
its final consummation (i.e. between death and resurrection) is
'Garden of Eden'.

Ezekiel (xxxvi. 35; cf. Is. li. 3) was the first to compare the
hoped-for time of deliverance with the golden age of the past,
but pre-Christian apocalyptic identifies them: the paradise of
the end is the primal paradise reappearing, offering the fruits
of the Tree of Life, living water, and living bread, the feast of
salvation, and fellowship with God (Rev. ii. 7).

Consistently, in the same literature, paradise is the home even
now, though hidden from men's eyes (cf. 2 Cor. xii. 4) of the
souls of dead patriarchs, and other elect and righteous men, as
Enoch and Elijah (who did not die). The souls of the ungodly
are in She'ol, a development from the ancient conception that
She'ol was the home of all departed souls.

These two conceptions are found side by side in the NT;
although the actual word occurs only here, at 2 Cor. xii. 4 and
Rev. ii. 7, the same idea is found in several passages: the 'bosom
of Abraham' (Luke xvi. 23) and the 'resting-places in my
Father's house' (John xiv. 2) are two examples from the
gospels.

The belief of the early church that paradise was now graced
by the presence of the risen Lord makes other phrases for going
to it or being in it natural. Cf. 1 Th. iv. 17; 2 Cor. v. 8; Phil. i.
23; 2 Tim. iv. 18; cf. Rom. viii. 38 f.; xiv. 7-9. Fellowship with
Christ is substituted for the more worldly attractions of paradise in apocalyptic speculation. For Luke Jesus is clearly the
Messiah of *Test. Levi* xviii, who makes paradise available for
the penitent. The criminal's humility wins for him the promise
of fellowship with Christ in paradise 'to-day', which has the

further significance that from now Christ has opened it, i.e. restored it.

with me. Cf. 'with Christ', Phil. i. 23.

the sixth hour. I.e. noon: Luke here follows Mark xv. 33 44 clearly, and the phrases added in verse 45 are justified from Mark's **darkness** and from Mark xv. 38.

the sun having failed. Strange, since the Greek would 45 naturally mean 'the sun being eclipsed', impossible at the time of full moon (which the Passover implies). But if we do not press the use of the Greek verb, the conjunction of the celestial sign with the beginning of the destruction of the temple emphasizes with perfect clarity Luke's eschatological conception: this destruction of Jerusalem begins those catastrophic events which inaugurate the kingdom. Cf. especially the close conjunction in ch. xxi of verses 24 and 25, where again the fate of Jerusalem is linked with celestial signs. In the Lord's death these events are set in motion.

crying with a loud voice. Luke omits the cry of dereliction 46 in Mark xv. 34 but takes the wordless cry of Mark xv. 37 and gives it articulate utterance in **Father, into your hands** . . . from Ps. xxxi. 5.

This man really was innocent. Nothing could illustrate 47 better Luke's anxiety to show Rome's virtual acquittal of the Lord than the form he has given to the utterance of the centurion; he has sacrificed the tribute in Mark xv. 39 ('This man was a son of God') which seems to concede so much more to the Christian claim.

this spectacle. The verse is peculiar to Luke, and may well 48 owe its inspiration to Zech. xii. 10-14 (cf. John xix. 37). In Zechariah the notes of looking on at a 'spectacle', and 'beating their breasts', and the activity of the women (verse 49) as something separate from the rest, are all present; and the mourning there is for a 'beloved [or 'only'] one' and as for a 'firstborn'. (See on ii. 7.)

at a distance. Cf. Pss. xxxviii. 11; lxxxviii. 8, 18.   49

Joseph of Arimathaea. Appears in all four gospels (Mark 50 xv. 43; Matt. xxvii. 57; John xix. 38) but nothing is known of the city. Like Symeon (ii. 25, q.v.) and Anna (ii. 38) he represents the older Israel in 'expecting the kingdom of God'.

54   **the day of preparation.** I.e. for the sabbath (not the Passover), the day of the week which we call Friday. (Cf. Mark xv. 42; John xix. 31, 42.)

was drawing on. As in Matt. xxviii. 1 and later ecclesiastical Greek, representing the Aramaic and Hebrew verbs idiomatically used of the 'breaking' of the Jewish day at sunset. The Greek verb is used normally of the actual dawn.

56   **on the sabbath they rested.** Luke conceals Mark's suggestion that the women bought the spices and myrrh on the sabbath (Mark xvi. 1), making their course of action more in accordance with religious custom and explaining why they took no action until the first day of the week. The sentence illustrates Luke's concern for his double audience of Jew and Gentile: both evangelists are aware that it was so late when the Lord was buried and so early when the women came to the tomb on the first day of the next week, that in preparing the perfumes they must have in fact broken the sabbath. Each gives a solution which is only partially satisfactory, while Matthew's version of the events avoids the difficulty altogether.

CHAPTER XXIV

1-53. THE EMPTY TOMB. EMMAUS. APPEARANCES
IN JERUSALEM

... but on the first day of the week very early they came 1
to the tomb carrying the spices which they had prepared;
and they found that the stone had been rolled away from 2
the tomb, and on entering they could not find the body. 3
And it happened that while they were at a loss about this, 4
suddenly two men stood over them in shining clothes;
when they were afraid and bent their faces towards the 5
earth, they said to them, 'Why are you looking for the
living one among the dead? Recall how he spoke to you 6
while he was still in Galilee, saying of the Son of Man 7
that he must be delivered up into the hands of sinful men
and be crucified and on the third day rise.' And they 8
recalled his words, and returned from the tomb and 9
reported these things to the eleven and to all the rest.
They were Mary Magdalene and Joanna and Mary of 10
James and the rest with them—they told the Apostles
these things, and it appeared in their judgment that their 11
words were nonsense, and they disbelieved them. But 12
Peter got up and ran to the tomb and stooped down and
saw the bandages lying by themselves and he went away
home wondering what had happened.

And see, two of them on the same day were making 13
their way to a village about seven and a half miles away
from Jerusalem, whose name was Emmaus, and they 14
were conversing with one another about all these things
which had happened. And it happened that in their con- 15
versation and discussion, Jesus himself approached and
went along with them; but their eyes were prevented 16
from recognizing him. And he said to them, 'What are 17
these words which you exchange with one another as
you walk?' And they stopped, looking downcast. And one 18

of them named Cleopas in answer said to him, 'Are you
the only one staying in Jerusalem and do not know of the
19 events of these days?' And he said to them, 'Which?' And
they said to him, 'Those connected with Jesus the Nazarene, who was a prophet mighty in deed and word before
20 God and the whole people, and how the high priests and
our rulers delivered him up to be condemned to death
21 and they crucified him. But we were hoping that he was
the one who was going to redeem Israel; yes, and with all
22 this it is the third day since this happened, and indeed
some women of our company astounded us, having been
23 early at the tomb, and not finding his body came saying
too that they had seen a vision of angels, who say that he
24 is alive. And some of those with us went off to the tomb
and found it just as the women had said but did not see
25 him.' And he said to them, 'Foolish men! How slow your
26 hearts are to believe in all the prophets said! Was it not
necessary for the Christ to suffer this and to enter into his
27 glory?' And beginning from Moses and from all the
prophets he interpreted to them in all the scriptures the
28 things about himself. And they approached the village
whither they were going, and he himself pretended to go
29 on further, and they held him back saying, 'Stay with us,
for it is nearly evening and the day has already declined'.
30 And he went in to stay with them. And it happened that
as he reclined with them he took bread and blessed it and
31 after breaking it gave them each part. And their eyes
were opened and they recognized him; and he became
32 invisible to them. And they said to one another, 'Were not
our hearts burning within us while he spoke to us on the
33 way, as he opened to us the scriptures?' And they rose up
that very moment and returned to Jerusalem, and found
34 gathered together the eleven and those with them, who
said, 'Indeed the Lord has risen and has appeared to
35 Simon'. And they narrated to them what had happened
on the way and how he was recognized by them in the
breaking of the bread.
36   While they were saying these things he himself stood
37 in their midst; startled and afraid they thought they were

seeing a spirit, and he said to them, 'Why are you dis- 38
turbed and why do questionings arise in your hearts?
Look at my hands and my feet, for it is really I myself. 39
Touch me and look, for a spirit does not have flesh and
bones as you see that I have.' And after saying this he 40
showed to them his hands and his feet. While they were 41
still disbelieving for joy and marvelling, he said to them,
'Have you anything to eat here?' And they gave him a 42
portion of cooked fish; and he took it and ate it before 43
them.

And he said to them, 'These were my words which I 44
spoke to you while I was still with you, that there must be
fulfilled all that had been written in the law of Moses and
in the prophets and psalms about me:—' then he opened 45
their minds to understand the scriptures and said to
them, 'Thus it was written that the Christ should suffer 46
and rise from the dead on the third day, and that there 47
should be proclaimed in his name repentance for the
forgiveness of sins to all the nations—beginning from
Jerusalem. You are witnesses of these things, and see, I 48
send out the promise of my Father upon you, but do you 49
wait in the city until you are endued with power from on
high.'

He led them out as far as Bethany, and he lifted up his 50
hands and blessed them; and it happened that as he 51
blessed them he was parted from them and was carried up
into heaven. And they returned to Jerusalem with great 52
joy, and were constantly in the temple blessing God.   53

    they found. The verb is constantly used in this narrative, the 2
reserve of which should be noticed: in neither Mark nor Luke
is there an account of the events constituting the actual resurrection (contrast Matt. xxviii. 2-4, which loses in credibility
while trying to gain in impressiveness). What is found or not
found makes the story.

    body. Omitting 'of the Lord Jesus' with D and Old Latin, 3
etc., as interpolation.

    two men. For the belief that Luke intends these to be Moses 4
and Elijah see on ix. 30 and Introduction, p. 71. It is this desire

to link the Resurrection with the Transfiguration that accounts for Luke's departure from Mark's 'young man' (Mark xvi. 5).

6   **Recall.** Verses 5-9 remind the reader that Jesus has prophesied all that has happened (ix. 18-22, 43-45; xviii. 31-33). Again, in the Emmaus story, in verses 25-27 and 32-35, and in the account of the Lord's appearance in Jerusalem (verses 44-49, peculiar to Luke), it is insisted that the scriptures prophesied it. This theme of prophecy fulfilled is of paramount importance in this chapter and is Luke's own chief contribution to his material; it is adumbrated earlier in the gospel at i. 11-20, 26-38, 39-45, 46-56, 67-80; ii. 8-20, 25-35, 36-40, passages showing similarities with this chapter. The theme is found also in iv. 16-30, where Luke makes it the main point of his narrative, and at vii. 18-23; ix. 28-36. (See P. Schubert in *Neutestamentliche Studien für Rudolf Bultmann*, Berlin, 1954, pp. 165 ff.)

while he was still in Galilee. Most probably a deliberate correction of 'he precedes you into Galilee' (Mark xvi. 7). Luke is determined that the gospel shall start from Jerusalem and nowhere else: see on xviii. 31. 'He is not here but is risen' is omitted as interpolation with D and Old Latin, etc.

7   **sinful men.** As in late Judaistic literature, equivalent to men 'without the law', i.e. Gentiles. Cf. especially LXX of Ps. ix. 18; 1 Macc. i. 34; ii. 48, 62; though this is of course only one of the uses. For Luke's attempt to avoid representing the action of delivering up Jesus into Roman hands as the supreme betrayal see on xxiii. 1.

10   **Mary Magdalene and Joanna.** See on viii. 2-3.

Mary of James. The only way to translate the phrase, since it is not clear whether this Mary was an unmarried daughter of a man named James or the mother of the same. Comparison of this verse in Luke with Mark xv. 40 and xvi. 1 suggests that this was James 'the small' who may be the same as the son of Alphaeus (vi. 15; cf. Mark iii. 18; Matt. x. 3; Acts i. 13) rather than the father of Judas (vi. 16; Acts i. 13; a James not found in Mark). For the custom of identifying women (not by their husband's name) see Bishop on 'Mary Clopas', *ET*, September 1954, pp. 382-383.

they told. The slight awkwardness of the English represents that of the Greek. The text adopted is that of the overwhelming majority of the oldest MSS.

but Peter got up. For a discussion of the authenticity of this 12 verse and its relation to the rest of the resurrection narrative, see Introduction, p. 28.

seven and a half miles. Taking a stade as about one-eighth 13 of a Roman mile (LS).

Emmaus. About thirty-four stades, in the direction of Joppa, if rightly identified with the modern Kulonieh (Jos. *B.J.* vii. 6. 6) rather than the place of 1 Macc. iii and iv (which is too far from Jerusalem, though thus taken by Eusebius, Jerome, and Sozomen).

but their eyes were prevented from recognizing him. 16 Like the servant of Elisha, 2 Kings vi. 8-23.

Cleopas. Cf. John xix. 25 for Clopas. The view that the 18 original tradition now represented by verse 12 may well have told of two disciples going to the tomb (Introduction, pp. 28 ff.) perhaps receives some support from the tradition in Origen (*Contra Cels.* ii. 62, 68) that the unnamed disciple with Cleopas was Simon. See also verse 24.

the one who was going to redeem Israel. Cf. Acts i. 6. 21 For the reasonableness of the Apostles' expectation of a literal restoration of Israel's independence see Introduction, pp. 34 and 71, and on i. 74; ii. 11; xxii. 36-38 and xxiii. 19.

angels. Although Luke had carefully called them 'two men' 23 (verse 4).

some of those with us. For the important significance of 24 this verse compared with verse 12 see Introduction, pp. 28 ff., and on verse 18 above.

was it not necessary. Part of the burden of Luke's gospel. 26 See Introduction, pp. 35 ff.

their eyes were opened. Apparently because the divine 31 gift inherent in the blessed bread restored their wearied physical and mental faculties: moreover, thus their fellowship with Jesus, broken by his death, was restored.

he became invisible to them. Eloquent of the fact that now they are once again with him and he with them, there is no need of their bodily fellowship with the Lord, who now enters into his glory.

34   **Indeed the Lord has risen and has appeared to Simon.**
Words which have naturally raised much curiosity and speculation. Cf. 1 Cor. xv. 5 which supports this order of the appearances, without knowledge of the two on the road to Emmaus.
For the explanation of the meagre reference see Introduction,
pp. 54 ff.

38   **why do questionings arise in your hearts?** I.e. of the kind
which produced the blasphemous accusation that the Lord was
in league with Beelzebub (xi. 15). See on ii. 35 and 52 for the
word translated here 'questionings'.

41   **Have you anything to eat here?** Verses 13-35, 44-47, if
taken as a whole, recall Tobit xii. 16-22, and it is particularly
striking that emphasis is laid upon the fact that the risen Lord
is not a spirit because he eats: the angel in Tobit confesses that
he has not eaten. Again it is not easy to judge whether Tobit
has influenced Luke or his source, but the affinity with comparatively late Judaistic literature is illustrated once more.

47   **Jerusalem.** See on xviii. 31. So closely does Luke adhere to
the scheme of the propagation of the gospel which makes Jerusalem its starting-place that he ignores altogether in Acts the
rise of Christianity in any local groups, such as seem to have
occurred at places such as Joppa, Lydda, Damascus, and no
doubt in Galilee.

48   **witnesses.** Reference to i. 2 reminds us how important the
idea is for Luke; he does not there claim that he has Apostles
among his witnesses, but that he relies on information handed
on by those who were 'eyewitnesses'. The vocabulary is different, but it is clear that Luke is claiming that he has for
informants the Apostles who were eyewitnesses of the Resurrection and witnesses of the Lord's teaching on the necessity of
his suffering and on the divine plan for the propagation of the
gospel. Cf. Acts ii. 32; iii. 15.

49   **the promise of my Father.** D's reading would give 'my
promise'; this is no doubt due to the influence of John xv. 16.
Within the sphere of Luke-Acts the only possible interpretation of these words must be founded on the clue given when
Luke narrates Pentecost (Acts ii. 17) and makes Peter see in the
outpouring of the Spirit the fulfilment of Joel iii. 1-5. Cf. Acts
i. 4 and ii. 39.

wait in the city. In contrast to the immediate gift of the Spirit by Jesus himself in John xx. 22. Just as the split in the temple veil was a foretaste of the fulfilment of the prophecy in xxi. 24-25 (see note on xxiii. 45), so in the outpouring of the Spirit at Jerusalem we must see a foretaste of the final redemption of xxi. 28 and perhaps an instance of the coming of the Son of Man (xxi. 27). Thus Pentecost is part of the redemption of Jerusalem, but does not save the actual city; like the Lord himself, it must suffer in order to be the starting-place of the gospel.

Bethany. According to Luke the old lodging-place at the 50 time of the Passover, and the place of arrest.

and was carried up into heaven. The text adopted is that 51 of the majority, and may be correct, since it is possible that the omission of these words was due to a desire not to anticipate the full account in Acts i. 9-11.

The theory that Luke xxiv. 50-53 with Acts i. 1-5 form an insertion made at a later time, when the whole work of Luke-Acts was divided, is argued at length by Sahlin (*op. cit.* pp. 11 ff.). But he admits that xxiv. 50-53 are Lucan in style, and we may claim that the real difficulties are raised by the double reference in Acts i. 2 and i. 9 to the Ascension, since the ending of the gospel is straightforward and contains no contradictions. Indeed, the whole of Acts i. 1-14 appears to retell the story of Luke xxiv. 50-53, adding details of the Ascension, but this may be held to throw suspicion on Acts i. 1-14 rather than on Luke xxiv. 50-53.

Perhaps the most probable solution would omit the words, 'and was carried up into heaven' with D, the Old Latin, and syr. sin. and omit also Acts i. 3-5. For it must be admitted that the verb translated 'was carried up' is unexpected: it is used in the active several times in the NT (especially in Hebrews) in connexion with the offering of sacrifice, and twice only (Mark ix. 2 and Matt. xvii. 1) in a general sense. There is no hint here that the Ascension is like the offering of a sacrifice, and the word is therefore apparently used colourlessly. This is strange in view of Luke's Ascension theology: at ix. 51 he uses the significant word 'assumption' to describe what the Lord was to accomplish in Jerusalem, including his death and entrance into glory; and by the use of the verb from the same root he links this with the actual Ascension which was the final means by which the Lord entered into his glory (Acts i. 2, 11, 22). It is probable that the 'going up' to Jerusalem (a phrase bearing the cultic connotation of going up to worship at the temple—see on xviii. 31; xix. 28) is also .deliberately linked to the Ascension (Acts ii. 34; cf. John xx. 17).

The phrase may therefore rightly be suspect on the ground that it dismissed too casually an event which has great importance in Luke-Acts. John xx. 17 reveals a conception of an Ascension as a return to the Father, typical of that Gospel, but Luke thinks of it as the entrance by the Messiah, after his suffering, upon the throne of the universe. The description of this event afforded by Acts i. 9-11 is linked to the gospel not only by the use of the verb mentioned but by the cloud (see on xxi. 27) and by the two men in white clothing (see on ix. 30). This part of the first chapter of Acts may then be confidently accounted Lucan, and suspicion allowed to fall rather on verses 3-5, which read in any case like an intrusion. On this view, Luke wrote both the preface to the gospel and that to Acts, and in the gospel took his story as far as the Lord's departure from the Apostles at Bethany (xxiv. 50-53); in the second volume, after a resumptive preface, he resumes also the story, not where the gospel had left it, but by a reference to the Lord's appearance to the eleven (Acts i. 6; cf. Luke xxiv. 36-49); from this point he continues his account, adding detail which he had designedly omitted in his gospel.

INDEX OF SUBJECTS

INDEX OF PROPER NAMES